Pressure Tennis

Paul Wardlaw
Head Women's Tennis Coach
University of Iowa

Human Kinetics

Library of Congress Cataloging-in-Publication Data

Wardlaw, Paul, 1959-
    Pressure tennis / Paul Wardlaw.
       p. cm.
    ISBN 0-7360-0156-5
    1. Tennis--Training. I. Title.

GV1002.9.T7 W27 2000
796.342'2--dc21   99-059765

ISBN: 0-7360-0156-5

Copyright © 2000 by Paul Wardlaw

All rights reserved. Except for use in a review, the reproduction or utilization of this work in any form or by any electronic, mechanical, or other means, now known or hereafter invented, including xerography, photocopying, and recording, and in any information storage and retrieval system, is forbidden without the written permission of the publisher.

Managing Editor: Melinda Graham; **Assistant Editor:** John Wentworth; **Copyeditor:** Barbara Field; **Proofreader:** Myla Smith; **Graphic Designer:** Nancy Rasmus; **Graphic Artist:** Dody Bullerman; **Photo Editor:** Clark Brooks; **Cover Designer:** Jack W. Davis; **Photographer (cover):** BONGARTS/Mark Sandten/SportsChrome USA; **Photographer (interior):** Tom Roberts; **Illustrator:** Sharon Smith; **Printer:** United Graphics

Human Kinetics books are available at special discounts for bulk purchase. Special editions or book excerpts can also be created to specification. For details, contact the Special Sales Manager at Human Kinetics.

Printed in the United States of America

10 9 8 7 6 5 4 3 2 1

Web site: http://www.humankinetics.com/

United States: Human Kinetics
P.O. Box 5076
Champaign, IL 61825-5076
1-800-747-4457
e-mail: humank@hkusa.com

Canada: Human Kinetics
475 Devonshire Road Unit 100
Windsor, ON N8Y 2L5
1-800-465-7301 (in Canada only)
e-mail: humank@hkcanada.com

Europe: Human Kinetics, P.O. Box IW14
Leeds LS16 6TR, United Kingdom
+44 (0)113-278 1708
e-mail: humank@hkeurope.com

Australia: Human Kinetics
57A Price Avenue
Lower Mitcham, South Australia 5062
(08) 82771555
e-mail: liahka@senet.com.au

New Zealand: Human Kinetics
P.O. Box 105-231, Auckland Central
09-523-3462
e-mail: humank@hknewz.com

Contents

Acknowledgments		iv
Drill Index		v
Introduction	Learning to Thrive Under Pressure	viii
Chapter 1	Winning Principles of Tennis Training	1
Chapter 2	Putting Pressure Intro Practices	12
Chapter 3	High-Percentage Tactics	19
Chapter 4	Court Position and Shot Selection	40
Chapter 5	Teaching Tactics	46
Chapter 6	Singles Drills	52
Chapter 7	Doubles Drills	114
Chapter 8	Warm-Up Drills	148
Chapter 9	The Performance Index	160
Chapter 10	Planning a Pressure Practice	172
Chapter 11	Proven Pressure Practice Plans	178
About the Author		203

Acknowledgments

My wife Katy lent her constant support, understanding, and love throughout this project. I hope my daughters Alexandra and Natalie will now see why "Daddy spends too much time on the computer." I am indebted to their encouragement and patience.

I've been fortunate to have three outstanding tennis mentors over the past ten years. B.E. Palmer and I worked closely together at Kenyon College, where the concepts and ideas for <u>Pressure Tennis</u> evolved and developed. B.E. has been a great friend and confidant in addition to being a master coach and psychologist. His presence is felt throughout the book. Jeff Moore at the University of Texas has been a true supporter, friend, and sounding board. His influence, wisdom, and knowledge have shaped my thinking more than he can imagine. Chuck Kriese at Clemson University made me realize as a young coach how little I had thought about tennis and actually knew about tennis. Chuck taught me I had only scratched the surface and that there was a depth to tennis and coaching I had yet to explore. This book is testament to Chuck's influence and inspiration.

Special thanks go out to my parents, Don and Ruth Wardlaw, and to Dick Maurer, Jeff Kutac, David Schilling, David Thornton, Charley Darley, Steve Houghton, Bob Hansen, Geoff Novak, Joaquin Lopez, Sasha Boros, Hayden Schilling, and the athletic departments at Benedictine University, Kenyon College, and The University of Iowa. Most important, I've had the pleasure to work with great players over the past fifteen years—the people who make coaching a joyful experience.

This project would not exist without the vision, expertise, and encouragement of Rainer Martens and Ted Miller and their staff at Human Kinetics. Thanks for all your help and guidance.

Drill Index

Singles Drills

First Exchanges

1	Two-Shot 20 Second Serves With Returns	53
2	Four-Shot 20 Second Serves With Returns	55
3	Four-Shot Pressuring Returns (X Marks the Spot)	57
4	Five-Shot 20 Second Serves—Serve and Volley	58
5	Four-Shot 20 Second Serves With Drop-Shot Returns	60
6	Four-Shot 20 Service Points	61
7	First-Serve Game	62
8	First-Strike Game	63
9	Pressuring Serve/Return Game	64

Point-Building Drills

10	Crosscourts—Deuce and Ad Court	65
11	Crosscourts—Inside-Out Forehands (Ad Court)	67
12	Crosscourts—With Inside Groundstroke Change of Direction	68
13	Crosscourts—With 90-Degree Change of Direction	70
14	Shifting-the-Court	71
15	Directionals—Coach-Fed Drill	73
16	Directionals—Inside Groundstroke Change of Direction	74
17	Directionals—Inside and 90-Degree Change of Direction	75
18	Directionals—Inside-Out Forehands	76
19	Directionals—Pressuring When Changing Direction	77
20	Directionals—Forehands Are Wild	78
21	Outside/Middle Game	79
22	Big Targets	80

Spin Drills

23	Drive vs. Loop	82
24	Drive vs. Slice	83
25	Slice vs. Slice	84
26	Loop vs. Loop	85
27	Random Spin	86
28	Offense/Defense	87

Pressuring Drills

29	Pinch Volleys	89
30	One-Player Closing Volleys	90
31	Three-Quarter-Court Closing Volleys	91
32	Two-Player Closing Volleys	93
33	Overhead Game	94
34	Wimbledon Points	95
35	Wimbledon Directionals	96
36	Drop-Shot Game	97

Recovery Drills

37	Inside Groundstroke Recovery Game	99
38	Inside Volley Recovery Drill Game	101
39	Short Inside Groundstroke Recovery Game	102
40	Short Outside Approach Shot Recovery Game	104

Singles Play

41	Two-Point Tennis	105
42	Tiebreaker Tournament	106
43	Eight-Game Pro-Sets	106
44	No-Ad Sets	107
45	Game-Point Sets	108
46	First Four Games	108

Crazy Drills

47	Crazy Groundstrokes	109
48	Crazy Returns	110
49	Crazy Volleys	111
50	Crazy Overheads	111
51	Crazy Overheads and Volleys	112

Doubles Drills

Doubles First-Exchange Drills

52	Doubles—20 Second Serves/Window Sequence (1v1)	116
53	Doubles—20 Second Serves/Lob Sequence (1v1)	117
54	Doubles—20 Second Serves/Short-Angle Volley Sequence (1v1)	118
55	Doubles—20 Second Serves/Returner Approach Sequence (1v1)	120

56	Doubles Crosscourt Serve and Volley (1v1)	121
57	20 Serves With Server's Partner (2v1)	122
58	20 Serves With Returner's Partner (2v1)	123
59	Returning Team vs. a Server (2v1)	125
60	Serving Team vs. a Returner (2v1)	126
61	Doubles Serve and Volley vs. Two Back (2v2)	127

Point Building

| 62 | Doubles Crosscourts (1v1) | 128 |

Pressuring

63	Doubles Two-Touch Crosscourt Serve and Volley (1v1)	130
64	Doubles Crosscourt Pinch Volleys (1v1)	132
65	Doubles One-Player Closing Volleys (1v1)	133
66	Doubles Two-Player Closing Volleys (1v1)	135
67	Doubles Overhead Game (2v1)	136
68	Doubles With Returner Pressuring (2v2)	137
69	Doubles With Returner's Partner Poaching (2v2)	138
70	Doubles Quick Volleys (2v2)	140
71	Doubles One-Team Closing Volleys (2v2)	141
72	Doubles One-Team Closing Volleys (2v2)	142
73	Doubles Overhead Game (2v2)	143

Doubles Play

74	1v1 Sets	144
75	Two-Touch Doubles (2v2)	145
76	Doubles Sets (2v2)	146
77	Doubles Tiebreakers (2v2)	146

Warm-Up Drills

A	5-Minute Warm-Up	149
B	Topspin Warm-Up	149
C	Volley Warm-Up	150
D	One-Up/One-Back Warm-Up	151
E	Directional Minitennis	151
F	Soft-Toss Drills	154
G	Soft-Toss Sequences	157
H	Doubles Warm-Up	158

Introduction

Learning to Thrive Under Pressure

Tennis is a game of pressure! Pressure situations occur constantly throughout a tennis match, offering continual tests and challenges as players respond to their opponents, playing conditions, and more often than not, themselves and their own game. Great players find ways to solve the problems pressure creates. However, greatness is not just reserved for Wimbledon, French Open, Australian or U.S. Open champions. Whether novices or seasoned veterans, players will be under pressure on the tennis court. Have their practice sessions prepared them to respond with greatness?

In 1991, I answered the above question with a no! My college team had just lost a quarterfinal match at nationals 5-4. We choked! We did not handle the pressure well. Leading 3-0 in the third set at second doubles, we opened the fourth game with two double faults. The momentum shifted and the match was lost. Why? I had not prepared my team for the pressure of the moment. I was responsible for not providing a practice environment that simulated match pressure. From that day in early May of 1991, I have worked to develop a training system that prepares players for the pressures of match play, a system that encourages and promotes responsibility and offers daily challenges in practice. The results have been extremely positive, as player and team productivity and improvement have become the norm and my team's capacity to handle pressure continues to expand. Pressure training works!

Pressure Tennis teaches players how to best prepare for the pressure of match play. Coaches will learn how to design and implement effective practice sessions using "pressure drills" that simulate matchlike conditions and matchlike pressure. When pressure training, players will notice immediate improvements in concentration, motivation, confidence, conditioning, and most important, the ability to handle the pressure of match play. In addition, practice sessions become purposeful and fun! *Pressure Tennis* offers maximum preparation for a player's journey to tennis greatness.

Chapters 1 and 2 explain in detail the benefits and principles behind training under pressure and the necessary structure for creating a pressure training environment. Chapters 3, 4, and 5 explore the tactical foundation and tactics used when designing pressure drills and when pressure training.

Chapters 6, 7, and 8 contain pressure training drills used in the sample practice plans. The drills include singles drills, doubles drills, and warm-up exercises, offering a comprehensive selection covering the most important aspects of match play. Chapters 9, 10, and 11 address how to plan and maximize a practice session. The Performance Index, a tool that measures practice performance, is also introduced here. Sample pressure practice plans are included and can be used immediately for a training session or can serve as a guide when designing pressure training practices.

Pressure Tennis will help players and teams reach their potential by providing a productive and fun practice environment. Players' capacity to handle pressure will increase, and tennis greatness will be within their grasp. As coaches and players will find, the only way to train is to pressure train. They can handle it!

Winning Principles of Tennis Training

As a coach, I've experienced euphoric wins and heartbreaking losses. My tennis teams have won national championships 5-4 and lost national championships 5-4. However, the match impacting my coaching the most occurred in the 1991 Division III national championships. We suffered through a difficult 5-4 quarterfinal loss against the eventual national champions. Neither players nor coaches were satisfied with each others' performance. We both felt more had to be done for the team to break through against the better teams. The players wanted to dictate points and not just react to their opponents. The coaches wanted the players to be more disciplined in their practice habits and take responsibility for their mental lapses in match play. Both coaches and players were correct in their assessments. Fortunately, I already knew the solution—we needed to pressure train.

The idea behind pressure training is simple—practices must simulate the pressures of match play if practice is to be beneficial. It's one thing to pound down-the-line forehands off a coach's feed but clearly another matter to hit the down-the-line forehand during a point in a match. Throw in another condition, say 5-4 in the third set, and the down-the-line forehand clearly becomes a challenge given the circumstances and pressures. Of course, we could even add that it's 5-4 in the third set of a national championship match with the team score tied at 4-4. Now that's pressure! But this was exactly the pressure my Kenyon College team succumbed to in 1991. The stakes were high, and we could not cope with the pressures associated with championship play. We had not trained to handle the pressure—we were not prepared.

Understanding Pressure

The true test of players is how they perform in competition under match pressure. When tennis players think of pressure, they commonly think only of the mental and emotional reactions the game produces when something is at stake—responses experienced in the mind. Pressure in these cases is purely the mind's response to the situation and circumstances surrounding the match. However, a closer look reveals there is more to pressure than just the psychological. There are the pressures of playing against an opponent whose strategies are difficult to attack or defend against or an opponent who rarely allows you to hit shots in your strike zone or an opponent who makes the match a survival of the fittest. Being prepared and willing to handle these various forms of pressure in match play is the aim of pressure tennis.

Players will find themselves under four types of match pressure:

- Psychological pressure
- Tactical pressure
- Technical pressure
- Physical pressure

If players are under pressure psychologically, tactically, technically, and physically in match play, a practice session must offer the same tests and challenges to really serve as preparation. For a practice session to have maximum benefit, these four core areas of development (psychology, tactics, technique, and conditioning) must be integrated throughout a training session and practiced at match speed, simulating match pressures.

Unfortunately, conventional tennis training does not prepare players for the pressures of match play. In fact, most tennis training avoids putting players under any type of pressure, with the possible exception of the physical. The average junior tennis player trains in a comfortable environment where emphasis is placed on technique and "feeling good" about one's strokes. Generally speaking, conventional tennis training is about grooving strokes (technique) and hitting lots of balls without consequences in a pressure-free, non-matchlike environment.

Having grown up playing and coaching tennis in a conventional environment, I continued this approach as a college coach. I structured most drills around technique, with occasional simulated point situations and match play. My teams hit a lot of tennis balls, grasped all the strokes technically, and there's no question we worked hard. But as I've learned, it's not just about working hard—it's about working intelligently, purposefully, and under pressure. Practice must be preparation for competition.

Our capacity to handle match pressure can be expanded and increased dramatically by practicing under pressure. A daily dose of pressure training allows players to deepen their experiential base in handling pressure. Being under pressure in practice takes players out of their comfort zone, exposing them to the unknown, the uncomfortable, and the unpredictable. Increasing players' ability to handle the pressures of tennis moves them closer to reaching their potential. Players become better able to compete and to adapt to changing match conditions and circumstances. In essence, they practice becoming comfortable with the uncomfortable! Ultimately, players who pressure train derive much more enjoyment from tennis as they become psychologically, tactically, technically, and physically stronger and more experienced. Pressure training is the best preparation for competition.

Benefits of Pressure Training

When pressure training, every drill realistically integrates and enhances the four major developmental areas—psychology, tactics, technique, and conditioning. Real psychological, tactical, technical and physical development can only occur when a player is under pressure, the type of pressure match play creates. Fortunately, pressure training simulates match play pressures, promoting player development at every practice. The benefits of pressure training are tremendous for each area of player development and are listed and explained below.

Benefits of Pressure Training

1. Psychology
   - motivation
   - concentration
   - competitiveness
   - willpower
   - accountability
   - responsibility
   - confidence
   - suffering
2. Tactics
   - decision making
   - problem solving
   - disciplined play
   - structured play
   - self-coaching
   - shot variety

- court position
- staying in range
3. Technique
    - random match-play situations
    - repetition at match speed
    - clearly revealed technical strengths and weaknesses
4. Conditioning
    - high physical intensity
    - realistic tennis-specific movements
    - nonstop action

Developing Mental Toughness

Pressure training prepares you to be mentally and emotionally tough—to be comfortable with the uncomfortable. The idea is to prepare in practice your psychological responses to match pressures. Experiencing psychological pressures during practice allows the coach and player to implement and practice mental and emotional toughness strategies before match play. When pressure training, players are well on their way to developing the psychological skills necessary to reach their potential as players.

Pressure training expands a player's mental and emotional capacities. How the player responds to the psychological pressures of match play is clearly revealed on a daily basis. Improvement in the following psychological areas will be immediate and dramatic.

- **Motivation.** Real, long-term motivation must come from within the player. In reality, though, it is difficult for players to maintain high levels of intensity and motivation during practice sessions. What is their motivation? Unless a player's practice performance has meaning, practice efforts will fluctuate. The solution is to pressure train. Players who pressure train are motivated to perform at match intensity because practices are challenging and are objectively measured by a Performance Index—everyone knows how you performed in practice. Most important, the practice environment, not the coach, becomes the dominant motivating force. The result is that pressure training fosters in players the most desired type of motivation: self-motivation.

- **Concentration.** A player's ability to concentrate is certainly taxed in match play. The longer the match, the more difficult it is to maintain a high level of concentration. By their nature, pressure practices require players to concentrate intently throughout the training session. Players often comment on how mentally exhausted they are after pressure training. This is especially true for players new to the program or during the first few practices of a semester for returning players. Players who pressure train will immediately improve their ability to concentrate for long periods.

Managing your emotions during practice will help you excel under match pressure.

- **Competitiveness.** Like concentration, competitiveness is a capacity that can be expanded by having to compete in practice. Using gamelike drills where the score is kept requires constant concentration and, of course, competitiveness. The idea here is not to create competitive monsters. Whether or not players are competitive by nature, they will be comfortable competing and prepared to compete when it is match time. There is no substitute for developing a mental base that allows you to concentrate and compete effectively during long and difficult matches.

Understanding Competition

The concept of *competition* is often misunderstood, especially given our culture's obsession with success and winning. *Compete* comes from the Latin *competere*, which means "to seek together." If you play your best, then I'll have to play my best to meet your challenge. Competitive environments promote athletic and personal development and provide opportunity for growth. Properly understood, competition is healthy and an ideal avenue for helping you reach your potential. It's no coincidence great athletes have teammates and opponents who bring out their best by "seeking together." Most recently, professional baseball's home-run race between Mark McGwire and Sammy Sosa comes to mind as an example of two players respectfully pushing each other to greatness. Tennis history reveals numerous healthy rivalries—Borg/McEnroe, Rosewall/Laver, Court/King, Evert/Navratilova, Edberg/Becker, Graf/Seles, and Sampras/Agassi, to name a few. Players and teams who understand that competition is about bringing out the best in each other have a tremendous advantage in maximizing their abilities.

- **Willpower.** A player's will is tested throughout a tennis match. Typically, there are two common scenarios that test a player's willpower. The first involves how players respond to temptations that arise throughout a match—temptations such as wanting to hit to the open court or playing how they want to play rather than how they need to play. The second scenario involves players' will to continue playing when uncomfortable. How will players respond when their opponents don't allow them to run their favorite play or hit their favorite shot? How will players respond when the match is difficult or they have lost the first set? Will the response be fight or flight? A player's will, or in essence, the ability to make choices and decisions about how to respond in competitive match play, must be exercised and developed in practice to prepare for the temptations and discomforts of match play. Once again, pressure training is about being prepared and willing to be comfortable with the uncomfortable. Are your players willing to do this?

- **Accountability.** Accountability can exist only when practice performance is measured objectively. Pressure training offers a tool, the Performance Index (discussed in chapter 9), which measures a player's performance on a daily, weekly, semester-long, and even career-long basis. When drills are games, the players know that every shot and point has value and that they are being held accountable for their performances. Players find it easier to take ownership for results that are of their own making. In addition to encouraging accountability, recording drill results improves motivation, concentration, competitiveness, and willpower.

- **Responsibility.** The language of players is very revealing. Players say things like "My forehand is off" or "My serve won't go in," as if their forehand and serve are separate entities that will not cooperate. Players who take responsibility for their games say things like "I'm not hitting my forehand well" or "I'm not hitting my serve in." They take ownership by saying "I," by making the subject of their difficulties themselves and not their strokes. And here, responsibility *(response ability)* concerns a player's ability to respond to circumstances, good or bad. When situations in match play are not to a player's liking, how does the player respond? Again, pressure training practice sessions mirror match conditions and produce situations where players have to respond, to take responsibility for their attitude and effort. As Viktor Frankl points out in *Man's Search for Meaning,* between stimulus and response, man has the freedom to choose. Players are not victims of their circumstances or strokes. Rather, players are free to shape outcomes and attitudes. They do so by choosing or deciding how to behave and respond.

  Pressure practices create circumstances whereby players have to respond and make choices. The attitudinal choices players make in practice are the same ones chosen in match play. If a player gives up when a match doesn't go her way, you'll see the same behavior in practice when the pressure drill doesn't go her way. Pressure training promotes growth as players take ownership for themselves and their own games by learning to control what they can control—their attitudes and behavior. Additionally, pressure drills and the objectivity of the Performance Index promote responsibility and discourage excuses and blame. A pressure training system encourages players to seek help and make necessary improvements. The freedom to choose, to respond accordingly, is theirs.

- **Confidence.** My favorite definition of *confidence* comes from former University of Florida Head Coach and Kenyon College Assistant Coach B.E. Palmer. Coach Palmer always says, "Confidence is hitting the ball in the court." If players lose confidence, they need to focus primarily on hitting the ball in the court. It is amazing how confidence returns when the ball is in play. Pressure training is a tremendous confidence booster because the nature of the drills emphasizes hitting a lot of balls in the court. After the first semester of pressure training, my Iowa team made comments like, "This is the most prepared I've ever felt going into a match" and "I feel so confident on the court." Their feelings of preparedness and confidence were not the result of hitting thousands of balls, but rather the result of hitting thousands of balls in the court.

- **Suffering.** Tennis is difficult! Once players and coaches accept that tennis is a difficult undertaking, it becomes manageable and enjoyable. That's why my teams have one goal, and that is to be a team of *players*. And here, a *player* is simply someone who is willing to suffer. Although typically not a positive concept in our culture, *suffering* means "to be put under," and what the players are under is pressure. When playing a worthy opponent, players expect to be under pressure. They expect the match to be difficult. They expect to suffer.

Pressure training produces *players,* people who are prepared and willing to be under pressure. Learning how to handle being under pressure is the essence of tennis and ultimately all sports (not to mention life). Pressure training definitely puts players under pressure, increasing their capacity to suffer.

Sharpening Your Tactics

Pressure training offers a clear and concise tactical progression designed around three main tactical decisions—when to change direction of the ball, what type of shot to use, and where to position yourself on the court. You'll see marked improvement in several areas.

- **Decision making.** Pressure training creates unpredictable situations that constantly tax a player's decision-making capabilities. With enough time in a pressure practice environment, a player's decision-making skills evolve into automatic and instinctual reactions. The result is that a well-trained player reacts to circumstances without having to think.

Athletes such as Andre Agassi and Pete Sampras bring out the best in each other in competition.

- **Problem solving.** Games are simply exercises in problem solving. Problems exist in abundance and constantly occur throughout a tennis match, offering continual tests and challenges as players respond to their opponents, playing conditions, drill restrictions, and more often than not, themselves and their own game. As most pressure training drills are games, problems to be solved constantly arise.
- **Disciplined shot selection.** Pressure training uses the Directionals as a tactical base. The Directionals (discussed in chapter 3) are a high-percentage tactical system that encourages and promotes disciplined shot selection.
- **Structured play.** Players crave structure and discipline in practice and in match play. The sense of security that structure provides is invaluable. This is especially true in pressure situations! Two of my team's national championships were a direct result of our ability to fall back on our structured patterns of play (Directionals). My players simply played the patterns and the ball rather than their opponents.
- **Self-coaching.** To learn from a mistake, a player has to understand that a mistake has been made. This means players must have a solid tactical foundation from which to play. Players who pressure train are well schooled in high-percentage tennis (Directionals) and are well aware of what constitutes sound tactics. Having proficiency in making the three main tactical decisions (when to change direction of the ball, what type of shot to use, and where to position yourself on the court) makes players instantly aware when they have erred in a shot or change-of-direction decision. By being tactically aware, players are able to coach themselves by making the necessary tactical adjustments and by not repeating poor decisions.
- **Shot variety.** Similar to a pitcher in baseball who must throw a variety of pitches to keep the batter honest, tennis players must be able to mix up spin, pace, location, and depth. Pressure drills provide opportunity to practice hitting spin and hitting against spin in unpredictable (random) live-ball situations. Players learn to hit with a variety of spin to make play less predictable and to keep the ball out of their opponent's desired hitting zone.
- **Court position.** Court position is king! Players who are aggressive with their court position control points and matches. Being able to play comfortably on or inside the baseline opens infinite tactical possibilities and promotes exciting all-court tennis. Every pressure training drill involves court position as a tactical element.

  Players must obviously be aware of their own court position. But just as important is an awareness of an opponent's court position. Where do they like to hit groundstrokes from? Where is their recovery spot on the court? Making opponents play from an uncomfortable and unfamiliar court position affects their timing and shot selection and ultimately produces errors and discomfort.
- **Playing within your abilities** (staying in your range). Each player has a comfort zone in which to play. I call this a player's range. A player's range

has a top end and a bottom end. Players must know their own capabilities to play in their range and to know when they are playing out of their range. I am amazed how often players play out of their range (above and below) when under pressure. If a player plays below that range, caution is usually the culprit and is typically brought on by fear of making a mistake. The desire to be out from under the pressure of a big point usually results in overaggressive, go-for-broke-type play—an example of playing above the range.

In conventional practice sessions, players train out of their range much of the time because there are no consequences. They can just grip it and rip it. Because pressure training performances are measured and indexed, players have to practice in their range. Teams that pressure train play exactly the way they practice—in their range!

Fine-Tuning Your Technique

The true test of technique is whether a player can execute a particular stroke under match pressure. Pressure training offers:

- **Random match-play situations.** In motor learning theory, drills that are unpredictable are called random, reflecting the random patterns that occur in match play. In studying the most effective learning environments for transference of practice habits to match habits, motor learning theorists conclude that random drills have the most benefit. Players do not feel as comfortable in random drills, but their ability to respond to the unpredictable nature of match play is heightened.

- **Repetition in match conditions at match speed.** Hitting off a coach's feed or ball machine in a controlled environment reveals little about a player's technique unless the player is learning a particular stroke. Once a player is fundamentally sound technically, repetition of strokes must occur at match speed under match pressure if there is to be value. Again, repetition in practice that is random and unpredictable promotes technically sound strokes that will hold up under match pressure.

- **Clearly revealed technical strengths and weaknesses.** If you want to learn about your players' strengths and weaknesses, watch them play a match. Because pressure training simulates match play, technical weaknesses and strengths are clearly exposed in practice. The result is that players know if their strokes are technically sound by their practice results. Pressure training definitely does not leave your players with a false sense of technical security. How your players stroke in a pressure training practice is how they will stroke in match play.

Getting the Most Out of Conditioning

The aim of a proper conditioning program is to prepare you for the actual physical rigors and demands of match play. Pressure training develops a strong aerobic and anaerobic foundation. In addition, functional strength is increased. Pressure training requires

- high physical intensity,
- realistic tennis-specific movements, and
- nonstop action.

Pressure training practices are *high energy* and *high intensity*, requiring a serious matchlike effort. Practicing at match intensity is physically demanding and has tremendous conditioning value.

Use *realistic tennis-specific movements*. Because pressure training takes place in a random learning environment, a player's movement and footwork patterns are taxed under match conditions. Again, players move in practice exactly the way they will move in a match.

Rely on *nonstop action*. A pressure training practice has very little downtime. Other than an occasional 90-second water break or time for an explanation, play is continuous and high intensity. Time flies when you are having fun, and I often hear players comment on how quickly practice seems to go by when pressure training.

Tennis is a game of pressure, and mastery can only occur when players are constantly exposed to the various pressures tennis offers. Without pressure in practice, players are denied an opportunity to experience the essence of tennis and a chance to grow and develop. *Pressure Tennis* shows you how to train players in an environment where they have the freedom to make choices, to take responsibility and ownership for their play, and to come to terms with their responses when under pressure. Pressure training promotes true development and empowerment by presenting daily risks and challenges and by encouraging players to be self-aware and open to change. What more can players ask for than having the opportunity to reach their potential, to experience the joy tennis has to offer? Tennis' greatness lies in its ability to test and challenge, to help players discover who they are and who they can be as tennis players and as people.

Pressure training is the ultimate preparation for competition. You will not find a more comprehensive, functional, or effective practice program—a beneficial training system that integrates and incorporates the four essential areas of player development. Players and teams that pressure train enter match play confident and assured that they are well prepared for the challenge at hand.

Putting Pressure Into Practices

I have pressure-trained my teams since 1992. Each year I learn more and more about the best ways to implement a pressure training program, and I am constantly adjusting and fine-tuning the system. I know for certain my pressure training program will continually evolve and develop in the years to come. Pressure training is certainly not a closed system. In fact, once coaches and players understand the general principles that shape the system, they will find avenues for their own personalities and tennis philosophies to emerge in a pressure training environment.

Pressure Training Practice Guidelines

When organizing a pressure training practice, I keep the following guidelines in mind:

- Emphasize a central theme
- Train effectively and efficiently
- Provide organization and structure
- Follow a logical progression
- Provide a tactical framework
- Compete in practice
- Keep score
- Test players' willpower
- Focus on playing

- Maximize practice time
- Challenge the players
- Use teaching aids
- Drill realistically
- Demand proper etiquette and behavior
- Have fun!

Emphasize and focus on a central concept or theme. Every practice revolves around a central theme that is developed and emphasized throughout the practice. A practice session might focus on approach shots and attacking, groundstroke patterns, or serving and volleying. Of course, the lesson plan is geared toward the needs of the team at a particular time of the year. For example, my teams will typically focus early in the season on building a foundation of strong groundstrokes and reliable serves and returns.

Train effectively and efficiently. Similar to match play, each drill incorporates tactics, technique, mental toughness training, and conditioning. The idea is to maximize your practice time by integrating these four player development areas whenever possible.

Provide organization and structure. Practices are organized and scripted to maximize available time. Players excel in structured and disciplined environments where there is a clear plan of action and purpose. Adopt a standard practice plan outline and type each practice plan. Organization and preparation speak volumes and provide a clear reflection of the coach's commitment.

Follow a logical progression from simple to complex. Drills should build upon each other, beginning with the simple and leading up to the complex. For example, a practice emphasizing volleys might follow a drill progression of

- minitennis volleys,
- crosscourt groundstrokes with one player volleying at the net,
- one-person closing volleys, and
- two-person closing volleys.

Although the above drills might not be self-explanatory, the idea here is for the drills to build progressively off each other, going from the simple, involving only technique (minitennis volleys), to the complex, involving technique, tactics, psychology, and conditioning (two-person closing volleys).

Provide a tactical framework. One important benefit when pressure training is that each shot in practice, just as in a match, has a purpose or tactical aim. Tactically, I focus on the *big three*, the three main tactical areas of tennis. The big three are

- when to change the direction of the ball,
- what type of shot (drive, slice, or loop) to use, and
- where to position yourself on the court.

Because the drills used in pressure tennis are segments of points that occur in a tactical framework, players must strategize and problem-solve each shot.

Compete in practice. Once the players have adequate technique and have grasped the team's singles and doubles strategies, practices can be beneficial only if they occur at match speed. Again, pressure training is about putting players in a match environment with match pressure. Competitive practices create matchlike pressure and daily challenges. Having something at stake, knowing that the next shot or point matters, is the only way to create pressure in practice.

Keep score. Keeping score in practice is difficult and requires mental effort. Having to expend physical energy on playing and mental energy on concentrating simulates a typical match environment. Keeping score also allows players to compare themselves to one another objectively.

Test players' willpower. Players obviously feel good and play well when allowed to play to their strengths; however, quality opponents often take away favorite shots and strategies. Is the player willing to be uncomfortable to do what needs to be done? Adopting a positive response to difficult circumstances is simply a matter of willpower.

Focus on playing. Tennis is a game of feet and head. For players to reach their potential, emphasis must be placed on playing and not just hitting. (Here *playing* refers to game situations where score is kept.) This is not to deny the value of technical work. Rather, technical work has its place in individual sessions, whereas play must be the focus of a team practice.

Maximize practice time. A well-scripted practice allows for little downtime. Time between drills is kept to a minimum, allowing for occasional water breaks and teaching time. Ninety seconds, the time allowed for changeovers, is a good standard. For maximum efficiency, drills on each court should end at the same time.

Challenge the players. Practice should be challenging and require players to train at the top of their range. Knowing the level and ability of the players is key to providing an environment that tests and pushes them to reach their potential.

Use teaching aids. Teaching aids (chalk, cones, hula hoops, ropes, twine, etc.) are vital and should be used whenever possible. I use a lot of chalk to highlight areas of the court and to mark spots (i.e., where to stand for returns). I've always liked Vic Braden's definition of tennis: "hitting targets with a score." With Braden's definition in mind, I use targets such as cones early in a practice session during warm-ups and when working on fundamentals. Teaching aids help players concentrate and focus on key aspects of the drill.

Drill realistically. Drills should be segments of points and should be as realistic or matchlike as possible for transference to match play to occur. Ideally, drills should begin with serves and returns.

Demand proper etiquette and behavior. Players must always exhibit proper behavior and etiquette when on a tennis court. Practice is certainly not the time to relax standards. What you see in practice is what you'll see in a match!

Have fun. Tennis is a game after all, so enjoy it. What could be more fun! It is important for coaches and players to keep the sport in perspective and to recall the sense of play—the sense of fun—that initially brought them to the game.

Drill Types

The question I am asked most often when talking about pressure training is, "How is technical work integrated into a pressure practice?" Technique (stroke work) and tactical concepts are best taught in a noncompetitive environment where the emphasis is on proper execution. The most effective technical and tactical teaching takes place one-on-one with the coach and player. Early in the season, players benefit from at least a couple of private or semiprivate hitting times per week. Team practices are better suited for team needs and for teaching team concepts. Of course, a teaching court (we call it our bullpen) can be set up during a team practice if individual needs warrant attention.

A pressure training program includes three types of drills:

- Stroke drills
- Tactical drills
- Pressure drills

Pressure drills are the dominant drill type in a pressure training practice and will be the focus of the rest of this chapter. Stroke and tactical drills are discussed briefly below.

Stroke and tactical drills are noncompetitive and are initially used for teaching technique and tactics. Stroke and tactical drills can serve as lead-ins to pressure drills and are also used to refresh and reinforce key technical and tactical aspects. For instance, if you are focusing on the volley, it might be helpful to begin with a volley drill emphasizing technique before practicing the volley in a pressure drill. Stroke and tactical drills do have a place in a pressure training environment, just not a large place.

Some stroke drills are extremely beneficial, however, and blend in well in a pressure training environment. I call these drills crazy drills. Jeff Moore at the University of Texas introduced me to two crazy drills (Crazy Overheads and Crazy Overheads and Volleys), and my assistant, Sasha Boros, and I have expanded the craziness to include groundstrokes, volleys, and returns of serve. Created to challenge and expand a player's range, crazy drills involve random feeding patterns. The crazy drills are designed to be unpredictable, taking players outside their comfort zone and beyond what they think they are capable of executing. Players make dramatic improvements in shot execution, making the abnormal the normal. Crazy drills take very little practice time and pay tremendous dividends with extended use.

I recommend a three-step process when teaching technique or tactics.

- **Step 1: Soft-toss feeds.** The feeder stands 5 to 10 feet in front of a player and tosses balls underhand. The slowness of the feed helps reveal players' technique, as they must generate pace from no pace. The feeder's proximity to the player makes coaching much more effective by allowing for ease of dialogue and close-up viewing. In a team practice, players can soft toss to each other, allowing the coach to roam and teach.
- **Step 2: Feeds from across the net.** After soft tossing, feed from the service line or baseline across the net. By feeding from across the net, the feeder can generate matchlike pace and simulate shots from realistic angles. Typically, the player's shots are not returned.
- **Step 3: Live-ball rally.** The final step in the instruction process is to play out the point as in a match, with shots being returned until the point or sequence ends. Live-ball rallies simulate match play and allow players to demonstrate their technique and tactics at match pace.

Once technique is established and tactics are understood, practice only has value under matchlike pressure. This is where pressure drills enter the picture. The rest of this chapter focuses on the essential characteristics and features of pressure drills.

Pressure Drills

Pressure drills create a competitive environment where players are challenged technically, tactically, psychologically, and physically. Pressure drills . . .

- **Are games.** Whether it is the number of serves made out of 20 attempts or the score between two players in a crosscourt forehand game, pressure drills involve some sort of counting. Pressure can only be created in a game environment where score is kept.
- **Are segments of points or situations that occur in match play.** Pressure drills must be as realistic as possible. A drill has maximum value when it simulates an actual match situation. Some drill sequences may involve only a few shots. For example, a four-shot sequence might be serve, return, groundstroke, and groundstroke. This drill emphasizes the first four shots of a point.
- **Use simple scoring that is easy to grasp.** The object is for the players to focus on playing rather than performing mental gymnastics when trying to keep score. You'll be amazed at the scoring possibilities you'll come up with. Believe me, I have learned the hard way on numerous occasions. Keep it simple!

- **Involve competition against teammates or a standard.** Pressure drills are competitive. Most pressure drills involve competition between teammates, but in some drills, the players are competing against a standard (when serving, for instance).
- **Start with a serve or a feed from a player.** If possible, pressure drills start with a serve; otherwise players feed the ball to start the point situation. There are only a few pressure drills in which coaches feed to start the point.
- **Are timed, have a certain number of repetitions, or end when a desired score is achieved.** Although tennis is not a timed sport, most pressure drills are timed. Timing drills not only maximizes court time, because all drills end at the same time, but it actually creates numerous pressure situations, because games are frequently tied and single points decide winning and losing. Tiebreaker scoring is often used in pressure drills by playing to 7 or even 11. Also, a certain number of repetitions might be stipulated, such as serving 20 serves, 10 to the deuce court and 10 to the ad court.
- **Have a consequence.** Players either win or lose a pressure drill. Winners move up a court and losers move down a court. I have known coaches in other sports where pressure training is used who have the players choose a physical consequence for the losers to perform after a drill (push-ups, sit-ups, or line drills, for example).
- **Have recordable results.** After each pressure drill, a score and result can be recorded. For example, players who win a drill or achieve a desired standard receive a "+" (plus) and players who lose a drill or fail to achieve a desired standard receive a "-" (minus). In addition, the score can be recorded. For example, if your standard for a "+" is making 17 or more serves out of 20, it is helpful to record the score to know how close the player comes to the standard. There is a big difference between making 8 of 20 and making 16 of 20 serves, even though both are recorded as a minus.
- **Have restrictions (including no restrictions) and stipulations.** Making players play within defined parameters teaches discipline, exercises their will, and forces them to problem-solve. For example, not being allowed to hit down the line in a crosscourt forehand drill promotes a point-building mentality and changes the focus from attacking the open court to patience. How will the player solve the problem of not being allowed to apply pressure down the line? Also, good opponents in match play can take away favorite preferences and options. Again, learning to be comfortable with the uncomfortable and unpredictable will pay tremendous dividends.
- **Have a tactical focus—every shot has a purpose.** The big three (Directionals, court position, and shot selection) provide a tactical focus for every shot. Forehands are no longer just forehands but might be point-building outside forehands or pressuring inside forehands. Depending on the shot, the player adopts a specific tactical aim and mind-set. Given this tactical focus, drills have to be realistic or segments of points.

Promote proper tennis behavior and etiquette. Because pressure drills are games won or lost, they evoke typical responses to winning and losing—some good, some bad. When pressure training, practice becomes a great opportunity to work on proper behavior and etiquette. Players will experience the same emotions they experience in match play, from anger to frustration to apathy to elation. There is no better preparation for good match behavior than having developed proper responses to difficult situations beforehand.

Require decision making and problem solving. Because pressure drills are segments of points that occur in a tactical framework, players must strategize and problem-solve each shot. Important factors affecting players' decisions are who their opponent is and their style of play and the drill restrictions. For example, it makes no sense to try to overpower an opponent in a crosscourt groundstroke drill. Each player knows where the ball is being hit, and very little open court is available in which to hit penetrating shots. In this case, it should be obvious that the crosscourt forehand game is a game of patience and errors rather than winners. As you will find, each pressure drill is clearly a problem to be solved.

Creating pressure drills appears to be as easy as turning drills into competitive games. However, a drill is not a pressure drill unless tactics are an essential part of it. In other words, the pressure drill reflects, instills, and reinforces a team's tactical system. The tactics are decided upon first, and then the drills are created to teach and reinforce those tactics. So before a pressure training system can be created, the coach must have a clear and detailed picture of the team's tactical approach. This leads to an explanation of the tactical system used to create the pressure drills in chapters 6 and 7.

3

High-Percentage Tactics

At the heart of *Pressure Tennis* lies a tactical system called the Directionals. The Directionals evolved from my work in 1992 with Kenyon College's number-two player, senior Kathryn Lane, who went on to earn All-America status in singles and doubles. Kathryn was a solid player with excellent groundstrokes. She had limited foot speed and used her aggressive strokes and serve to dictate matches and compensate for her lack of court coverage. Kathryn maintained excellent court position, playing on or inside the baseline, but she had a tendency to rush points and gave herself little room for error when attacking or closing out points. Most of her errors were wide or in the net. Tactically, Kathryn needed a way of playing that enhanced the following:

- High-percentage shot selection
- Aggressive attacking play
- Court coverage and anticipation
- Natural stroking—using natural hip and shoulder rotation

Kathryn's tactical decision on each shot became whether or not to change the direction of the ball. At the heart of the Directionals is the question Kathryn learned to ask on each shot: "Do I change direction, or do I hit the ball back to where it came from?"

Chuck Kriese pointed out in his book *Total Tennis Training* that not changing the direction of the ball (holding the angle) creates the greatest margin of error and ensures that the racket contacts the ball at a right angle—the most forgiving angle on contact. However, a major tactical goal is to hit shots that are biomechanically sound; that is, shots that allow your hips and shoulders to rotate naturally. As you will soon see, for some shots, changing the direction of the ball is the more natural, preferred, and advantageous option, regardless of the racket's angle at contact.

Tactical Tennis—The Big Three

Trailing 3-0 in the third set of her 1998 match against the University of Michigan's number-six player, the University of Iowa's Carolina Delgado was at a tactical loss. She was frustrated by her opponent's error-free tennis and by her own numerous errors. With the team match on the line, Carolina was definitely feeling the pressure to produce. During the changeover, I strongly encouraged her to refocus by following the Directionals, maintaining aggressive court position on the baseline, and driving her backhand instead of looping it. Heeding my advice, Carolina proceeded to win the next five games in a row and eventually the set and match by a score of 7-5 in the third set. Needless to say, her win was crucial in Iowa's 4-3 team victory.

But what really happened from a tactical standpoint in Carolina's third-set comeback? The answer is simple: Carolina played from her tactical base, a foundation established and built daily in practice. Carolina lost her way in the third set by focusing on her opponent rather than on her own game and her own strengths. My coaching tip on the changeover was just a reminder to play as she had trained in practice—follow the Directionals, keep good court position (on or inside the baseline), and select the appropriate shot. In other words, focus on the big three.

The big three—Directionals, court position, and shot selection—form the general framework for tactical tennis by addressing the following three tactical decisions:

- When to change direction of the ball
- Where to position yourself on the court
- What type of shot to use

Regardless of their specific game style—baseliner, aggressive baseliner, serve-and-volleyer, counterpuncher, or all-courter—players must be aware of the big three and the tactical implications for their games. Again, the big three address tactical decisions and provide a strategic framework from which players build their tactical games.

Inside and Outside Groundstrokes

The essence of the Directionals is found in the difference between inside and outside groundstrokes. Forehands and backhands are no longer just forehands and backhands. Forehands are either outside forehands or inside forehands, and backhands are either outside backhands or inside backhands.

- **Outside groundstrokes.** Examples of outside groundstrokes occur when two players are in a crosscourt rally. The groundstrokes are called outside groundstrokes because the ball crosses in front of a player's body and is moving away or to the outside.

The players in figures 3.1 and 3.2 are in crosscourt rallies hitting forehand to forehand and backhand to backhand. They are hitting outside groundstrokes or, more specifically, outside forehands (figure 3.1) and outside backhands (figure 3.2).

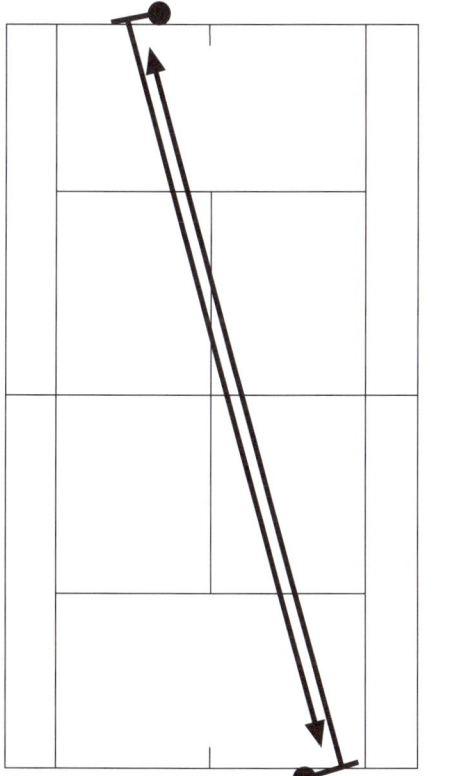

Figure 3.1 Outside forehands

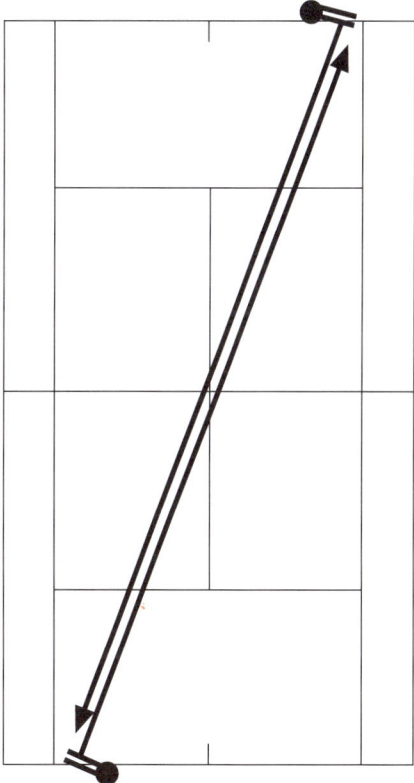

Figure 3.2 Outside backhands

- **Inside groundstrokes.** Inside groundstrokes occur when the ball does not cross in front of a player's body. An example of an inside forehand is the following: P1 and P2 are in a crosscourt rally hitting outside backhands (figure 3.3) until P2 hits a ball that doesn't cross P1's body and P1 must hit a forehand (figure 3.4). The forehand in figure 3.4 is an inside groundstroke because the ball is coming into or inside the body and doesn't cross P1's body.

The outside forehand

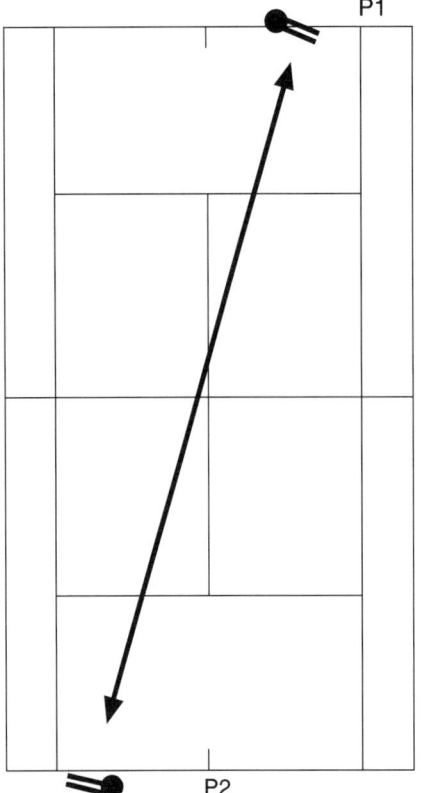

Figure 3.3 Player 1 and Player 2 in a crosscourt rally hitting outside backhands

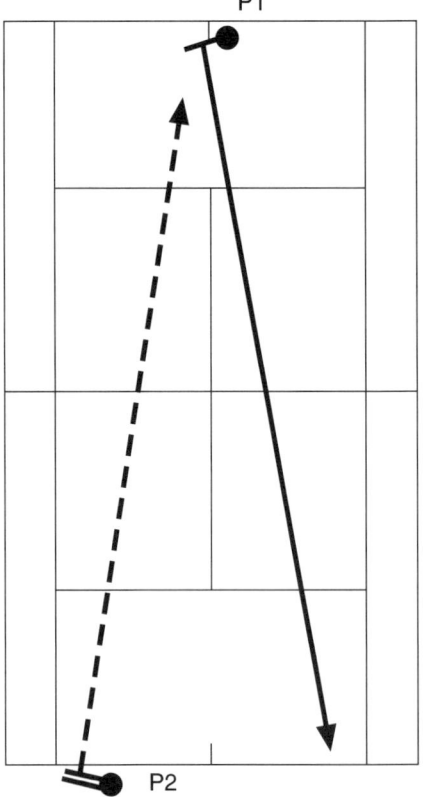

Figure 3.4 Player 1 hitting an inside forehand

An example of an inside backhand is the following: P1 and P2 are in a crosscourt rally hitting outside forehands (figure 3.5) until P2 hits a ball that doesn't cross P1's body and P1 must hit a backhand (figure 3.6). The backhand in figure 3.6 is an inside groundstroke because the ball is coming into or inside the body and doesn't cross P1's body.

The relationship between the ball and the player (not the ball and the court) determines whether an inside or outside groundstroke will be hit. If the ball crosses in front of a player's body, an outside groundstroke will be hit. If the ball does not cross in front of a player's body, an inside groundstroke will be hit.

The inside backhand

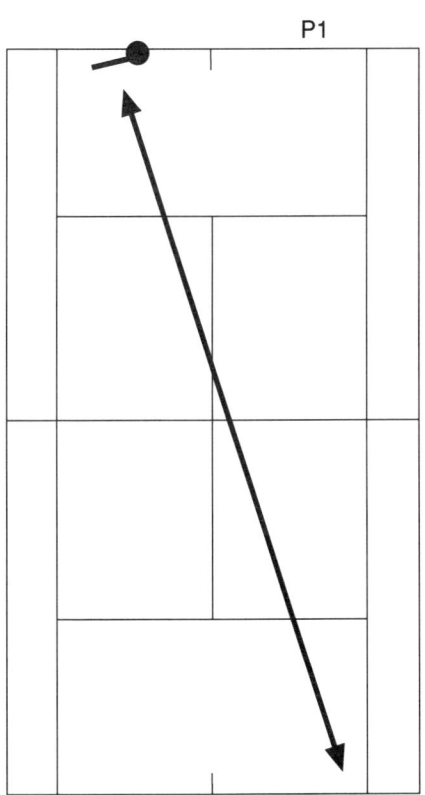

Figure 3.5 Player 1 and Player 2 in a crosscourt rally hitting outside forehands

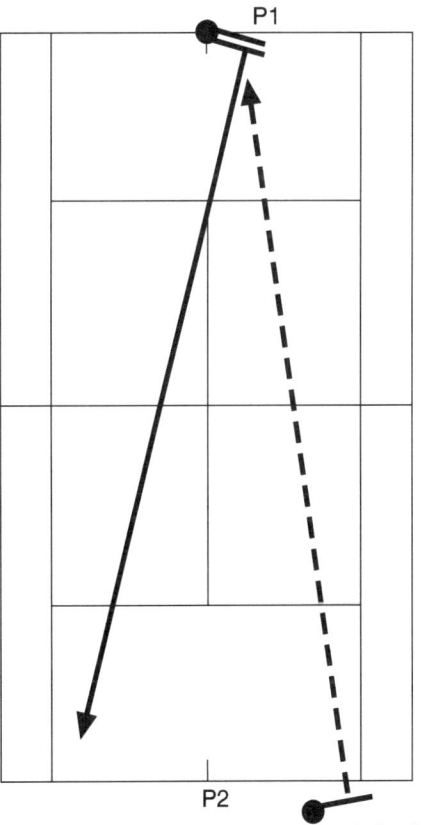

Figure 3.6 Player 1 hitting an inside backhand

Understanding the difference between outside and inside groundstrokes is the novel insight that led to the development of the Directionals. In fact, if you are not clear on the distinction between the outside and inside groundstroke, I advise you to reread the previous section before proceeding.

Warning—a clear understanding is necessary!

It's important to remember there are two types of modern players—those who split the court in half (players who equally play forehands and backhands) and those who play with a weapon (players who overplay a strength, usually the forehand). The following three tactical guidelines are for those who split the court in half. Directionals for players with a weapon will follow.

Guideline One: Outside Groundstrokes/ No Change of Direction

The most natural and most high-percentage shot is to hit the ball back crosscourt by not changing the direction of the ball (figures 3.7 and 3.8) — making a shot that leaves the strings at a right angle. Significantly fewer errors will be made, and your opponents will have fewer openings from which they can attack.

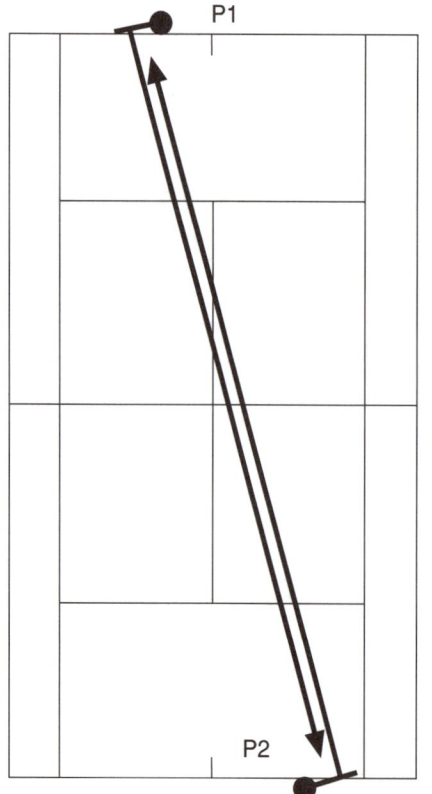

Figure 3.7 Outside forehands, no change of direction

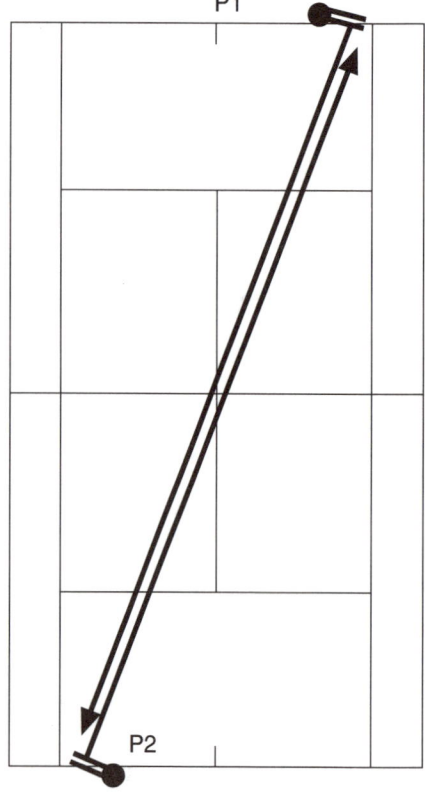

Figure 3.8 Outside backhands, no change of direction

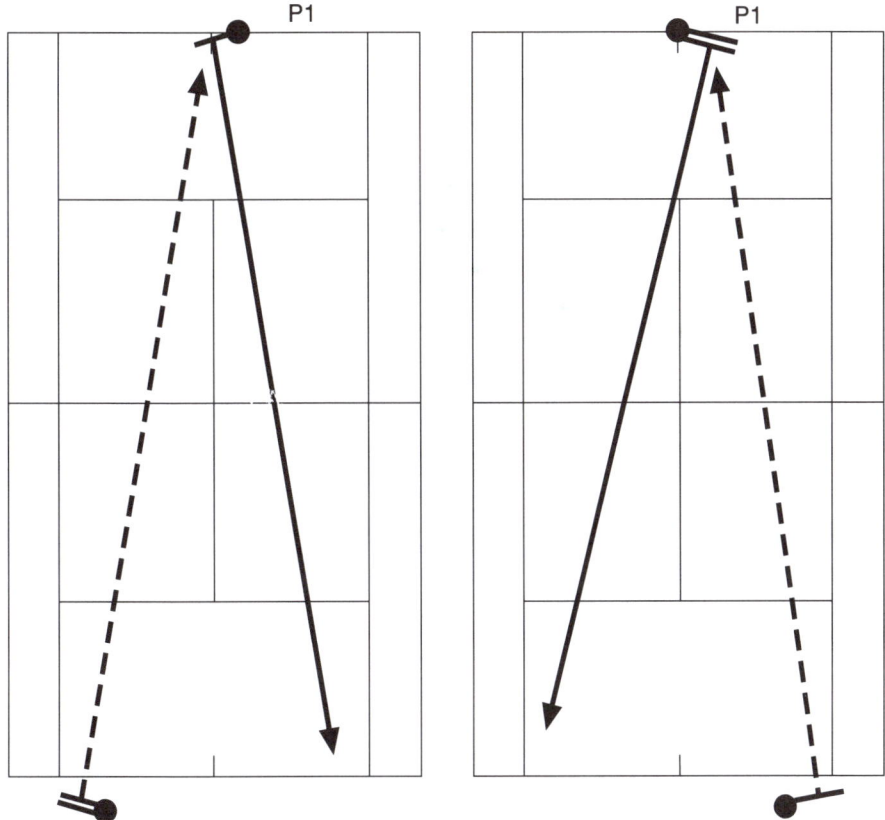

Figure 3.9 Player 1 changing direction on an inside forehand

Figure 3.10 Player 1 changing direction on an inside backhand

Guideline Two: Inside Groundstrokes/Change Direction

Because your hips and shoulders rotate, it is far more natural to change direction on inside groundstrokes and hit to the open court.

Inside groundstrokes (see figures 3.9 and 3.10) are the shots that give you offensive control of the point. Players should be alert to step into the court on inside groundstrokes, taking the ball on the rise. Court position inside the baseline is the key to taking offensive advantage of an inside groundstroke.

The initial difficulty in hitting an inside groundstroke crosscourt is that you can't see your target as you prepare to hit the ball. Because you can't see your target, mastering inside shots becomes a matter of gaining a feel for the court and a sense of the width of the court.

Guideline Three: Changing Direction on Outside Groundstrokes—The 90-Degree Change of Direction

Again, on deep outside groundstrokes, the high-percentage shot is to stroke the ball back to where it came from (not changing direction). However, there are times when it's important to be able to change direction on outside groundstrokes—the most obvious being on crosscourt shots landing short.

When changing direction on an outside groundstroke, hit the ball so that it crosses your opponent's baseline perpendicular (90 degrees) to the baseline (figures 3.11 and 3.12). In nongeometric terms—if you contact the ball 3 feet from the sideline, the ball should cross your opponent's baseline 3 feet from the sideline. Because the baseline (not the sideline) is the referent, the ball crosses the baseline at a 90-degree angle. This is called a 90-degree change of direction (90 COD).

The 90-degree change of direction

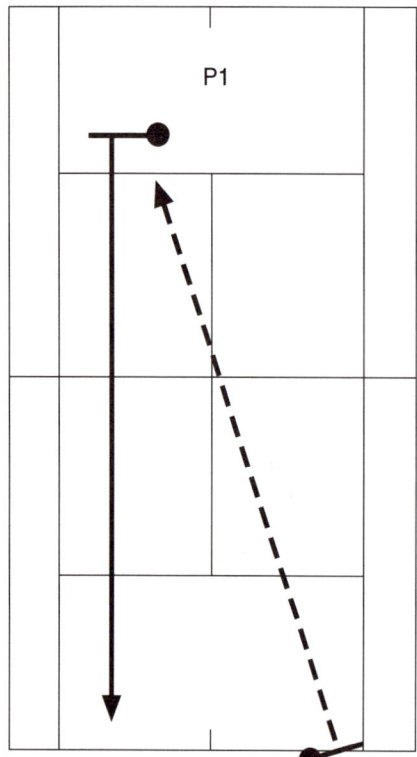

Figure 3.11 Player 1's 90-degree change-of-direction forehand

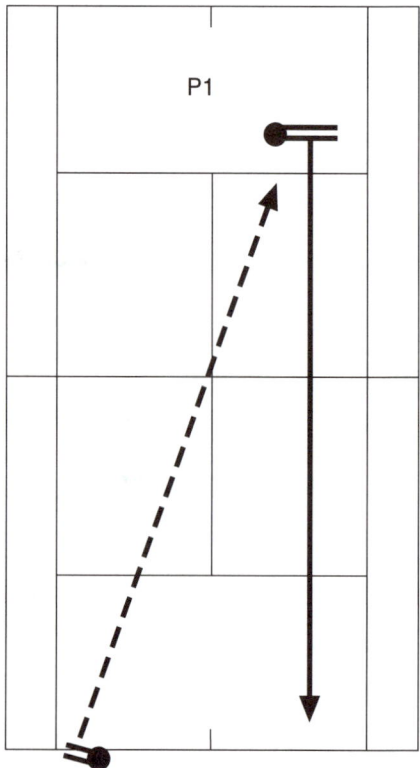

Figure 3.12 Player 1's 90-degree change-of-direction backhand

Typically, when players change direction on outside groundstrokes, they think, "Hit the ball down the line." By thinking "line," they aim at the line, reducing all margin of error. By changing their reference point from "line" to "90 degrees," the player has room for error, and since most 90 COD shots are forcing, the player has at the very least initiated an attacking sequence without taking a huge gamble. In addition, the player can concentrate on depth, as width or angle ceases to be a factor. Increased depth then makes the shot more forcing or penetrating.

Guidelines for Playing With a Weapon

Most top players in the game have at least one thing in common. They all play to their strengths by setting up and controlling points with their forehand weapon. By overplaying their forehands, running around their backhands, and being able to penetrate the baseline with their weapon, top players create many more inside groundstroke opportunities to capitalize on. Two types of inside forehands must be developed and used when playing with a weapon.

Inside Forehand One: Inside-Out Forehand— No Change of Direction

To play successfully with a weapon, the player has to be able to hit inside-out forehands. Inside-out forehands are simply inside forehands hit with no change of direction (see figure 3.13). Inside-out forehands are usually hit off deep shots and are used to create opportunities for shorter inside forehands from which to attack.

Inside Forehand Two: Inside Forehand— 90-Degree Change of Direction

Because the weapon player is playing from the ad court, the inside forehand is hit as a 90-degree change of direction. The emphasis is on depth and penetration rather than width. This shot is usually hit off three-quarter-court-depth or shorter shots. Having court position inside the baseline is the cue for when to hit the inside forehand—90-degree change-of-direction shot (see figure 3.14).

The inside/out forehand

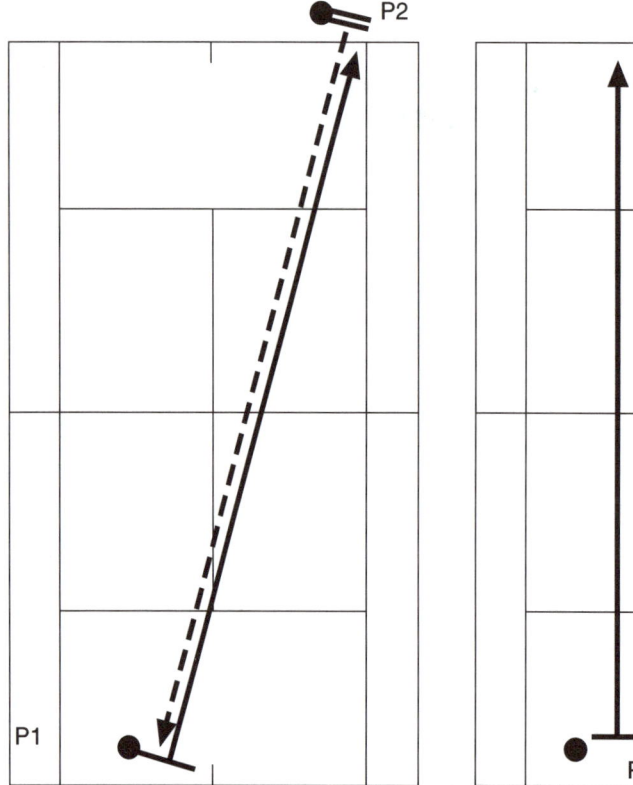

Figure 3.13 Inside forehand by P1 is hit with no change of direction.

Figure 3.14 Inside forehand by P1 is hit as a 90-degree change of direction.

First Exchanges—Serves and Returns

The aim of both the server and the returner is to take control of the point by applying pressure and creating weak replies on which to pressure. On first serves, the server can strike first with a pressuring serve while the returner aims to just start the point. If the first serve is missed, the returner has first opportunity to apply pressure off the usually weaker second serve. Awareness of the tactical implications of the Directionals when serving and returning leads to more predictable and controllable outcomes and creates more pressuring opportunities. Always a great way to start a point!

First Serves

Servers have three location options when serving—wide, at the body, or down the middle (the "T"). Each location has advantages and, used in combination, keeps the returner off balance and out of rhythm.

- **Wide serve.** Serving wide forces the returner wide of the singles court and, if the serve is penetrating enough, creates inside shots for the server to turn on. Rule of thumb: Forcing wide serves creates inside shots for the server.

- **At the body.** Serving at the body neutralizes players with long, sweeping strokes and makes it difficult for the returner to set up properly. Rather than moving to the ball, the returner must move away from the ball to hit the return. Serves at the body, however, will either be inside or outside balls for the returner, depending on what side of the body the serve comes to and which way the returner moves. The server should anticipate returns accordingly.
- **Down the middle.** Serving down the middle or at the T creates late returns and short outside shots off which the server can approach and apply pressure.

Second Serves

Ideally, the server should remain aggressive but under control when hitting second serves and always be wary of the returner's ability to apply pressure off the second serve. The server should also be cognizant of the tactical options of the returner when the Return-of-Serve Guidelines are followed (discussed next). Understanding the returner's best options will make your service game much stronger as court coverage and anticipation improve.

Return-of-Serve Guidelines

Every point begins with a serve and a return of serve. These first exchanges dictate how points take shape and, more than any other area, affect the outcome of a match. The importance of serves and returns is often overlooked. In professional tennis, the server has a clear offensive advantage, and it's understandable why set analysis focuses on breaks of serve—the true measure of server and returner effectiveness. Using the Directionals on returns of serve will give structure to a difficult task and produce higher percentage returns.

Return of First Serves

Imagine having to return one of Pete Sampras's 120-mile-an-hour first serves. With his pace and aim, it's no wonder it's difficult to break his serve. As the top professionals show, first-service opportunities are the chance for a player to go for an immediate offensive strike.

The server and the returner

Because the server has the advantage and typically tries to take the initiative on first serves, the job of the returner when returning first serves is to neutralize the point. Neutralizing the point means that the server is not in a position to pressure the returner off the return.

Deuce-Court Returns

On all first-service returns except inside returns, there is no change of direction (figures 3.15 and 3.16). By not changing direction, you'll create a larger margin of error on a difficult shot. On inside returns (serves at the body and to the backhand), a 90 COD return is recommended (figure 3.17).

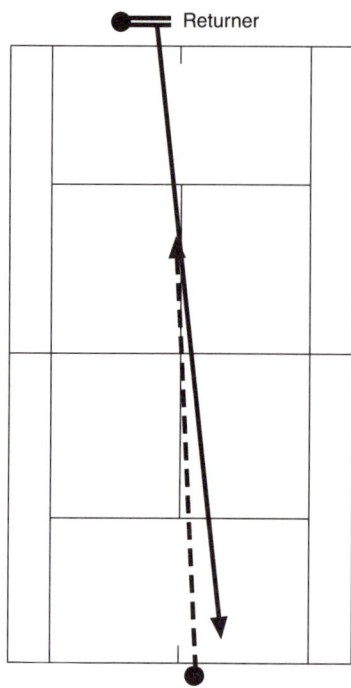

Figure 3.15 Return serves up the middle with no change of direction

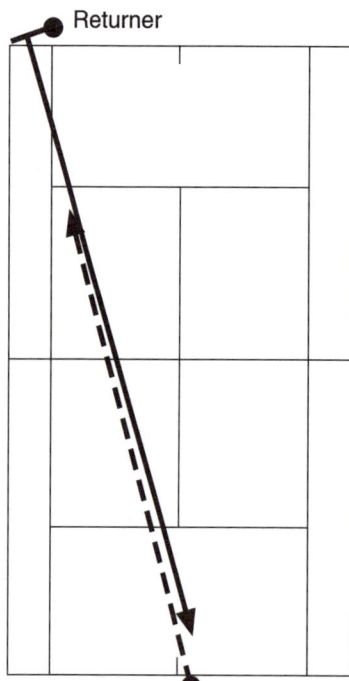

Figure 3.16 Return wide serves with no change of direction

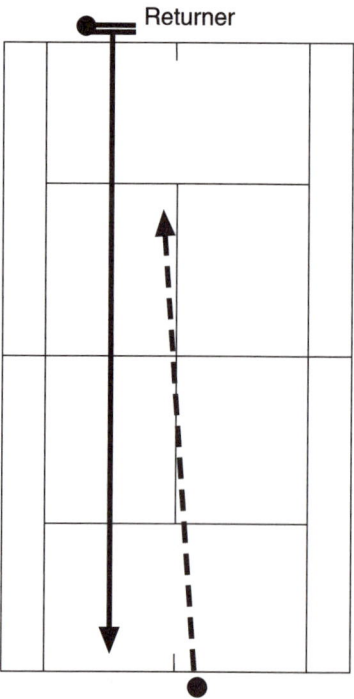

Figure 3.17 Inside backhand return with a 90-degree change of direction

Ad-Court Returns

On all first-service returns except inside returns, there is no change of direction (figures 3.18 and 3.19). Again, by not changing direction, you'll create a larger margin of error on a difficult shot. On inside returns (serves at the body), a 90-degree COD return is best. Ad-court returners with a forehand weapon will hit either a 90-degree COD or an inside-out forehand on inside returns (figures 3.20 and 3.21).

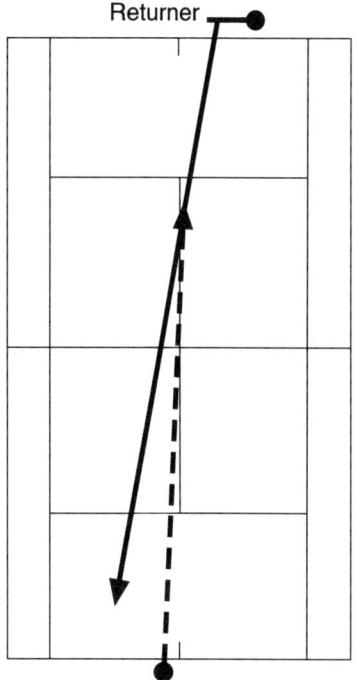

Figure 3.18 Return serves up the middle with no change of direction

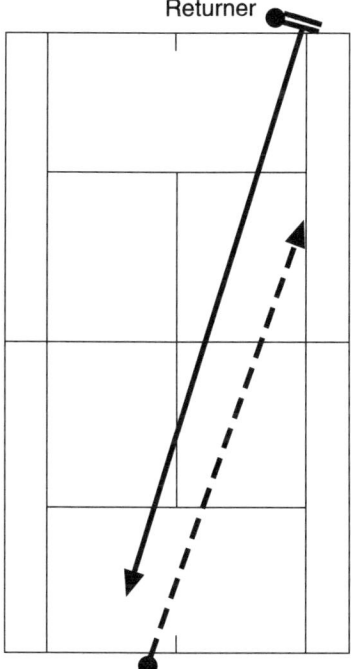

Figure 3.19 Return wide serves with no change of direction

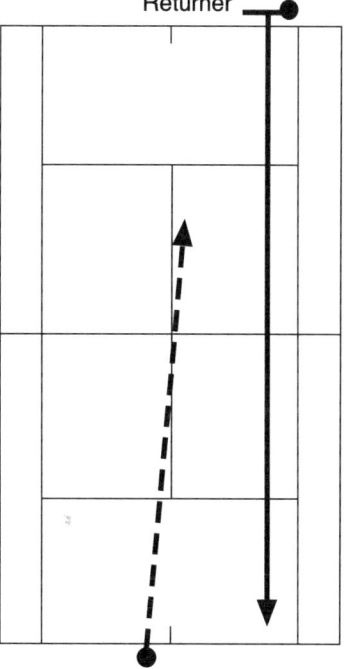

Figure 3.20 Inside forehand return with a 90-degree change of direction

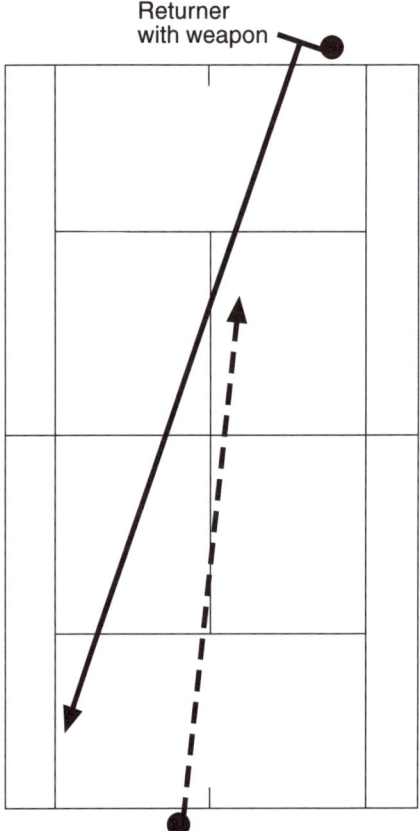

Figure 3.21 Inside-out forehand return with no change of direction

Second-Serve Returns

When returning second serves, the job of the returner is to take advantage of the reduced pace of the serve and pressure the server by shifting the court (forcing with location) or by pressuring with pace and penetration. Usually, the smart play when forcing with pace or penetration is to hit through the middle of the net (the center strap makes an excellent target) with no chance for wide errors.

Advanced players look to take immediate control of a point with their forehands off second-serve returns. This is done by positioning themselves almost at the center of the baseline when returning from the deuce court and with the left foot in the ad-court alley when returning from the ad court. The inside-out forehand return is most effective from the ad court. Returning a second serve is a perfect opportunity to apply pressure immediately and take control of a point.

Another successful return off the second serve involves chipping (slicing) and charging the net. Two interesting and predictable plays can be run. On

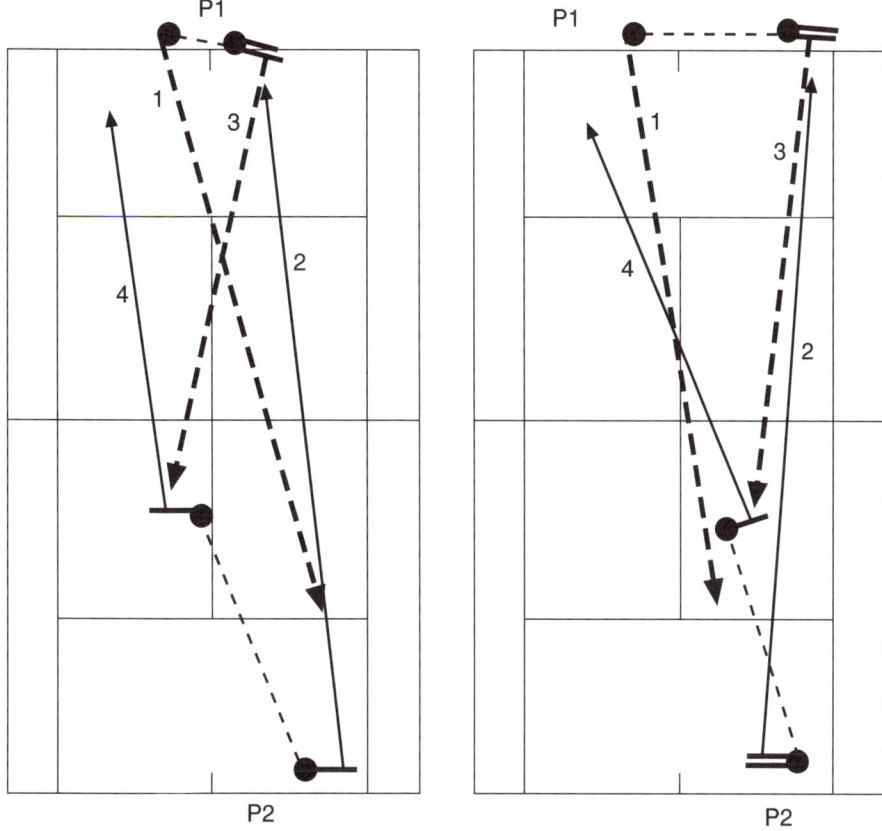

Figure 3.22 On outside serves, chip down the middle and cover the crosscourt passing shot.

Figure 3.23 On inside serves, chip down the line and cover the down-the-line passing shot.

outside serves, chip the return down the middle (giving the server an inside ball to turn on) and cover the crosscourt passing shot (figure 3.22). On inside serves, chip down the line and cover the down-the-line passing shot (figure 3.23).

Approach Shot Guidelines

Approach shots create volley opportunities and should be thought of as part of a two-shot sequence—approach, volley. Approach shots are hit off three-quarter-court-deep balls or shorter, and typically two situations arise—the player approaches off a short outside ball or a short inside ball. Besides following the Directionals, the key to approaching successfully is to remember that baseline groundstrokes and midcourt groundstrokes are technically completely different strokes (on approach shots, the backswing is to shoulder level and the stroke is down and through the ball).

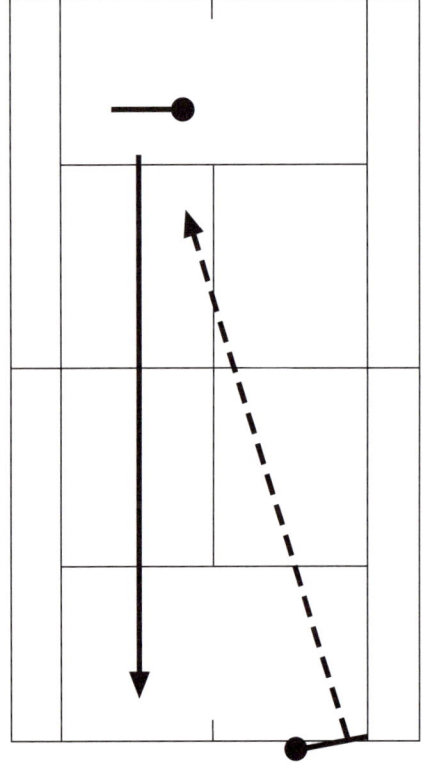 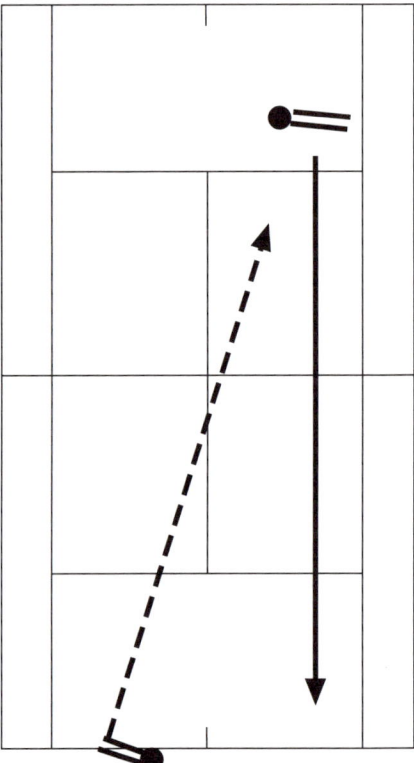

Figure 3.24 A 90-degree change of direction is used on the outside forehand approach shot.

Figure 3.25 A 90-degree change of direction is used on the outside backhand approach shot.

Outside Approach Shots

On outside groundstroke approach shots, hit a 90-degree change of direction (see figures 3.24 and 3.25).

Inside Approach Shots

On inside groundstroke approach shots, players who split the court will change direction (figures 3.26 and 3.28). Players with a weapon will either change direction or not change direction on the inside-out forehand (figure 3.27).

Passing Shot Directionals

Opponents typically approach either down the line off short outside balls (figure 3.29) or crosscourt off inside balls (figure 3.30). Given the reduced time between shots when a player is approaching, it is most advantageous to pass by not changing the direction of the ball. The only exception is when a player approaches down the middle of the court and the passer has an

High-Percentage Tactics **35**

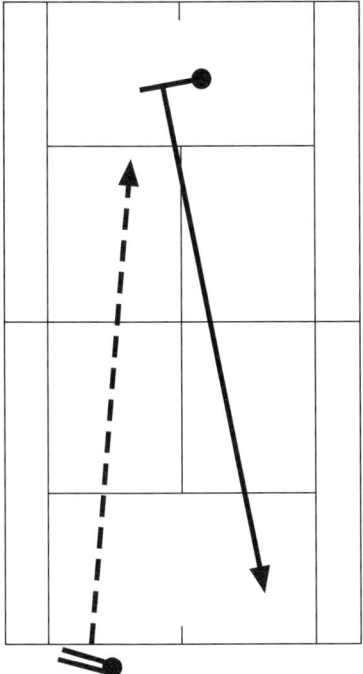

Figure 3.26 Players who split the court will change direction on an inside forehand approach shot.

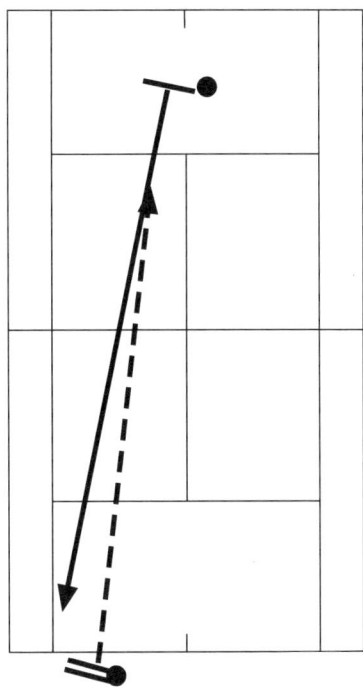

Figure 3.27 Inside-out forehand approach with no change of direction

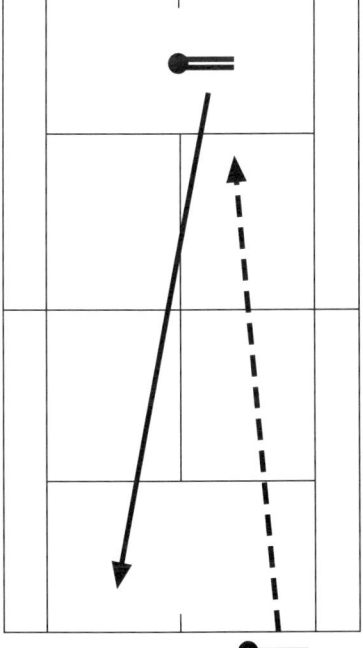

Figure 3.28 Players who split the court will change direction on an inside backhand approach shot.

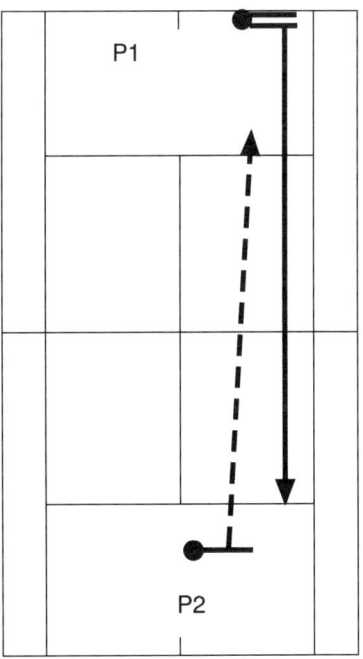

Figure 3.29 Player 1 passing with no change of direction

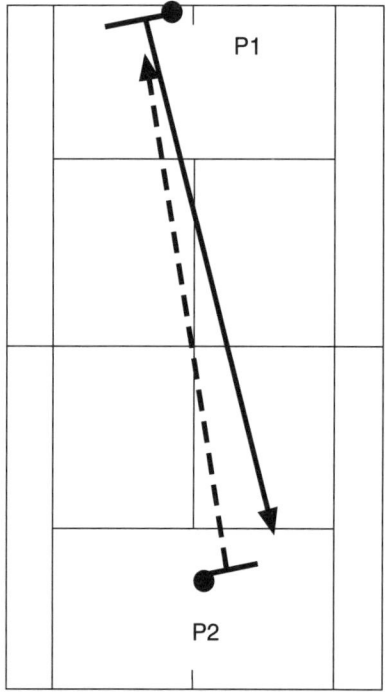 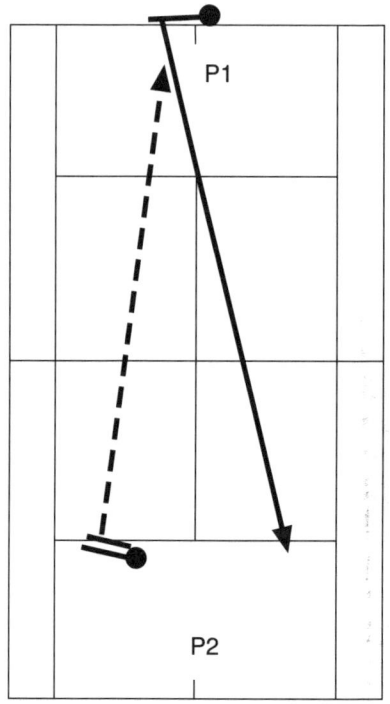

Figure 3.30 Player 1 passing with no change of direction

Figure 3.31 Player 1 passes with a change of direction off an approach through the middle.

inside ball that can be turned on (figure 3.31). Passing shots are hit behind the approaching player when following these passing shot guidelines. By not changing direction, the passer focuses on the ball and holding the angle (not changing direction), rather than focusing on the volleyer.

These passing shot guidelines are the first option when an opponent attempts to approach, especially early in a match. Being passed can be very discouraging to an opponent and can cause the approacher to try for too much when approaching again or alter the approacher's pressuring zone, making the approacher wait for an even shorter ball. Of course, at some point your opponent will catch on to your passing shot patterns, and you might have to change direction occasionally to keep the approacher honest.

Volley Directionals

The Directionals also apply to volleys with some minor modifications based on the type of passing shot hit.

Outside Volleys

Three situations typically occur on outside volleys:

- The player can control the volley because the passing shot is hit high or not very hard.

- The player cannot control the volley because the passing shot is hit low or with a lot of pace.
- The passing shot is hit hard and away, resulting in a stab or reflex volley.

Note. On passing shots hit hard and away from the volleyer that result in a stab or reflex volley, the easiest play is to volley down the line, which is usually the only option, given the difficulty of such a volley. In this case, the volleyer is off balance, and it is important to keep the ball in front of the volleyer for coverage of the next shot.

On outside volleys that can be controlled, players have the option to

- not change direction (figure 3.32) or
- hit a 90-degree change of direction (figure 3.33).

On balls hit above the net that can be controlled, players must choose the best shot taking into consideration their opponent's court position, whether or not their opponent is moving, the own court position and closeness to the net, and the need for being less predictable (players can't always hit to open court, as opponents will begin to cover accordingly).

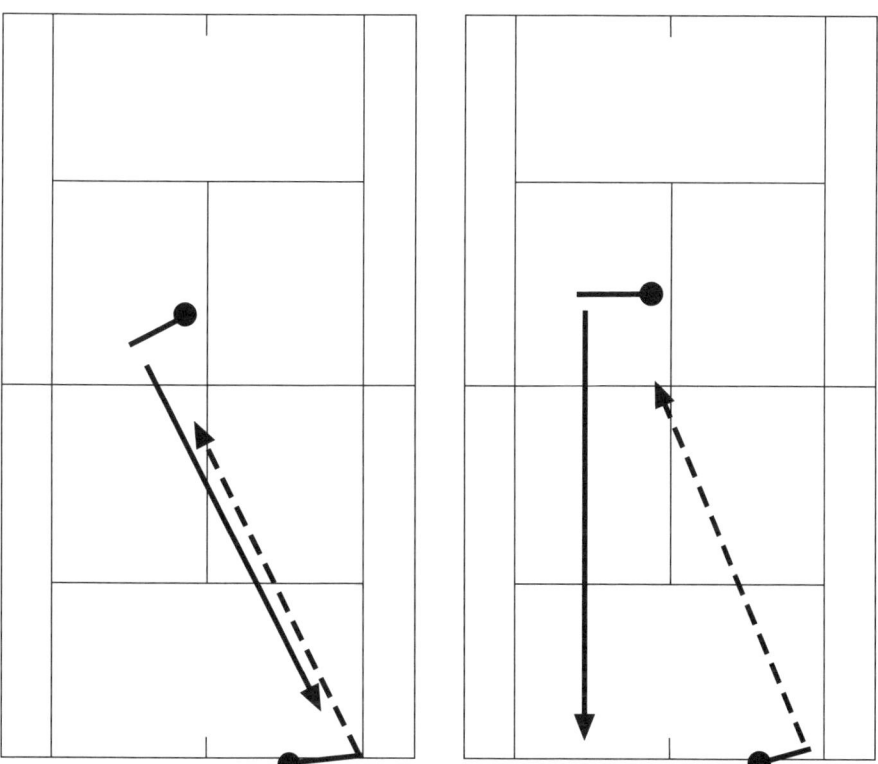

Figure 3.32 Outside volley with no change of direction

Figure 3.33 Outside volley with 90-degree change of direction

Note. Outside backhand volley options mirror the forehand examples.

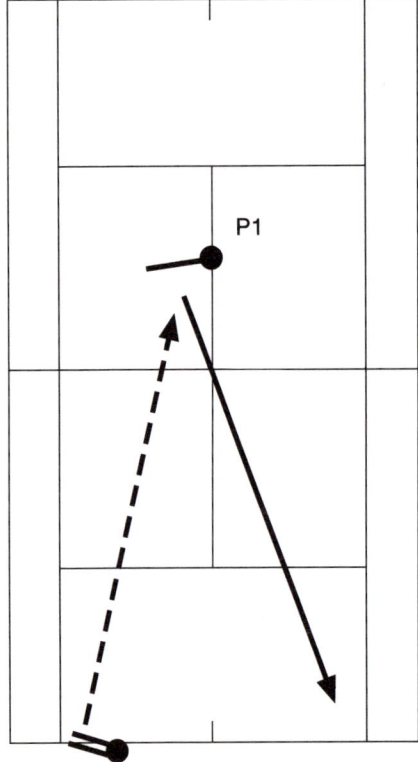

Figure 3.34 Change direction on inside forehand volleys

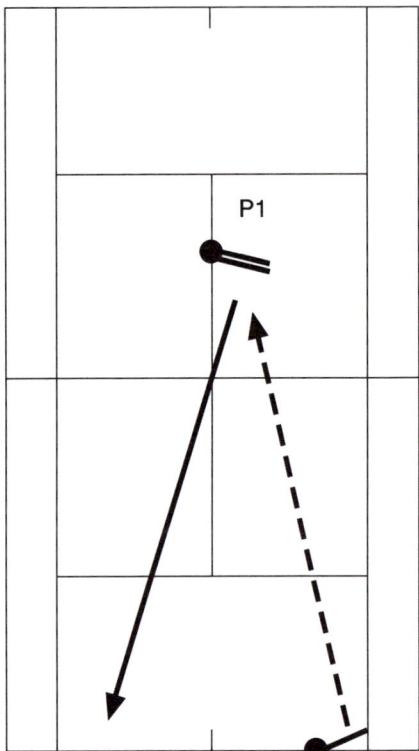

Figure 3.35 Change direction on inside backhand volleys

On outside volleys that players cannot control (low or heavy-paced outside passing shots), no change of direction is preferred. The player is in essence acknowledging that the opponent has hit a good shot, and as he or she is not in a position to control the ball, not changing direction allows him or her to close farther to the net, cutting down the passing angles. The hope is that the player will get a better volley opportunity on the next shot.

Inside Volleys

As with inside groundstrokes, inside forehand and inside backhand volleys require changing direction (see figures 3.34 and 3.35).

Recovery

Under pressure, players strive to get the rally back to neutral or, ideally, to gain an offensive advantage. The idea here is to recover what has been lost—the offensive. Maintaining composure and proper shot selection when being attacked takes discipline and practice. Again, the aim is to react to the ball and not to the situation. When pressured, players normally have two responses—counter with groundstroke drives or take the air out of the ball.

- **Groundstroke drives.** When countering with a groundstroke drive, follow the Directionals—no change of direction on outside groundstrokes and change direction on inside groundstrokes. It is very important not to change direction on outside balls where the recoverer is wide of the singles court. Following these guidelines when recovering will force opponents to change direction to win points and will create more inside opportunities on which the recoverer can regain the offensive.

- **Take the air out of the ball.** When pulled wide, players need to buy time to recover. This can be done by lobbing or looping the ball deep, which also forces opponents to choose the more difficult option of playing the ball out of the air from mid- or three-quarter court.

Anticipation

In 1993, Kenyon College had a first-year player with world-class speed based on the United States Tennis Association (USTA) fitness testing standards. She could fly on all the standardized tests, but when on the tennis court, her court coverage was average at best. Her problem was not her ability to move, but rather her ability to know when to move—she lacked anticipation. Slower, less athletic players with good anticipation covered the court much better than the speedy, athletic freshman.

The question for me became, "How do you teach anticipation?" Because anticipation relies on intuition and experience, the common wisdom has been that the more you play, the better you'll anticipate—exposure to repetitive situations will help you react more quickly as these situations occur in match play. Although this is true to some extent, there is an option to waiting and hoping for better anticipation. Anticipation can be enhanced and taught.

How do you teach anticipation? Instruct your players to react to their opponent as if the opponent plays by the Directionals. Most players use these patterns because the Directionals mirror natural play. If your opponent is hitting an inside groundstroke, move to cover the crosscourt return. If your opponent is hitting a deep outside groundstroke, move to cover the crosscourt return. If your opponent is hitting a deep outside groundstroke, expect the opponent to not change direction and return the ball back crosscourt. Watch the professionals and you will see how common these patterns are.

Reading the play, moving and covering areas of the court before the ball is hit is the key to developing anticipation. The Directionals give players sound reasons to base their court coverage options on and the immediate result is improved anticipation.

4

Court Position and Shot Selection

A French Open match between André Agassi and Michael Chang paints a vivid picture of the benefits of maintaining good court position. The match began with both players trading shots from the baseline. As the first set wore on, Agassi began playing inside the baseline while Chang moved back 2 to 3 feet behind the baseline. Agassi took immediate control of the match with his aggressive court position, and the first set and match were his.

Agassi's change in court position caused Chang to concede his own court position because of the change in spacing and timing. As a result, Chang lost depth, angle, and versatility.

- spacing,
- timing,
- depth,
- angle, and
- versatility.

• **Spacing.** Because players are used to a certain amount of spacing between themselves and their opponents, one player's change in court position has an opposite effect on the other player—Agassi moves up, Chang moves back.

• **Timing.** In addition to spacing, timing is affected by an opponent's court position. If Chang had elected to hold his court position, he would have had less time to prepare for Agassi's shots and an even more difficult time controlling points. Chang moved back to give himself more time to react to Agassi's penetrating groundstrokes.

Court Position and Shot Selection

Michael Chang playing behind the baseline

- **Depth.** Another by-product of Agassi's change in court position was improved depth for Agassi and decreased depth for Chang. Again, similar to being comfortable with spacing and timing between shots, players are also consistent with their shot length. For example, Chang's shots travel on the average between 68 and 75 feet to land consistently on the 78-foot-long tennis court. As Chang retreated, his shot length remained between 68 and 75 feet but his depth decreased by the amount of his lost court position, allowing Agassi to continue his assault from within the baseline.

- **Angle.** The closer a player is to the net, the greater the angle available. As Agassi moved inside the baseline, he created more angle to use in opening the width of the court. Chang, of course, gave himself even less angle to play with by moving behind the baseline.

- **Versatility.** With Chang camped out behind the baseline, he had very few tactical options other than just retrieving and defending. On the other hand, Agassi's court position offered a wide variety of effective tactical choices, from drop shots to approach shots to angled shots. Agassi's court position clearly allowed him to play a versatile all-court game.

Finding Your Zone

All-court tennis requires players to be comfortable playing from different areas of the court. The court can be divided into three tactical zones—a point-building zone, a pressuring zone, and a point-ending zone—that require different tactical decisions, strokes, and shot selections (see figure 4.1). The dimensions of each zone are relative to each player and his or her strokes; that is, Pete Sampras can easily pressure from the baseline with his forehand, whereas someone like Michael Chang is more comfortable pressuring from midcourt. The point here is that where a tactical zone begins and ends depends on the abilities of the player.

Point-building Zone

Note. I've adopted "point building" from the University of Texas women's coach, Jeff Moore. The concept of point building descriptively captures the essence of modern baseline play—build the point until pressure can be applied. Thanks Jeff!

This zone typically begins just in front of the baseline and extends behind it. As the zone's name indicates, point-building shots take place here and can

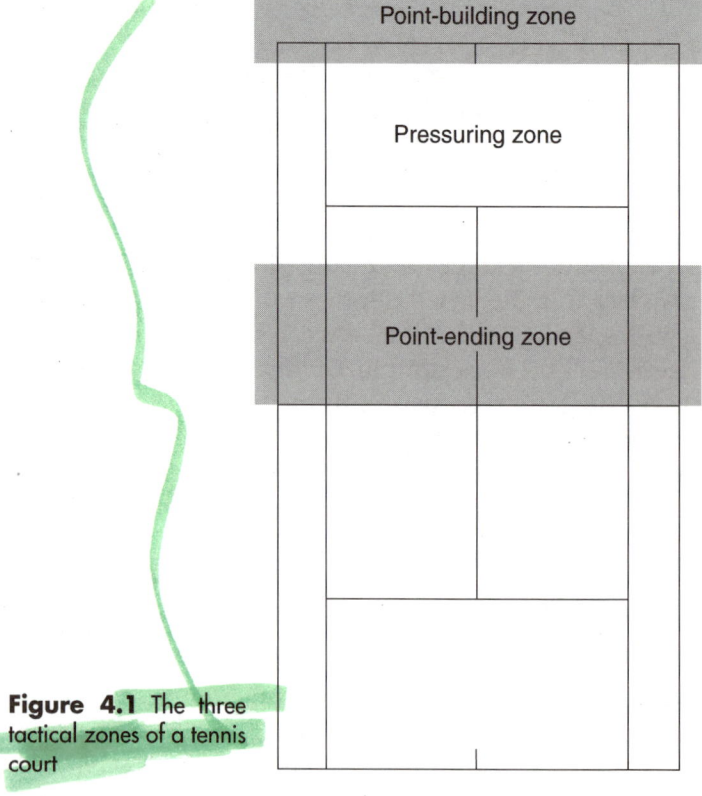

Figure 4.1 The three tactical zones of a tennis court

best be described as aggressive, controlled groundstrokes. When playing from the point-building zone, players try to create weak replies that allow them to apply pressure. Players remain aggressive when playing from the point-building zone, but a premium is placed on penetration through the baseline and net clearance (especially on outside groundstrokes). From a coaching standpoint, net or wide errors are inexcusable when hitting point-building shots.

Inside groundstrokes are one of the most productive forcing shots when playing from the point-building zone. Typically, an inside groundstroke creates other inside groundstrokes or short balls that can be used to apply pressure.

Pressuring Zone

The object of playing from this zone is to pressure an opponent, not to end the point. Forcing shots from three-quarter court, approach shots, and approach volleys are all hit from the pressuring zone. This is the beginning of at least a two-shot sequence—usually the pressuring shot and then the point-ending shot. By moving forward and playing the ball on the rise, a player can turn a point-building shot into a pressuring opportunity just by changing their court position.

Point-Ending Zone

After a pressuring shot, the player has an opportunity to end the point, usually with a volley, an overhead, or a combination of the two. Ideally, after a pressuring shot, the point should end in one shot, but players must be prepared for the ball to be returned. Losing a point after thinking it has been won can be a huge momentum shifter.

As the Agassi/Chang match reveals, the player with the best court position controls the match and most likely will be the winner. Of course, it is also a lot more fun to be controlling and dictating a match rather than just reacting.

From a tactical standpoint, players should not only be aware of their own court position, but of their opponent's court position as well. Although this sounds obvious, it is amazing how players become self-absorbed and think their difficulties are always of their own making. In the Agassi/Chang match, it would have been easy for Chang to blame his loss on poor play or his failure to maintain his court position. The lesson here, though, is that Chang lost his court position because of Agassi's aggressive court position. Future match preparation for Chang would include practicing having to maintain his own court position when his opponent changes court position. Court position is definitely a two-way street!

Shot Selection

Arantxa Sanchez Vicario's 1998 French Open fourth-round win against Serena Williams revealed the value of having a multidimensional shot selection. Williams slugged her way to a set and 5-2 lead with penetrating topspin drives before Sanchez Vicario rallied for the victory by looping, slicing, and selectively choosing her opportunities to drive balls and pressure. The unpredictability of Sanchez Vicario's pace, spin, and bounce unsettled the young Williams, leading to numerous unforced errors and the loss of the match.

The modern game of tennis is an athletic game of racket head acceleration and topspin. With high-tech rackets and open stances, players generate enormous pace and spin on groundstrokes and serves. Although topspin and power rule the day, it is still important for players to develop a variety of useful shots, as evidenced by Sanchez Vicario.

At a minimum, players must be able to hit three types of shots: the topspin drive, the slice, and the loop.

Arantxa Sanchez Vicario

- **Topspin drive.** Everyone's favorite, forehand and backhand drives, are usually the first strokes learned in tennis. Hit with topspin, drives are the predominant shots hit in a tennis match because it is the topspin drive that allows players to play offensive tennis. Typical aggressive groundstroke drives have a net clearance of 1 to 3 feet.

  Preferences: Best used when point building and when pressuring. A pressuring drive is hit flatter and with less topspin than a point-building drive.

- **Slice.** Hit with underspin, the slice bounces low and forces opponents to hit up to clear the net. The slice is necessary for hitting drop shots, very effective on approach shots, and excellent for neutralizing topspin drives.

  Preferences: Versatile shot used when point building, on approach shots (groundstrokes or volleys) when pressuring, and on volleys when ending the point. Most slices are hit with the backhand when point building and pressuring.

- **Loop.** Not to be confused with the lob, a loop is struck as aggressively as a drive but with more topspin and more net clearance. A looped groundstroke crosses an opponent's baseline at least at shoulder height.

  Preferences: An excellent choice when point building. The loop makes it difficult for opponents to maintain court position and creates short replies on which to apply pressure.

Not only should players be comfortable hitting these three shots, but they should also be comfortable hitting against these shots. Each player has an ideal hitting zone that suits their game and grips. Typically, the modern hitting zone is from thigh height to chest height. To keep shots out of an opponent's hitting zone, common sense dictates that good tactical players make their opponents play shots either below the knees (slice) or at shoulder height or above (loop). Alas, common sense rarely prevails in junior tennis, as players tend to hit what feels best, and that is the drive. The drive looks good and feels good, but unfortunately offers opponents the perfect ball to hit. The lesson here is that what a player desires does not always produce the most effective result. Imagine how many home runs Mark McGwire would have hit if pitchers threw only balls to his ideal hitting zone. I think that's called batting practice!

Tactically, sound tennis players, like baseball pitchers, keep balls out of their opponents' ideal hitting zones. All players are capable of playing their best when they feel comfortable. Tactically speaking, players keep opponents off balance and uncomfortable by making them hit against a variety of shots and spins that are out of the ideal hitting zone. As the old saying goes, variety is the spice of life, not to mention good tactical tennis. Just ask Arantxa Sanchez Vicario.

5

Teaching Tactics

It's one thing to have sound tactics, but it's another to effectively teach players these tactics and create a practice environment where the tactics are actually transferred to match play. The following tips and suggestions were gathered over the past seven years as I taught tactics at tennis camps, coaching clinics, and to my teams.

As mentioned in chapter 2, I recommend a three-step process when teaching technique or tactics.

- **Step 1: Soft-toss feeds.** Feeders stand 5 to 10 feet in front of a player and toss balls underhand. The slowness of the feed helps reveal players' technique, as they must generate pace from no pace. The feeder's proximity to the player makes coaching much more effective by allowing for ease of dialogue and close-up viewing. In a team practice, players can soft toss to each other, allowing the coach to roam and teach.

- **Step 2: Feeds from across the net.** After soft tossing, feed from the service line or baseline across the net. Feeding from across the net allows the feeder to generate matchlike pace and creates realistic angles from which to feed. Typically, the player's shots are not returned.

- **Step 3: Live-ball rally.** The final step in the instruction process is to play out the point as it would be in a match, with shots being returned until the point or sequence ends. Live-ball rallies simulate match play and allow players to demonstrate their technique and tactics at match pace.

Coach soft tossing to a player

Thinking-Out-Loud Training

It's easy to assume players will learn tactics after being shown the concepts and patterns on the court or chalkboard. The reality is that players must learn how to think tactically. I find this is best accomplished by what I call "thinking-out-loud" training. For example, if players are learning to distinguish between inside and outside groundstrokes, have them say "outside" when hitting outside groundstrokes and "inside" when hitting inside groundstrokes. In this example, having the player verbalize the stroke being hit tells the coach whether the player is grasping the concept and makes the player mentally aware of what he or she is doing.

Whenever players are learning a concept for the first time—whether Directionals, court position, or shot selection—have them "think out loud." There is no better way to know what players are really thinking, or even if they are thinking at all.

Teaching the Directionals

Putting the pieces of the Directionals together requires a reasoned progression so that tactical development coincides with technical development and match results are not sacrificed. The best way to proceed is by teaching and emphasizing the Directionals in the following order:

- Outside groundstrokes
- Inside groundstrokes
- Ninety-degree change-of-direction shots

Outside Groundstrokes

Points typically unfold in the following manner. Crosscourt shots are exchanged until an inside groundstroke or a short outside groundstroke opportunity arises. Crosscourt groundstrokes, including the inside-out forehand, are the bedrock of most offensive and defensive games. The first step in becoming a tactical player is learning how to hit outside groundstrokes with emphasis on patience, placement, depth, spin, and pace—in that order. Even though outside groundstrokes are the least offensive-oriented shots of the Directionals, hitting deep crosscourt shots is high-percentage tennis and entices opponents into change-of-direction errors. Players won't hit many crosscourt outside groundstroke winners, but their opponents will at least have to hit a lot of balls and make many more low-percentage winners.

Initially, location and depth are the essential areas of concern when hitting outside groundstrokes. Outside groundstroke rallies need to be diagonal rather than vertical, with shots landing out of the middle third of the court (figure 5.1). The concept of changing the rally from a vertical to a diagonal rally is called "shifting the court" (figure 5.2). Tennis is a diagonal game, not a vertical one. Typically, less advanced play involves vertical rallies—ones

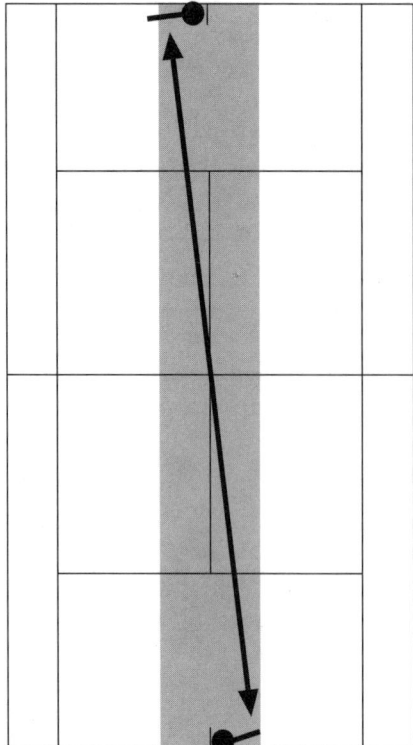

Figure 5.1 Vertical forehand rally in the middle third of the court

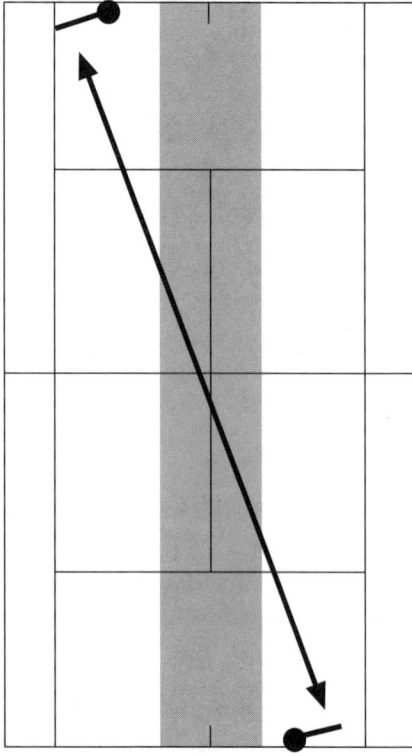

Figure 5.2 Court shifted to diagonal forehand rally

that take place in the middle third of the court. Effective high-level tennis requires diagonal rallies—ones that take place outside the middle third of the court. Shifting the court is simply a matter of hitting away from the middle third of the court. The concept is important in communicating to players that the rally is too vertical. Most important, the Directionals are more effective when the court has been shifted diagonally. Playing high-level points involves a shifted court with groundstrokes being hit through the baseline, not the sideline. Again, the emphasis is on penetration and not width.

Inside Groundstrokes

Hitting outside groundstrokes well will generate numerous inside groundstroke opportunities. The key is learning to take control of the point and advantage of these inside opportunities by making inside groundstrokes pressuring shots. The pressure is created by penetrating the baseline and not worrying about width. Also, the inside groundstroke is a player's opportunity to change direction and hit to the open court, making his or her opponent hit while moving.

As discussed earlier, the inside ball is one of the shots whereby players can't see their target as they hit the ball. Therefore, learning to judge and develop a feel for where to hit the ball is half the battle in becoming proficient on inside groundstrokes. Players typically hit inside groundstrokes well from the baseline, since the inside groundstroke tends to be natural. Inside groundstrokes from the three-quarter-court area are more difficult to hit, since the ball is hit on the rise and played from an unfamiliar court position in no-man's-land. Establishing court position inside the baseline during rallies and taking the ball on the rise are the two key areas to develop for most players. Again, players should remember to focus on penetrating the baseline rather than striving for width or angle.

Changing Direction on Outside Groundstrokes

Hitting outside and inside groundstrokes well is one of the essentials of a backcourt-based game. The next area to focus on is the 90-degree change-of-direction (COD) shot on short outside shots. The first step is for players to eliminate the mental image of aiming at the line when hitting 90-degree COD shots. Like inside groundstrokes, 90-degree COD shots should cross the baseline before the sideline. Again, the emphasis is on penetration and not width. These shots are usually part of a sequence and not point-enders. Players must also realize that hitting from the three-quarter-court area or shorter requires a different stroke than hitting from the baseline. Players typically make deep errors on approach shots because they use their baseline groundstroke from the midcourt.

Court shifted to diagonal forehand rally.

Following the above progression will produce a tactically sound player. Individuality will develop as players gravitate toward their particular style and physical, mental, emotional, and technical strengths and weaknesses become apparent. Will the player split the court in half or play with a weapon? Will a weapon be developed later? Will the player be an all-court player, a baseliner, or a serve-and-volleyer?

Directional Temptations

Following the Directionals makes play natural and uncomplicated and creates numerous change-of-direction temptations for opponents. As players consistently make correct change-of-direction decisions, they find their opponents continually taking the bait by hitting to the open court, making change-of-direction errors—usually on deep outside groundstrokes. However, two temptations arise for the player using the Directionals.

   1. **Going for too much angle on inside groundstrokes.** Inside groundstrokes cannot be missed wide! The inside groundstroke gives a player control of the point and should be thought of as part of a sequence and rarely a point-ender. Ensuring that inside groundstrokes cross the baseline before the sideline will aid in resisting this temptation. Again, emphasis should be on penetration through the baseline, not on width.

   2. **Changing direction on deep outside groundstrokes.** The shot may look easy and the court may be open, but the player is hitting a difficult, low-percentage groundstroke. If the player misses the 90 COD shot, he or

she will either hit wide or more to the middle, giving the opponent an inside groundstroke and control of the point. Players must know their limitations and carefully choose when to change direction on outside groundstrokes. The shorter the outside ball to change direction on, the better!

Tactics shape a pressure training system and give each drill and shot in practice a purpose. The difficulty lies not in creating tactics, however, but in teaching players how to use the tactics, especially when under pressure. The pressure drills that follow have been designed to develop players in a systematic and progressive fashion, regardless of level of ability. From singles drills to doubles drills, one thing is certain—players will be under pressure.

6

Singles Drills

Now we finally get to the fun part, the heart and soul of a pressure training system—the drills. Organized by tactical areas, the singles drills are games in which score is kept and players win or lose (just as in a tennis match). The drills create an environment whereby the game teaches the game by putting players into situations where they must problem-solve and make decisions, ultimately figuring out how to get the job done given the parameters of the drill. Challenging, instructive, pressuring, crazy, and fun—the singles drills are all that and more.

The singles drills are organized into five tactical categories:

1. First exchanges
2. Point building
3. Spin
4. Pressuring
5. Recovery

First-exchange drills. At the most elementary level, players must be able to start points by hitting their serves in and their returns in play. As obvious and as easy as this sounds, the serve and return present numerous problems. Like shooting free throws in basketball and putting in golf, the server has complete control over the outcome of the task and unfortunately plenty of time to think about the various possibilities—positive and negative. Regardless of the level of play, serving can be a pressure-packed experience. The sheer number of double faults on big points at major tournaments serves as testament to the psychological pressure servers are under.

From a server's standpoint, I stress the second serve first, the doubles first serve second, and finally the singles first serve. From a returner's standpoint, I stress getting the point started on first-serve returns and pressuring the server on second-serve returns.

Surprisingly few points last beyond four shots, including the serve and return. Making players aware of the importance of the first few shots is vital and the reason many of the service drills are from two- to five-shot sequences.

At a more advanced level, first exchanges—the serve and return—dictate how a point unfolds. Players look to take control of points by immediately pressuring with their first serve or off a second-serve return.

Point-building drills. The foundation of a tennis game, point-building or baseline drills focus on the effective use of groundstrokes in creating pressuring opportunities. Players are under control yet remain aggressive, waiting to capitalize on short replies or inside groundstrokes.

Spin or shot-selection drills (loop, slice, or drive). At a minimum, players should be proficient at hitting and hitting against each of these three shots. Being able to hit a variety of spin enables players to adjust comfortably to different playing styles and, most important, keep shots out of opponents' ideal hitting zones.

Pressuring drills. Putting opponents under pressure by approaching the net off penetrating groundstrokes and volleys from three-quarter court and in, pressuring drills are high energy and action packed.

Recovery drills. The recovery drills are very popular with players, not to mention a lot of fun. Although improving recovery and defense is the aim, recovery drills also involve pressuring and are very beneficial in developing and improving pressuring and point-ending skills.

In addition to the tactical drills, there are sections on singles play and crazy drills. The singles drills are fun and beneficial alternatives to playing regular sets and matches of singles in practice. There is an endless variety of creative ways to play sets and tiebreakers; however, remember to keep these drills productive and purposeful. The crazy drills blend in well with a pressure practice, and although they are not competitive and last only a minute or less, there is no better return on the practice time invested.

First-Exchange Drills— Serves and Returns

1 Two-Shot 20 Second Serves With Returns

Purpose

To practice second serves and Directional returns of second serves

Time

Untimed (Approximately 10 minutes).

Procedure—Full Singles Court

1. P1 serves 10 second serves to the deuce court and 10 second serves to the ad court while P2 returns using Directional patterns.
2. Drill repeats with P2 serving 20 second serves and P1 returning.
3. Points end after the return.

   P1 serves and P2 returns.

   P1: Serves second serve.

   P2: Returns second serve using Directionals (outside ball, no change of direction or inside ball, change directions).

   Inside-out forehand returns are allowable from the ad court.

Scoring

Count number of serves made. For example, P1 makes 18 out of 20 second serves. My standard for success is for the server to make at least 17 or more serves out of 20.

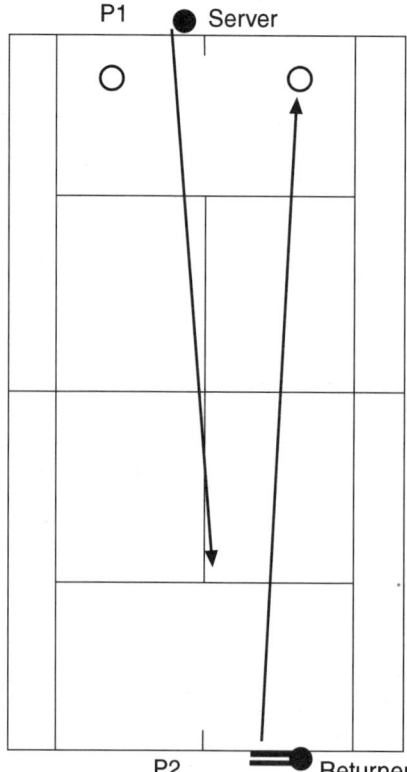

Drill 1 Two-Shot 20 Second Serves With Returns

Key Points

- The returner emphasizes shifting the court (starting the point on a diagonal) and forcing the server to move.
- The returner uses the Directionals for return guidelines—outside groundstroke, no change of direction and inside groundstroke, change directions.
- This is an excellent drill for the returner to learn return patterns before proceeding to more advanced return drills.

Variations

1. Targets for returner are helpful.
2. Server can be assigned location for second serve.
3. Server may serve and volley the entire drill or occasionally.
4. Returner has to hit all returns with the forehand, looking to pressure immediately.
5. Inside-out forehand returns are allowable from the ad court.

2 Four-Shot 20 Second Serves With Returns

Purpose

To practice second serves and Directional returns of second serves.
To practice the first four shots of a point.

Time

Untimed (Approximately 15 minutes).

Procedure—Full Singles Court

1. P1 serves 10 second serves to the deuce court and 10 second serves to the ad court while P2 returns using Directional patterns.
2. After the serve and return, each player hits a groundstroke.
3. Drill repeats with P2 serving 20 second serves and P1 returning.

   P1 serves and P2 returns.

   P1: Serves second serve.

   P2: Returns second serve.

   P1: Hits groundstroke.

   P2: Hits groundstroke.

   Point is stopped after fourth shot (P2's second shot).

Scoring

Count number of serves made. For example, P1 makes 18 out of 20 second serves. My standard for success is for the server to make at least 17 or more serves out of 20.

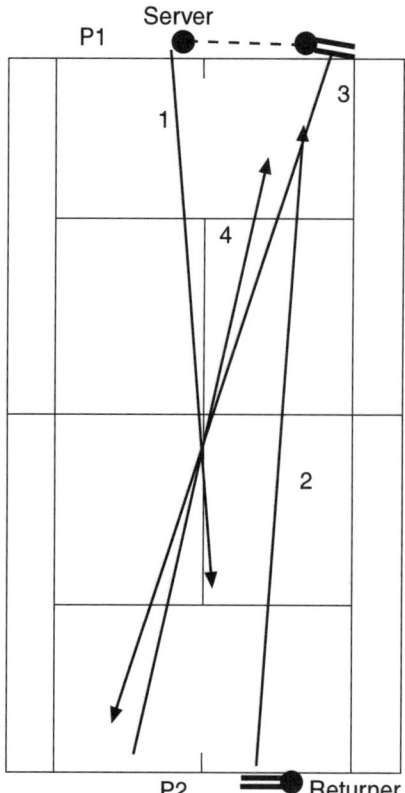

Drill 2 Four-Shot 20 Second Serves With Returns

Key Points

- This is a great drill for working on second serves and returns of second serves while reinforcing the need to react quickly to aggressive, penetrating returns.
- As very few points in a match even make it past the first four shots, players learn to begin points.

Variations

1. Server can be assigned location for second serve.
2. Server may serve and volley the entire drill or occasionally.
3. Returners may approach off returns.
4. Returner has to hit all returns with the forehand, looking to pressure immediately.

3 Four-Shot Pressuring Returns (X Marks the Spot)

Purpose

To teach returners how to take control of a point by pressuring off the second serve with their forehands.

Time

Untimed (Approximately 15 minutes).

Procedure—Full Singles Court

1. P1 serves 10 second serves to the deuce court and 10 second serves to the ad court while P2 returns.
2. After the serve and return, each player hits a groundstroke.
3. The returner hits all returns with the forehand.
4. Returners must stand on the chalked X with the left foot when the server tosses. (The X is on the center mark on the baseline on deuce-court returns and in the alley on ad court returns.)

   P1 serves and P2 returns.

   P1: Serves second serve.

   P2: Pressures with forehand.

   P1: Recovers with a groundstroke.

   P2: Pressures again.

   Point is stopped after fourth shot (P2's second pressuring shot).

Scoring

Count number of serves made. For example, P1 makes 18 out of 20 second serves. My standard for success is for the server to make at least 17 or more serves out of 20.

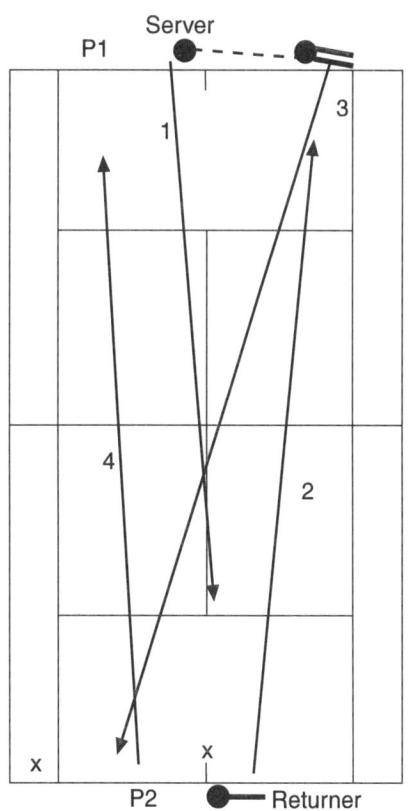

Drill 3 Four-Shot Pressuring Returns (X Marks the Spot)

Key Points

- Inside-out forehands are recommended for ad court returns.
- Showing forehand puts tremendous pressure on the server, and returners are surprised how effectively they return when starting at the X.

Variations

1. Server can be assigned location for second serve.
2. Returners may approach off returns.

4 Five-Shot 20 Second Serves—Serve and Volley

Purpose

To practice serving and volleying.
To simulate the first five shots of a serve-and-volley point beginning with a second serve.

Time

Untimed (Approximately 15 minutes).

Procedure—Full Singles Court

1. P1, serving and volleying, serves 10 second serves to the deuce court and 10 second serves to the ad court while P2 returns.
2. After the serve and return, the server hits two volleys and the returner hits one groundstroke. Serve returns are hit directly at the server ensuring a first volley is hit.
3. After the first volley, the returner may pass the server. The sequence ends on P1's second volley.

   P1 serves and P2 returns.

   P1: Serves second serve.

   P2: Returns second serve to server.

   P1: Volleys.

   P2: Hits passing shot.

   P1: Volleys.

   Point is stopped after fifth shot (P1's second volley).

Scoring

Count number of serves made. For example, P1 makes 18 out of 20 second serves. My standard for success is for the server to make at least 17 or more serves out of 20.

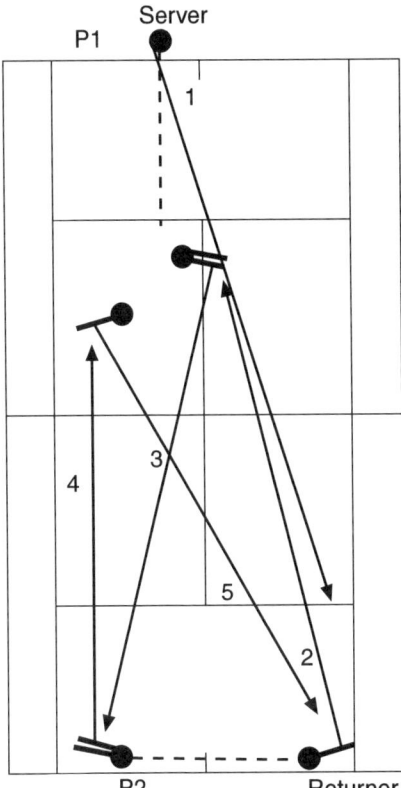

Drill 4 Five-Shot 20 Second Serves—Serve and Volley

Key Points

- This is a great drill for developing serving and volleying skills and practicing returning against an attacking player.
- The volleyer learns to penetrate the baseline on first volleys creating point-ending opportunities on the second volley.
- Excellent drill for practicing Directional volley guidelines.

Variations

1. Server can be assigned location for second serve.
2. Returner must use Directional patterns.
3. Volleyer uses Directional volley guidelines.
4. First volley is deep and second volley is angled short.

5 Four-Shot 20 Second Serves With Drop-Shot Returns

Purpose
To practice hitting drop-shot returns off second serves.

Time
Untimed (approximately 15 minutes).

Procedure—Full Singles Court

1. P1 serves 10 second serves to the deuce court and 10 second serves to the ad court while P2 hits drop-shot returns.
2. After the serve and drop-shot return, the server hits whatever shot is possible and the returner either passes or lobs the server.

   P1 serves and P2 returns.

   P1: Serves second serve.

   P2: Hits drop-shot return.

   P1: Returns drop shot.

   P2: Hits passing shot or lob.

   Point is stopped after fourth shot (P2's second volley).

Scoring
Count number of serves made. For example, P1 makes 18 out of 20 second serves. My standard for success is for the server to make at least 17 or more serves out of 20.

Key Points
- Returner drop-shots using Directional patterns.
- Server returns drop-shot return down-the-line to limit the returner's passing shot angles.

Variation
1. Server can be assigned location for second serve.

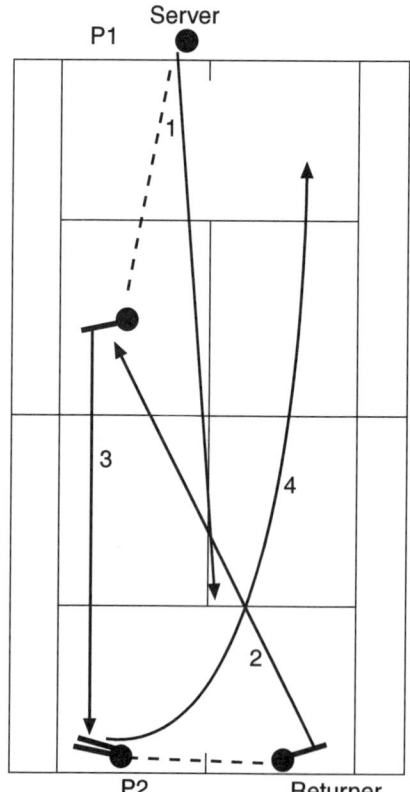

Drill 5 Four-Shot 20 Second Serves With Drop-Shot Returns

6 Four-Shot 20 Service Points

Purpose

To practice pressuring with the first serve and return of the second serve.

Time

Untimed (approximately 15 minutes).

Procedure—Full Singles Court

1. Servers have a first and second serve for each point sequence.
2. Each player serves 20 points—10 to the deuce court and 10 to the ad court.
3. After the serve and return, each player hits a groundstroke.

   P1 serves and P2 returns.

   P1: Serves first serve and then second serve, if needed.

   P2: Returns serve.

   P1: Hits groundstroke.

   P2: Hits groundstroke.

   Point is stopped after fourth shot (P2's second shot).

   Four-shot sequence begins with P1's serve.

Scoring

Count number of first serves made or double faults. Two or fewer double faults are desirable.

Key Points

- With a first and second serve, servers can work on pressuring with the first serve and returners with the second serve.
- Servers learn the value of making first serves and taking immediate control of the point.
- Returners focus on starting the point when returning first serves and pressuring off second serves.

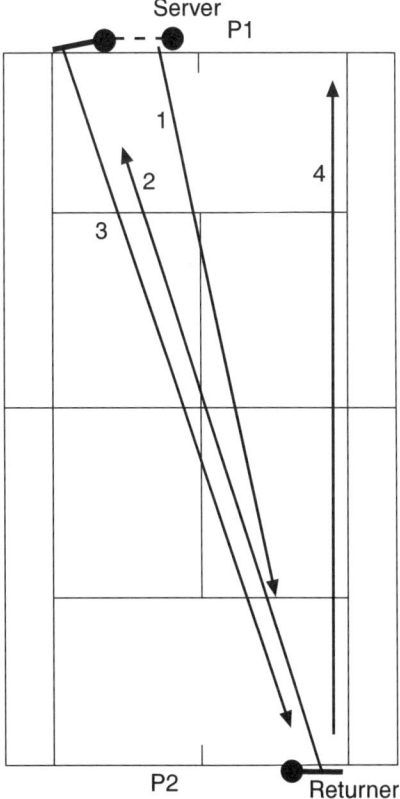

Drill 6 Four-Shot 20 Service Points

Variations

1. Server can be assigned location for first and/or second serve.
2. Returner must use Directional patterns.
3. Server may serve and volley the entire drill or occasionally.
4. Returners may approach off second-serve returns.
5. Returner has to hit all second-serve returns with the forehand, looking to immediately pressure.

7 First-Serve Game

Purpose

To practice pressuring with the first serve.
To practice returning aggressive first serves.

Time

Three-, 4-, or 5-minute games.

Procedure—Full Singles Court

1. With an emphasis on pressuring with the first serve, each server is allowed two first serves and a second serve per point.
2. P1 serves two points, one to the deuce court and one to the ad court. P2 then serves two points, one to the deuce court and one to the ad court. Repeat sequence until time is called.

    P1 serves and P2 returns.

    P1: Serves first serve, then another first serve (if needed), and then a second serve (if needed).

    P2: Returns serve.

    Point is played out.

Scoring

One-point scoring.

Key Points

- Location on first serves is as important as pace.
- Servers create openings by serving wide or down the middle.
- Return difficult first serves down the middle of the court to keep the court closed and to start the point.
- Use Directional return patterns when returning.

Variations

1. Server can be assigned location for first and/or second serves.
2. Server may serve and volley.
3. Returner must use Directional patterns.
4. Returners win two points off second-serve points.
5. Returners may approach off second-serve returns.
6. Returner has to hit all second-serve returns with the forehand, looking to pressure immediately.

8 First-Strike Game

Purpose

To develop the first serve as a weapon.
To practice creating pressuring opportunities with the first serve.

Time

Six-minute games divided into two 3-minute segments.

Procedure—Full Singles Court

1. Hitting only first serves, servers score a point if they achieve a first strike—serve an ace or service winner, force a return error or short reply that is put away, or hit a serve-and-volley winner.
2. P1 serves to the deuce court until achieving a first strike, then serves to the ad court until achieving another first strike, and then it's back to the deuce court.
3. After P1 serves for 3 minutes, P2 serves for 3 minutes.

    P1 serves and P2 returns.

    P1: Serves only first serves.

    P2: Returns serve.

    Point is played out.

Scoring

One point for each first strike.

Key Points

- A Jeff Moore original from the University of Texas, the First-Strike Game emphasizes developing the first serve as a weapon.

- Server adopts an aggressive attitude—"I will strike first."
- Location on first serves is as important as pace.
- Servers create openings by serving wide or down the middle.
- Return difficult first serves down the middle of the court to keep the court closed and to start the point.
- Returners use Directional returns.

Variations

1. Server can be assigned location for first serves.
2. Returner must use Directional patterns.

9 Pressuring Serve/Return Game

Purpose

To create a pressuring mindset when serving first serves and returning second serves.

To practice pressuring with first serves and pressuring when returning second serves.

Time

Three-, 4-, or 5-minute games.

Procedure—Full Singles Court

1. Servers have two serves, a first and a second.
2. Servers pressure with their first serves while returners pressure with their second serve returns.
3. P1 serves two points, one to the deuce court and one to the ad court. P2 then serves two points, one to the deuce court and one to the ad court. Repeat sequence until time is called.

    P1 serves and P2 returns.

    P1: Serves a pressuring first serve or a second serve, if needed.

    P2: Returns first serve or pressures off second serve.

    Point is played out.

Scoring

Players score two points if they win the point as a direct result of pressuring with either the first serve or the return of a second serve. One-point scoring otherwise. Again, pressuring means to put the server or returner on the defensive by taking the offensive. Also, "direct result" can be ambiguous, and players will have to use their judgment here. Whether the point lasts two or five shots, the question to ask is, "Did the pressuring serve or pressuring return dictate the outcome of the point?"

Key Points

- The primary focus is on adopting the right attitude when serving and returning—"I will create an attacking opportunity."
- This drill is also very helpful so players can become aware of how points unfold as direct result of their pressuring initiatives.

Variations

1. Returners may approach off second-serve returns.
2. Returners have to hit all second-serve returns with the forehand.

Point-Building Drills

10 Crosscourts—Deuce and Ad Court

Purpose

To practice building points with outside groundstrokes.

Time

Three- or 4-minute games.

Procedure—Half a Singles Court on the Diagonal

1. The game is played diagonally on either the deuce or ad court.
2. Players must recover to a chalked line one pace from the baseline center mark by touching the line with the inside foot (left foot on the deuce court). Recovery ensures players move realistically as if playing the entire singles court.
3. Ideally, only forehands should be hit from the deuce court and backhands from the ad court.
4. P1 serves two points, then P2 serves two points. Players have only one serve per point.

    P1: Serves second serve.

P2: Returns crosscourt.
P1: Hits forehand crosscourt.
P2: Hits forehand crosscourt.
Point is played out crosscourt.

Scoring

One-point scoring for net, wide, or deep errors, or a combination of the three, depending on the level of play or where you are in the season.

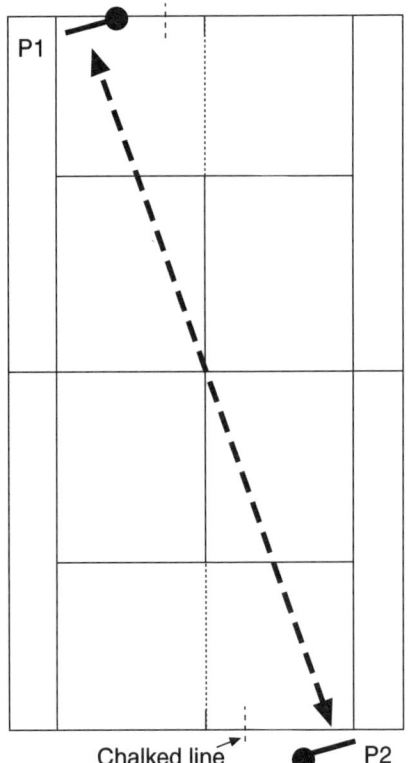

Drill 10 Crosscourts—Deuce and Ad Court

Key Points

- Tactical tennis, especially when using the Directionals, must begin with a proper foundation in crosscourt play.
- These crosscourt games are tennis' most essential drill.
- Effective crosscourts create pressuring opportunities by producing inside and short outside groundstrokes.
- Players should focus on high net clearance and avoid wide errors.
- Point-Building is most effective when players use aggressive topspin drives and loops.

Variations

1. Two-point errors for net or wide errors.
2. Feeds rather than second serves to start point.

11 Crosscourts—Inside-Out Forehands (Ad Court)

Purpose

To practice building points with inside-out forehands from the ad court.

Time

Four-minute game with two 2-minute segments. For example, P1 hits inside-out forehands for 2 minutes, then P2 hits inside-out forehands for 2 minutes.

Procedure - Half A Singles Court On the Diagonal

1. Point is played out crosscourt from the ad court with the server hitting backhands and the returner hitting inside-out forehands.
2. P1, hitting backhands, aims at a chalk mark one pace from the center mark of P2's baseline, making the drill more realistic for the inside-out player.
3. P1 must recover to a chalked line one pace from the baseline center mark by touching the line with her inside foot (right foot).
4. Players have only one serve per point.

    P1: Serves second serve to the ad court.

    P2: Returns crosscourt, ideally with an inside-out forehand.

    P1: Hits backhand crosscourt.

    P2: Hits inside-out forehand crosscourt.

Point is played out crosscourt from the ad court.

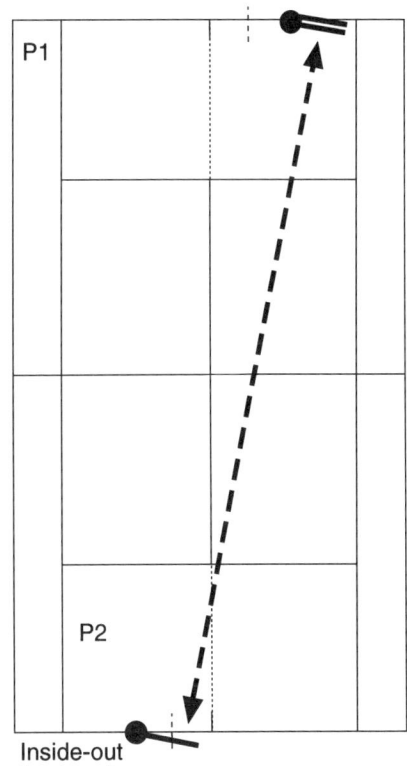

Drill 11 Crosscourts—Inside-Out Forehands (Ad Court)

Scoring

One-point scoring.

Key Points

- Players who play with a weapon must practice hitting point-building inside-out forehands from the ad court.
- Inside-out forehands should penetrate the baseline with ample net clearance.
- The focus is on creating short replies from which to pressure.

Variations

1. Two-point errors for net or wide errors.
2. If the inside-out forehand player is inside the baseline, he or she may hit to the deuce court by turning on the inside ball (90 COD). The point is then played out on the full singles court.
3. Feeds rather than serves to start point.

12 Crosscourts With Inside Groundstroke Change of Direction

Purpose

To practice creating and capitalizing on inside groundstroke opportunities when building points.

Time

Three- or 4-minute games.

Procedure—Full Singles Court

1. The drill begins as either a deuce-court or an ad-court drill.
2. When an inside groundstroke change of direction occurs, the point is played out on a full singles court.
3. Players must recover to a chalked line one pace from the baseline center mark after hitting an outside groundstroke to make the drill realistic.
4. P1 serves two deuce-court points, then P2 serves two deuce-court points. Players have only one serve per point.

    P1: Serves second serve.

    P2: Returns crosscourt.

    P1: Hits forehand crosscourt (inside groundstroke COD is allowed).

P2: Hits forehand crosscourt (inside groundstroke COD is allowed).
Point is played out on a full singles court after an inside COD occurs.

Scoring

One-point scoring.

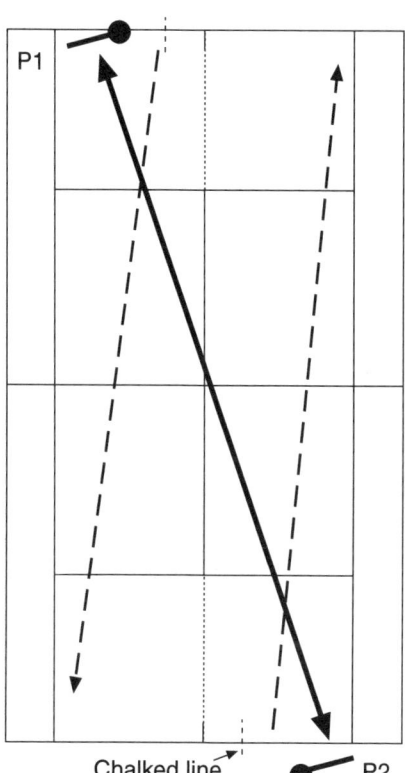

Drill 12 Crosscourts With Inside Groudstroke Change of Direction

Key Points

- This Crosscourt drill allows the players to hit to the open court on inside groundstrokes using the Inside Groundstroke Change of Direction guidelines.
- To change direction on the inside groundstroke, players should be aggressive with their court position and look to take the ball on the rise.
- To generate more inside opportunities, the focus must be on aggressive, penetrating outside groundstrokes. The outside creates the inside!

Variations

1. Two-point errors for net, wide, or change-of-direction errors.
2. Feeds rather than serves to start point.

13 Crosscourts With 90-Degree Change of Direction

Purpose

To practice building points and pressuring on short outside groundstrokes. To practice changing directions on outside groundstrokes using the 90-degree change-of-direction guideline.

Time

Three- or 4-minute games.

Procedure—Full Singles Court

1. The drill begins as either a deuce-court or an ad-court drill.
2. When a 90-degree COD occurs, the point is played out on a full singles court.
3. Players must recover to a chalked line one pace from the baseline center mark by touching the line with the inside foot (left foot on the deuce court) to make the drill realistic.
4. Ideally, only forehands should be hit from the deuce court and backhands from the ad court.
5. P1 serves two points, then P2 serves two points. Players have only one serve per point.

    P1: Serves second serve.

    P2: Returns crosscourt.

    P1: Hits forehand crosscourt (90 COD is allowed with proper court position).

    P2: Hits forehand crosscourt (90 COD is allowed with proper court position).

    Point is played out on a full singles court after a 90-degree change of direction occurs.

Scoring

One-point scoring.

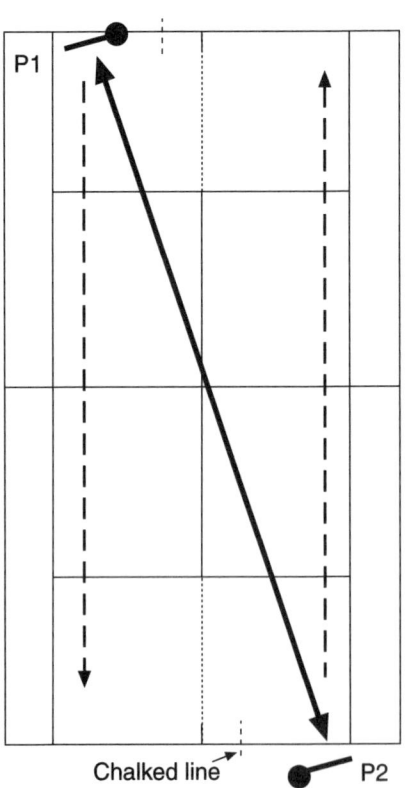

Drill 13 Crosscourts With 90-Degree Change of Direction

Key Points

- Players learn to recognize outside change-of-direction opportunities by focusing on their court position (on or inside the baseline), ability to retain balance and the degree of pressure they are under.
- Each player will have his or her own range with 90-degree change-of-direction shots. Learning their limitations is essential.
- When changing direction on outside groundstrokes use the principle of 90-degree COD, regardless of court position.
- To generate more short outside opportunities, the focus must be on aggressive, penetrating outside groundstrokes. Pressuring outside groundstrokes create 90-degree COD opportunities!

Variations

1. Two-point errors for net, wide, or change-of-direction errors.
2. Feeds rather than serves to start point.

14 Shifting-the-Court

Purpose

To practice making a vertical baseline rally a diagonal baseline rally.

Time

Three- or 4-minute games.

Procedure—Full Singles Court

1. Drill is played either on a deuce or ad court, depending on how the court is shifted off the feed.
2. Players must recover to a chalked line one pace from the baseline center mark by touching the line with the inside foot (left foot on the deuce court).

   P1: Feeds ball up the middle.

   P2: Shifts court with either forehand or backhand (forehand shifts to deuce court, backhand shifts to ad court).

   Point is played out on the diagonal.

   P1 feeds two points, then P2 feeds two points.

Scoring

One-point scoring.

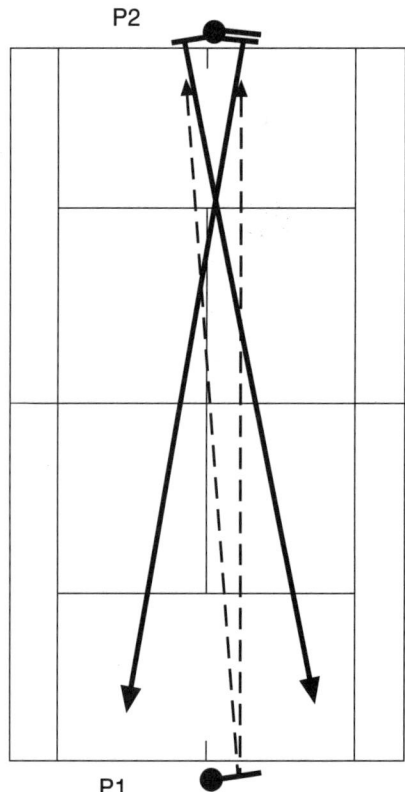

Drill 14 Shifting-the-Court

Key Points

- Tennis is a diagonal game, not a vertical one.
- Effective high-level tennis requires diagonal rallies—rallies that take place outside the middle third of the court.
- Shifting the court is just a matter of hitting away from the middle third of the court. The concept is important in communicating to players that the rally is too vertical.

Variations

1. Two-point errors for net or wide errors.
2. Play full-court points once court has been shifted (Directionals can be used).

15 Directionals—Coach-Fed Drill

Purpose

To teach players Directional concepts in a controlled live-ball point situation.

Time

Six-minute games with two 3-minute segments. Games can also be played to 11 rather than for time.

Procedure—Full Singles Court

1. A player is fed either an inside, deep outside, or short outside groundstroke and the point is played out on a singles court, with players only allowed to change direction on inside groundstrokes or short outside groundstrokes.
2. The player receiving the feed calls out "inside," "outside," or "90" to indicate that the concepts are grasped.
3. The coach feeds from the deuce- or ad-court alley about three-quarter-court depth.

   Coach: Feeds either inside ball, outside ball, or short outside ball to P1.

   P1: Uses Directional patterns calling out "inside, outside, or 90" depending on feed.

   P2: Uses Directional patterns.

   Point is played out on a full singles court with both players following the Directionals.

Scoring

One-point scoring.

Drill 15 Directionals—Coach-Fed Drill

Key Points

- A Chuck Kriese original, this is the first live-ball drill I use when teaching players the Directionals.
- This is an excellent drill for applying Directional concepts at match speed.
- Naming the shot verifies that the Directional concepts are being grasped.

Variations

1. Two-point errors for net or wide errors.
2. Coach feeds from random places behind the baseline.

16 Directionals—Inside Groundstroke Change of Direction

Purpose

To practice the first two Directional patterns—outside groundstroke, no change of direction and inside groundstroke, change direction.

Time

Five-minute games.

Procedure—Full Singles Court

1. Point is played out with players changing direction only on inside groundstrokes.
2. After hitting outside groundstrokes, players must recover to a chalked line one pace from the baseline center mark by touching the line with the inside foot (left foot on the deuce court).
3. P1 serves two points, one to the deuce court and one to the ad court. P2 then serves deuce and ad court points.
4. Players have only one serve per point.

    P1: Serves second serve.

    P2: Returns serve crosscourt if outside, changes direction if inside.

    P1: Hits groundstroke crosscourt following Directional patterns.

    Point is played out with players changing directions only on inside groundstrokes.

Scoring

One-point scoring.

Key Points

- This Directional drill allows the players to change direction only on inside groundstrokes.
- Players may hit through the middle on purpose to give opponents inside balls on which to change direction.
- When returning, returners can change direction only on inside serves.

Variations

1. Two-point errors for net or wide errors.
2. Players have a first and a second serve.
3. Players call out "inside" when changing direction.

17 Directionals—Inside and 90-Degree Change of Direction

Purpose

To practice Directional patterns and changing directions on inside and short outside groundstrokes.

Time

Five-minute games.

Procedure—Full Singles Court

1. Point is played out with players changing direction only on inside and short outside groundstrokes.
2. After hitting outside groundstrokes, players must recover to a chalked line one pace from the baseline center mark by touching the line with the inside foot (left foot on the deuce court).
3. P1 serves two points, one to the deuce court, one to the ad court. P2 then serves deuce and ad court points.
4. Players have only one serve per point.
5. When returning, returners can change direction only on inside serves.

    P1: Serves second serve.

    P2: Returns crosscourt if outside, changes direction if inside.

P1: Hits outside groundstrokes crosscourt following Directional patterns.

Point is played out with players changing directions only on inside groundstrokes and short outside groundstrokes.

Scoring

One-point scoring.

Key Points

- This Directional drill allows the players to change direction on inside groundstrokes and on short outside groundstrokes whereby the player has both feet inside the baseline.
- Points will be long and predictable but with a structured flow.
- Players may play through the middle to force their opponent to change directions off the inside ball.

Variations

1. Two-point errors for net or wide errors.
2. Two-point errors for 90 COD shots.
3. Players have a first and a second serve.

18 Directionals—Inside-Out Forehands

Purpose

To practice Directional patterns when playing with a weapon.
To develop inside-out forehands.

Time

Five-minute games.

Procedure—Full Singles Court

1. Point is played out with change of direction allowable only on inside groundstrokes and with inside-out forehands.
2. P1 serves two points, one to the deuce court, one to the ad court. P2 then serves deuce and ad court points. Players have only one serve per point.
3. When returning, returners can change direction only on inside serves, but may hit inside-out forehand returns from the ad court.

P1: Serves second serve.

P2: Returns crosscourt if outside, changes direction if inside (inside-out from ad court allowed).

P1: Hits groundstroke using Directional patterns.

Point is played out with change of direction allowable only on inside groundstrokes.

Scoring

One-point scoring.

Key Points

- This Directional game allows players to hit inside-out forehands, developing their forehand weapons.
- The inside-out forehand is used to build the point from the ad court or until a short inside forehand is created.

Variations

1. Two-point errors for net or wide errors.
2. Players have a first and a second serve.
3. 90-degree COD allowed.

19 Directionals—Pressuring When Changing Direction

Purpose

To practice pressuring when changing directions on inside and short outside groundstrokes.
To become aware of necessary court position from which to attack.

Time

Five-minute games.

Procedure—Full Singles Court

1. Point is played out following the Directionals, with players having to approach the net after changing direction. Players must approach off inside and short outside groundstrokes.
2. When returning serves, returners can change direction only on inside serves.
3. P1 serves two points, one to the deuce court, one to the ad court. P2 then serves deuce and ad court points. Players have only one serve per point.

P1: Serves second serve.

P2: Returns crosscourt if outside, changes direction if inside.

P1: Hits groundstroke crosscourt or approaches net if changing directions.

Point is played out.

Scoring

One-point scoring.

Key Points

- Court position on or inside the baseline when changing direction is crucial in allowing the approacher to achieve good first-volley position.
- A player's ability to quickly move forward will be revealed in this fast-paced drill.

Variations

1. Two-point errors for netted or wide shots.
2. Two-point errors for 90-degree COD shots.
3. Players have a first and a second serve.

20 Directionals—Forehands Are Wild

Purpose

To practice playing with a forehand weapon while following directional patterns with the backhand.

Time

Five-minute games.

Procedure—Full Singles Court

1. Players hit unrestricted with their forehands (including returns).
2. Backhand change of direction is allowed only on inside groundstrokes.
3. P1 serves two points, one to the deuce court, one to the ad court. P2 then serves deuce and ad court points. Players have only one serve per point.

    P1: Serves second serve.

    P2: Returns with forehand. Use Directional patterns on all backhands.

    P1: Hits groundstroke—forehands are wild and backhands follow Directional patterns.

    Point is played out.

Scoring

One-point scoring.

Key Points

- Players look to play as many forehands as possible.
- Backhands follow Directional patterns, creating a free (forehands) but structured (backhands) environment.

Variations

1. Two-point errors for netted or wide shots.
2. Two-point errors for 90-degree COD shots.
3. Players have a first and a second serve.

21 Outside/Middle Game

Purpose

To practice creating and hitting pressuring inside groundstrokes.
To become aware of necessary court position to capitalize on inside groundstroke opportunities.

Time

Four-minute games with two 2-minute segments.

Procedure—Full Singles Court

1. Point is played out with P2 hitting every shot through the middle and P1 turning on inside shots or hitting with no change of direction on outside groundstrokes.
2. P1 feeds for 2 minutes, then P2 feeds for 2 minutes.

   P1: Feeds through the middle of the court.

   P2: Hits groundstroke through the middle of the court.

   P1: Hits an inside groundstroke.

   P2: Hits groundstroke through the middle of the court.

   P1: Hits an inside groundstroke (may have to hit an outside groundstroke).

   Point is played out.

Scoring

One-point scoring.

Key Points

- The aim of this drill is to practice creating, hitting, and turning on inside groundstrokes.
- Players hitting the inside shot are aggressive with their court position, ideally taking the ball on the rise and playing either on or inside the baseline.
- Players feeding balls through the middle work on recovery footwork and reading the play—this drill requires a high work rate.

Variation

1. Two-point errors for net or wide errors.

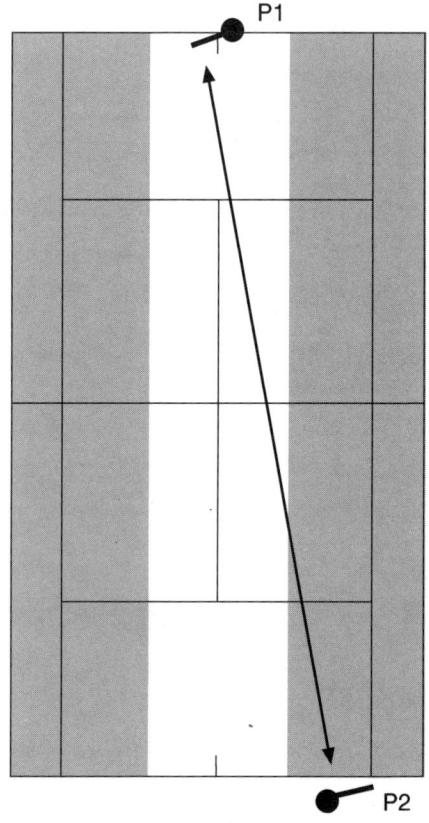

Drill 21 Outside/Middle Drill

22 Big Targets

Purpose

To practice rallying with a large margin of error—high net clearance and a safe distance from sidelines and baselines.

Time

Three-minute games.

Procedure—Full Singles Court

1. Targets (small disk cones) are placed in the deuce and ad court corners three paces from the sideline and three paces from the baseline.
2. Players aim at the "big targets" in either the deuce or ad court throughout the rally.
3. P1 or P2 feeds. Who feeds should have no bearing on the drill.

P1: Feeds groundstroke to P2.

P2: Aims for deuce or ad "big target," hitting a heavy, aggressive topspin shot.

P1: Aims for deuce or ad "big target," hitting a heavy, aggressive topspin shot.

Point is played out.

Scoring

One-point scoring.

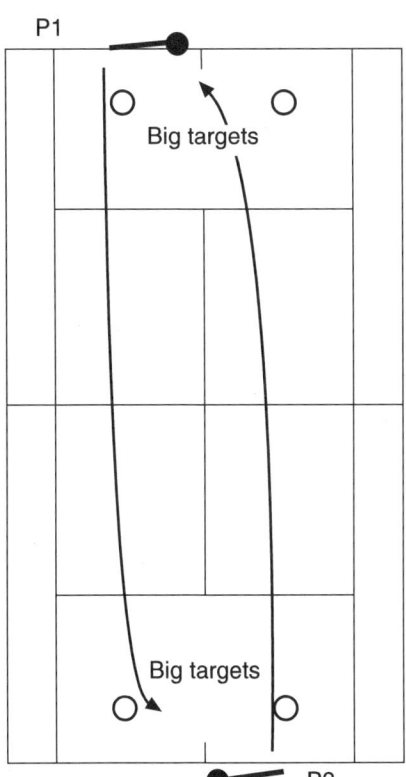

Drill 22 Big Targets

Key Points

- I call the targets "big targets" because by aiming at the cones, players have a big area into which to hit—guaranteeing a large margin of error.
- Big Targets is the ultimate clay-court drill, as the players hit heavy, aggressive topspin shots.
- Balls should clear the net by a large margin and should rarely be wide or deep. It is not unusual for good players to play only two or three points during a Big Targets drill.

Variations

1. Net and wide errors are two-point errors.
2. Hitting the disk cone is a two-point bonus.

Spin Drills

23 Drive vs. Loop

Purpose

To practice driving groundstrokes off looped shots.
To practice looping groundstrokes off driven shots.

Time

Four-minute games with two 2-minute segments, allowing each player to drive and loop.

Procedure—Half a Doubles Court

1. The driver is always the feeder.
2. After 2 minutes, the driver becomes the looper and the looper the driver.

   P1: Feeds to three-quarter court.

   P2: Loops groundstroke.

   P1: Hits topspin drive.

   Point is played out with P1 driving and P2 looping.

Scoring

One-point scoring.

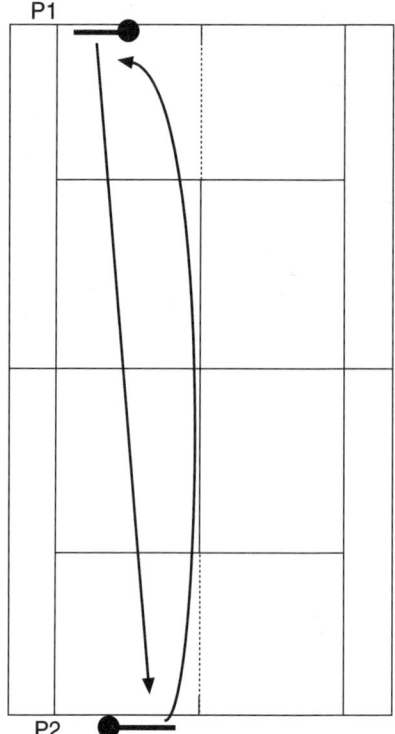

Drill 23 Drive vs. Loop

Key Points

- The aim of this drill is to learn how to hit a loop off a topspin drive and how to hit a topspin drive off a loop.
- For the drill to be most productive, players driving should remember that a drive is just a normal topspin groundstroke and not a kill shot.
- An ideal loop is a shot that crosses the baseline at shoulder height or higher, forcing the player to hit out of their ideal hitting zone.

Variations

1. Play crosscourt with the option of starting with a serve.
2. Net errors are two-point errors.
3. Play on a full singles court.

24 Drive vs. Slice

Purpose

To practice groundstroke drives off underspin shots.
To practice undersping shots off driven groundstrokes.

Time

Four-minute games with two 2-minute segments, allowing each player to drive and slice.

Procedure—Half a Doubles Court

1. The driver is always the feeder.
2. After 2 minutes, the driver becomes the slicer and the slicer the driver.

   P1: Feeds to three-quarter court.

   P2: Slices groundstroke.

   P1: Hits topspin drive.

   Point is played out with P1 driving and P2 slicing.

Drill 24 Drive vs. Slice

Scoring

One-point scoring.

Key Points

- The aim of this drill is to learn how to slice off a topspin drive and how to hit a topspin drive off a slice.
- An ideal slice is a shot that forces the player to hit from knee height or lower and at least forces the player to lift the ball up and over the net.
- Both forehands and backhands are sliced.

Variations

1. Play crosscourt with the option of starting with a serve.
2. Play crosscourt using only the ad court, as most modern players slice only their backhands.
3. Play on a full singles court.

25 Slice vs. Slice

Purpose

To practice hitting underspin off underspin shots.

Time

Three-minute games.

Procedure—Half a Doubles Court

1. P1 feeds two points, then P2 feeds two points.

    P1: Feeds to three-quarter court.

    P2: Slices groundstroke.

    P1: Slices groundstroke.

    Point is played out with both P1 and P2 slicing.

Scoring

One-point scoring.

Drill 25 Slice vs. Slice

Key Points

- The aim of this drill is to learn how to slice off a slice. The best counter to a low slice is to reply with a slice until a better shot to drive becomes available.
- Both forehands and backhands are sliced.

Variations

1. Play crosscourt with the option of starting with a serve.
2. Play crosscourt using only the ad court, as most modern players slice only their backhands.
3. Play on a full singles court.
4. Slice approach on any balls landing in the service box. Player may now pass with a topspin drive or underspin lob.
5. If a drop shot is hit and the player wins the point as a direct result of the drop shot, he or she wins two points.

26 Loop vs. Loop

Purpose

To practice looping off a looped groundstroke.

Time

Three-minute games.

Procedure—Half a Doubles Court

1. P1 feeds two points, then P2 feeds two points.
2. To ensure depth, the service boxes are out of bounds.

    P1: Feeds to three-quarter court.

    P2: Loops groundstroke beyond service box.

    P1: Loops groundstroke beyond service box.

    Point is played out with both players looping.

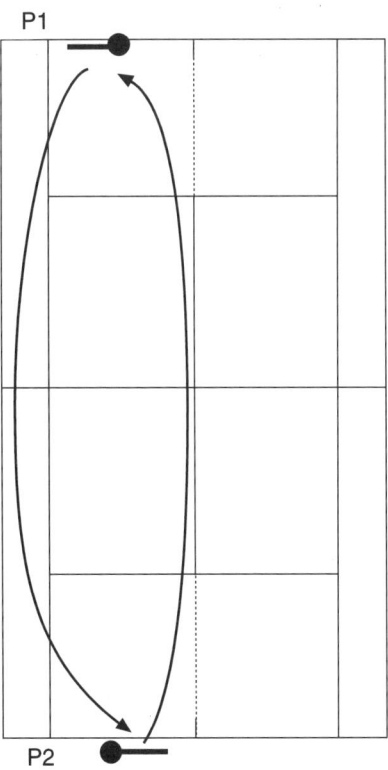

Drill 26 Loop vs. Loop

Scoring

One-point scoring.

Key Points

- A loop is an aggressively hit topspin shot with high net clearance that bounces at or above shoulder height and pushes the opponent behind the baseline.
- The best counter to a high, bouncing loop is to reply with a loop until a better shot to drive becomes available.
- Depth is essential to an effective loop.

Variations

1. Play crosscourt with the option of starting with a serve.
2. Play on a full singles court.
3. Either player may attack a short loop by driving an approach shot and playing out the point.

27 Random Spin

Purpose

To practice using a variety of spin shots (drive, slice, loop) in order to keep the ball out of an opponent's ideal hitting zone.

Time

Three-minute games.

Procedure—Half a Doubles Court

1. P1 feeds two points, then P2 feeds two points.
2. Players hit a variety of spin shots (loop, slice or drive) and never the same spin twice in a row.
   P1: Feeds to three-quarter court.
   P2: Hits either a drive, slice, or looped groundstroke.
   P1: Hits either a drive, slice, or looped groundstroke.
   Point is played out.

Scoring

One-point scoring.

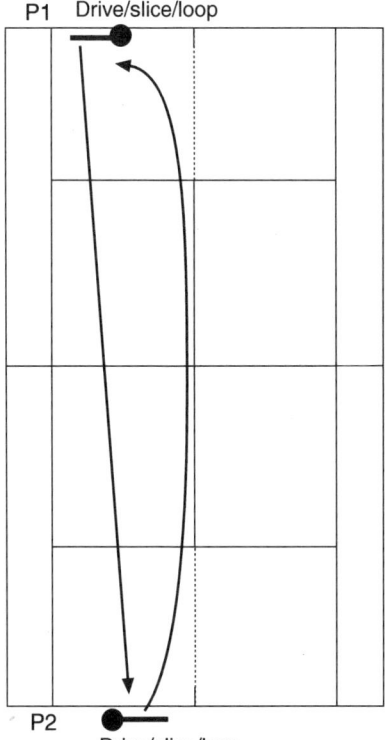

Drill 27 Random Spin

Key Points

- Players focus on keeping the ball out of an opponent's ideal hitting zone.
- Not hitting the same two consecutive shots prevents players from becoming grooved.

Variations

1. Play crosscourt with the option of starting with a serve.
2. Play on a full singles court.

28 Offense/Defense

Purpose

To practice pressuring against defensive players.
To practice defending against and neutralizing an offensive player when under pressure.

Time

Four-, 5- or 6-minute games with two segments.

88 Pressure Tennis

Procedure—Half a Doubles Court

1. Offensive player always feeds.
2. Players switch roles after 2 or 3 minutes.
   P1: Feeds straight ahead.
   P2: Hits defensive shot (loop or slice).
   P1: Hits offensive groundstroke.
   P2: Hits defensive shot (loop or slice).
   Point is played out.

Scoring

One-point scoring.

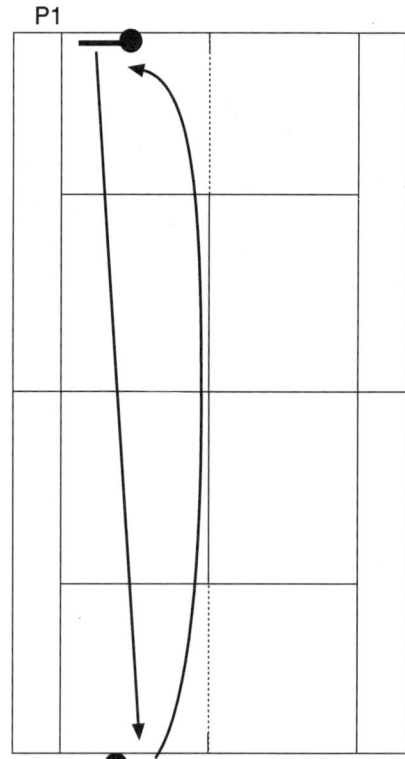

Drill 28 Offense/Defense

Key Points

- In this drill, the offensive player is able to play as aggressively as he or she wants, allowing the offensive player to play at the top of their range.

- Playing on half a doubles court leaves little space to hit winners and reveals much about a player's offensive prowess.
- The defensive player loops or slices but may lob or pass with a drive if the offensive player approaches the net.

Variation

1. No lobs allowed.
2. Defensive player may attack if short reply is created.

Pressuring Drills

29 Pinch Volleys

Purpose

To practice volleying and defending from on or inside the baseline.

Time

Four-minute games with two 2-minute segments.

Procedure—Half a Singles Court

1. P1 begins at the service line with P2 on or inside the baseline.
2. Players switch roles after 2 minutes.

    P1: Feeds straight ahead and stays on the service line.

    P2: Hits groundstroke at P1.

    P1: Volleys and then closes.

    P2: Plays out point by staying on or inside the baseline. No lobs are allowed.

Scoring

One-point scoring; only the volleyer scores. After each player has a turn volleying, the volleyer with the most points is the winner. Baseline player loses a point if he or she moves behind the baseline; must be on or inside the baseline.

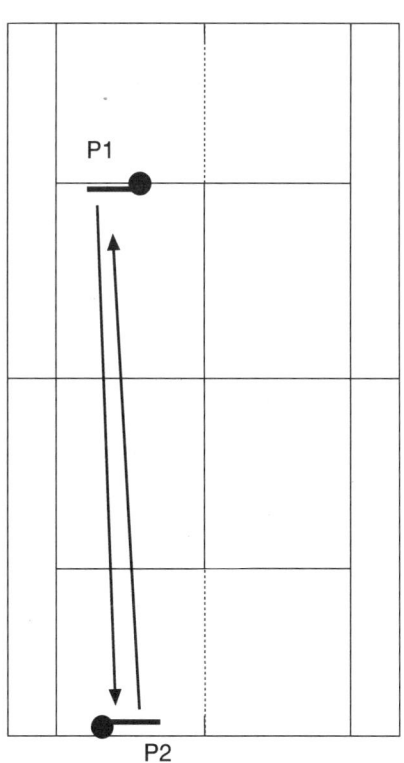

Drill 29 Pinch Volleys

Key Points

- From Clemson's Chuck Kriese, Pinch Volleys is great for improving volleys as well as building quick hands from on or inside the baseline when the groundstroker has been "pinched."
- Given the pace of the modern singles and doubles game, it is essential for players to develop quick hands from the baseline and net.
- Pinch Volleys forces players to counter deep penetrating shots and quickly returned volleys effectively. Having to play on half a singles court makes the drill one of control, as there is no open court to hit to. Who will break down first, the volleyer or the groundstroker?

Variations

1. Two-point errors for unforced netted shots—volleys or groundstrokes.
2. Groundstroker may lob after net player has hit two volleys.
3. Baseline player hits balls to volleyers feet off feed making them half-volley (good opportunity to practice rolling balls to feet).
4. Play on half a doubles court.

30 One-Player Closing Volleys

Purpose

To practice approach shots, first volleys, and point-ending volleys and overheads.
To practice neutralizing attacking players.

Time

Three- or 4-minute games.

Procedure—Half a Doubles Court

1. Both players begin at the baseline.
2. P1, as the baseliner, feeds two points, then P2 becomes the baseliner and feeds two points.
   P1: Feeds straight ahead to the service line and stays on the baseline.
   P2: Approaches hitting back to P1.
   P1: Hits groundstroke, making P2 volley or half-volley.
   P2: Volleys and plays out point.

Scoring

One-point scoring.

Key Points

- Players work on approaching off a short ball.
- Emphasis is on the baseliner making the volleyer hit a first volley and on the volleyer hitting controlled, deep first volleys to establish good court position for a point-ending volley or overhead.
- One Player Closing Volleys is a player favorite and used almost daily.

Variations

1. Lobs or no lobs can be stipulated.
2. Unforced baseline or volley net errors are two-point errors.
3. Volleyer slices the approach shot.

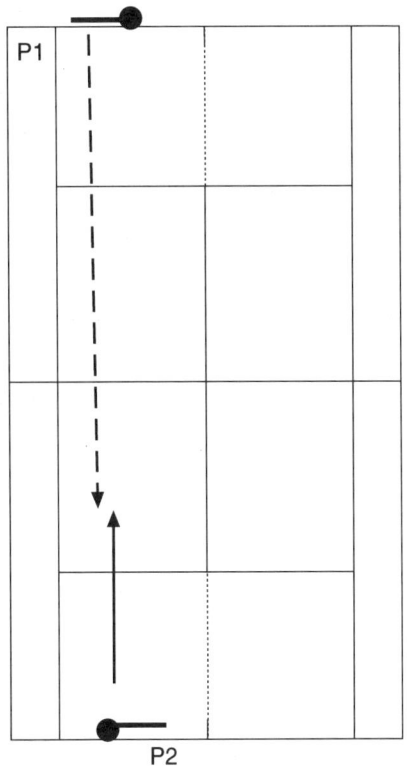

Drill 30 One-Player Closing Volleys

31 Three-Quarter-Court Closing Volleys

Purpose

To practice approach volleys, closing volleys, and point-ending volleys and overheads.
To practice neutralizing attacking players.

Time

Three- or 4-minute games.

Procedure—Half a Doubles Court

1. Both players begin at the baseline.
2. P1, as the baseliner, feeds two points, then P2 becomes the baseliner and feeds two points.

P1: Loops feed to the three-quarter court.
P2: Hits approach volley back to P1.
P1: Hits groundstroke, making P2 volley or half-volley.
P2: Volleys and plays out point.

Scoring

One-point scoring.

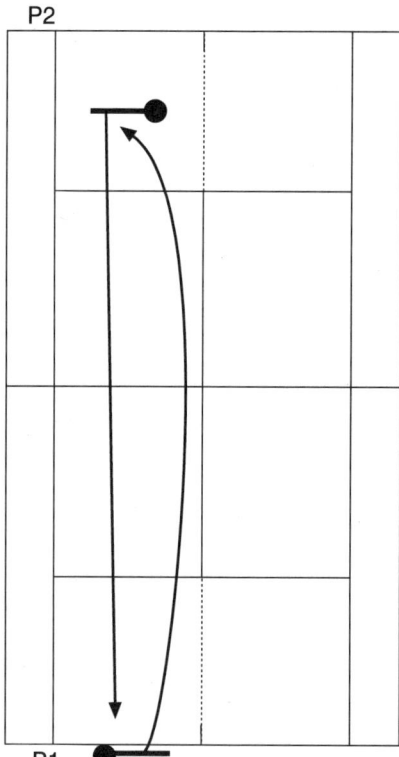

Drill 31 Three-Quarter-Court Closing Volleys

Key Points

- Players often fail to capitalize on looped or floated shots landing in the mid- or three-quarter-court area.
- Learning to play out of the air from no-man's-land allows players to maintain their court position and counter players who loop or lob.
- Three-quarter-court volleys are rarely point-ending shots and should be considered part of at least a two-shot point-ending sequence.

Variations

1. Lobs or no lobs can be stipulated.
2. Unforced baseline or volley net errors are two-point errors.

32 Two-Player Closing Volleys

Purpose

To practice quick volley exchanges when closing to the net.

Time

Three- or 4-minute games.

Procedure—Half a Doubles Court

1. Both players begin at the baseline.
2. P1 feeds two points, then P2 feeds two points.

   P1: Feeds straight ahead to the service line and closes to the net.

   P2: Approaches, hitting back to P1 (P2 must hit shot at P1 and cannot pass off the feed).

   P1: Volleys back to P2.

   P2: Volleys and plays out point.

Scoring

One-point scoring.

Key Points

- Players work on quick volley exchanges while both players close toward the net.
- Keeping volleys low is at a premium, as whoever pops up a volley is in serious trouble.

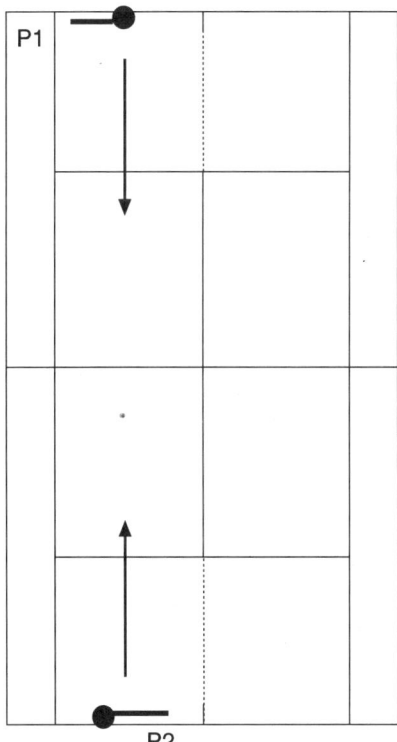

Drill 32 Two-Player Closing Volleys

Variations

1. Lobs or no lobs can be stipulated.
2. First volleys must touch the court in front of closing feeder.
3. Player slices approach shot.
4. Play on half a singles court.

33 Overhead Game

Purpose

To practice controlling the pressuring zone and ending points in the air. To practice neutralizing attacking players and defending against the overhead.

Time

Untimed (approximately 15 minutes).

Procedure—Half a Doubles Court

1. P2 begins at the baseline and P1 begins at the service line.
2. P1 feeds three points, then P2 feeds three points. A point cannot begin until an overhead is hit.
3. Once the overhead is struck, the point is played out (P2 does not have to lob again). If a shot is missed or the lob is unplayable, restart the sequence. Again, the point doesn't officially begin until the overhead is hit.
4. Play to 7 or 11, with each player having an equal number of opportunities. (If P1 starts out as the feeder, P2 will end as the feeder.)

    P1: Feeds ball to P2 and stays on the service line.

    P2: Hits groundstroke to P1.

    P1: Volleys back to P2 (P1 may now close).

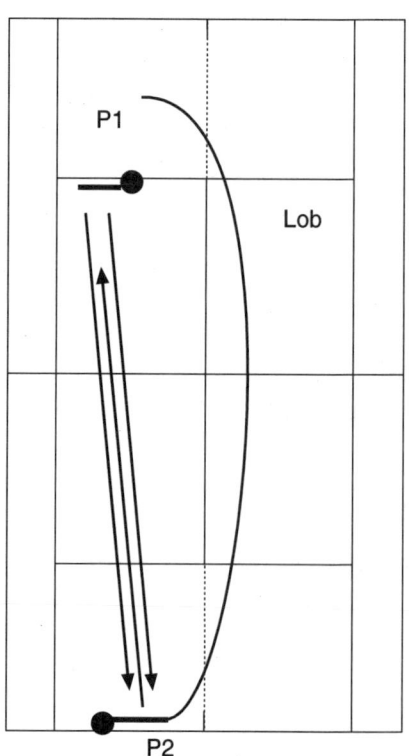

Drill 33 Overhead Game

P2: Lobs P1.

P1: Hits overhead.

Point begins when overhead is hit and is played out.

Scoring

One-point scoring; only the overhead hitters may score (similar to volleyball scoring).

Key Points

- The Overhead Game is an excellent drill for practicing the overhead in a matchlike environment.
- Attacking players learn to close after hitting overheads and to finish the point from the front court.
- The game also develops a player's ability to defend against an overhead by countering with either a lob or a groundstroke. The defending player learns to exploit space behind the attacking player (by lobbing) in order to exploit space in front of the attacking player (by hitting topspin groundstrokes to the feet). A fun but challenging drill.

Variations

1. P2 can hit a half-volley to P1 off the feed (good practice for hitting to the feet of an attacking player).
2. The baseline player may earn a point if he or she somehow gets to the net and hits an overhead winner.

34 Wimbledon Points

Purpose

To practice pressuring by playing from court position on or inside the baseline.

Time

Three- or 4-minute games.

Procedure—Half a Doubles Court

1. Both players begin on or inside the baseline. approaching on any ball that lands in the service box.
2. Players must come to the net on any shot landing in the service box, including the feed.

3. P1 feeds two points, then P2 feeds two points.
   P1: Feeds straight ahead beyond the service line.
   P2: Hits groundstroke from on or inside the baseline.
   P1: Hits groundstroke from on or inside baseline.
   Point is played out.

Scoring

One-point scoring.

Key Points

- As with grass-court points, players look to move forward in this quick-exchange drill.
- The emphasis is on court position, taking advantage of short shots, approaching, and closing.

Variations

1. Lobs or no lobs can be stipulated.
2. Player slices approach shot.
3. Allow players to approach off any shot.
4. Net errors are two-point errors.
5. Players must slice all shots except when passing net player.

35 Wimbledon Directionals

Purpose

To develop an aggressive mentality and to practice pressuring from on or inside the baseline using Directional patterns.

Time

Three- or 4-minute games.

Procedure—Full Singles Court

1. Both players use the same Directional patterns (outside shot, no change of direction, inside shot, change directions), but only the returner plays on or inside the baseline throughout the point.
2. The returner must also approach on any ball that lands in the service box (not including the serve).

3. P1 feeds two points (one to the deuce court, one to the ad court), then P2 feeds two points.

   P1: Serves second serve.

   P2: Returns serve from on or inside baseline.

   Point is played out. Returner loses point if he or she goes behind the baseline.

Scoring

One-point scoring.

Key Points

- The emphasis is on having the returner maintain aggressive court position and consciously look to take advantage of short shots.
- The returner's mind-set throughout the point should be "I want to move forward."

Variations

1. Player slices approach shot.
2. Returner may approach off any shot including serve.
3. Server also plays on or inside the baseline.
4. Ninety-degree change of direction allowed.

36 Drop-Shot Game

Purpose

To practice drop shots.
To practice controlling and directing an opponent's court position.

Time

Three- or 4-minute games.

Procedure—Half a Doubles Court

1. Both players begin at the baseline.
2. Point is played out. Player being drop shotted may also reply with a drop shot, and lobs are allowable.
3. P1 feeds two points, then P2 feeds two points.

   P1: Feeds straight ahead.

98 Pressure Tennis

P2: Hits topspin groundstroke to service line.
P1: Moves inside the court and hits drop shot.
P2: Moves forward after (not before) P1 hits drop shot.
P1: Lobs or passes.
Point is played out.

Scoring

One-point scoring.

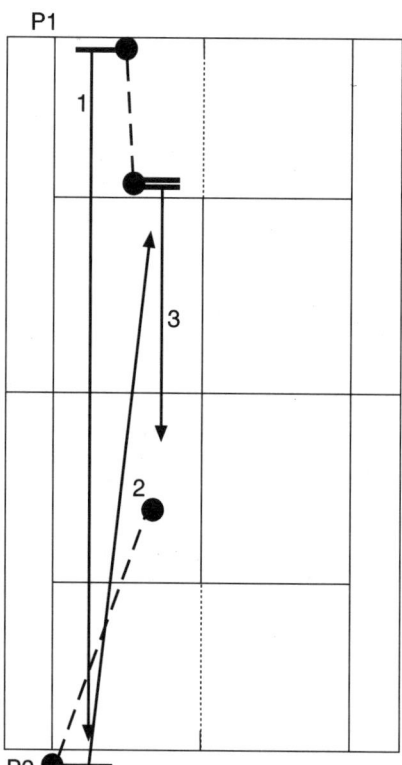

Drill 36 Drop-Shot Game

Key Points

- Pressuring is not limited to pace and penetration. Altering an opponent's court position, making him or her play from an unfamiliar area, puts players under tremendous pressure.
- The Drop-Shot Game reminds players to exploit the whole court and to make players play from less desirable places—in this case, the front court.
- Player hitting drop shot should establish court position inside the baseline.

Variation

1. No lobs allowed.
2. Player may either drop shot or approach and go to net off the feed. Game becomes a combination of the Drop-Shot Game and One-Player Closing Volleys.

Recovery Drills

Recovery drills work best with two teams of two players on each court, but they may involve three players, one player pressuring and two players recovering. I prefer to have coaches feed recovery drills, but player feeds are adequate.

37 Inside Groundstroke Recovery Game

Purpose

To practice recovering against and neutralizing pressuring inside groundstrokes.
To practice hitting pressuring inside groundstrokes from 3/4 court.

Time

6-minute games with two 3-minute segments.

Procedure—Full Singles Court

1. With two teams of two players, one team pressuring and the other recovering, players alternate playing singles points beginning with a coach's feed.
2. Recovering players should begin outside the doubles court and may release once the feed is made. Adjust starting position depending on players' abilities.
3. Coach feeds are from either the deuce or ad court depending on whether working on inside backhands or forehands.

Note. In this example feeds are from the deuce court.

    Coach: Feeds three-quarter-court inside backhand groundstroke to P1.

    P1: Plays feed on or inside the baseline and changes direction to the ad court (P1's shot should penetrate the baseline).

    P3: Runs to play P1's inside groundstroke and tries to recover by hitting back crosscourt.

    Point is played out. Players may come to net if possible.

    P2 and P4 play the next point.

Scoring

Keep track of the pressuring team's score only, using one-point scoring. The team with the highest total after the two rotations wins the drill.

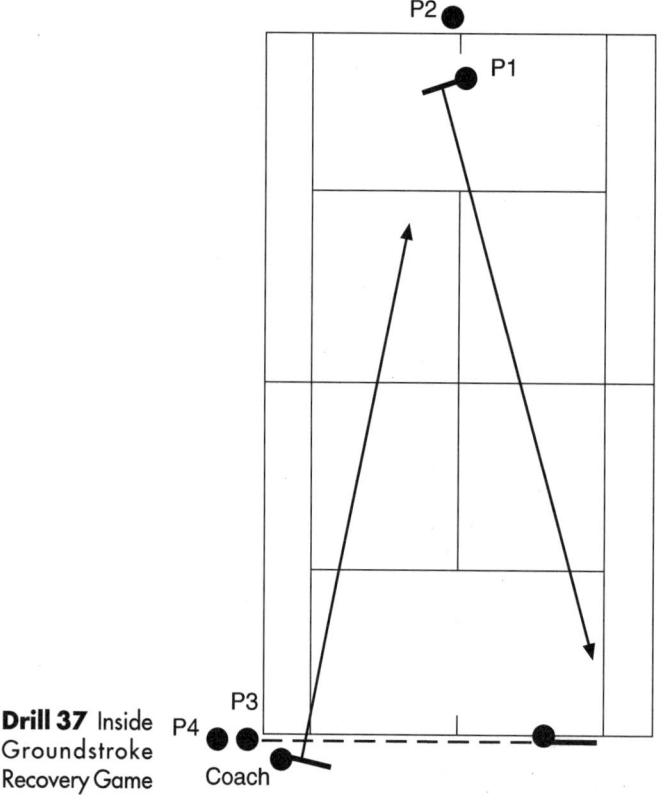

Drill 37 Inside Groundstroke Recovery Game

Key Points

- Inside groundstrokes are usually the first opportunity for players to take control of a point.
- Court position is crucial in capitalizing on the three-quarter feed, so the player moves on or inside the baseline to take the ball on the rise.
- The recovering player aims to neutralize the point or even regain the offensive by hitting crosscourt and behind the pressuring player.

Variation

1. Feed point from ad court for work on deuce-court recovery and inside forehands.

38 Inside Volley Recovery Game

Purpose

To practice recovering against and neutralizing pressuring inside volleys. To practice hitting pressuring inside volleys from 3/4 court.

Time

6-minute games with two 3-minute segments.

Procedure—Full Singles Court

1. With two teams of two players, one team pressuring and the other recovering, players alternate playing singles points beginning with a coach's feed.
2. Recovering players should begin outside the doubles court and may release once the feed is made. Adjust starting position depending on players' abilities.
3. Coach feeds are from either the deuce or ad court depending on whether working on inside backhands or forehands.

Note. In this example feeds are from the deuce court.

Coach: Feeds three-quarter-court inside backhand volley to P1.

P1: Plays feed between 3/4 court and the service line and changes direction to the ad court (P1's volley should penetrate the baseline).

P3: Runs to play P1's shot and tries to recover by hitting back crosscourt.

Point is played out.

P2 and P4 play the next point.

Scoring

Keep track of the pressuring team's score only, using one-point scoring. The team with the highest total after the two rotations wins the drill.

Key Points

- Players pulled wide will often float or lob shots down the line or through the middle to three-quarter-court depth. Being able to play an inside volley from three-quarter court is essential in capitalizing on the floated or lobbed shot.

- The inside volley is played to the open court. The recovering player aims to neutralize the point or even regain the offensive.

Variation

1. Feed point from ad court for work on deuce-court recovery and inside forehand volleys.

39 Short Inside Groundstroke Recovery Game

Purpose

To practice recovering against and neutralizing pressuring inside groundstrokes.
To practice hitting pressuring inside groundstrokes from the midcourt.

Time

6-minute games with two 3-minute segments.

Procedure—Full Singles Court

1. With two teams of two players, one team pressuring and the other recovering, players alternate playing singles points beginning with a coach's feed.
2. Recovering players should begin outside the doubles court and may release once the feed is made. Adjust starting position depending on players' abilities.
3. Feeds are from either the deuce or ad court depending on whether working on inside backhands or forehands.

Note. In this example feeds are from the deuce court.

Coach: Feeds midcourt inside groundstroke to P1.

P1: Plays feed from the midcourt and changes direction to the ad court and closes to the net.

P3: Runs to play P1's shot and tries to recover by hitting back crosscourt or by lobbing.

P1: Looks to end point.

Point is played out.

P2 and P4 play the next point.

Scoring

Keep track of the pressuring team's score only, using one-point scoring. The team with the highest total pressuring wins the drill.

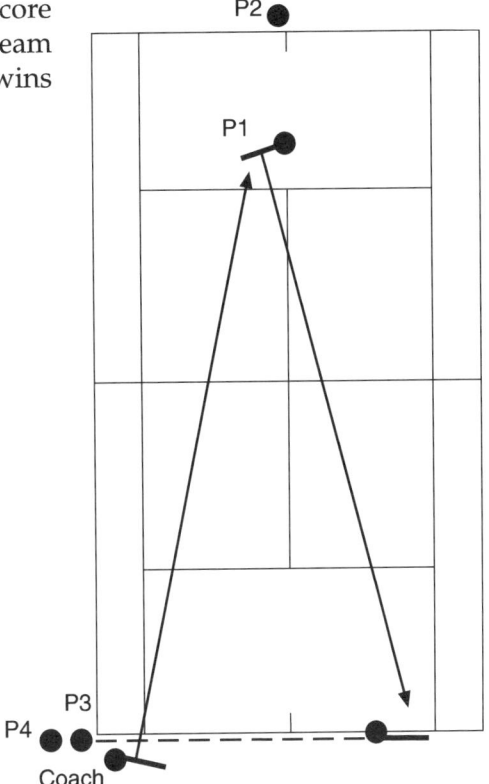

Drill 39 Short Inside Ground-stroke Recovery Game

Key Points

- Inside groundstrokes hit from the midcourt are difficult to recover against, given the pressuring player's proximity to the net and the potential angle.
- The recovering player should pass crosscourt, if possible, without changing the direction of the approach shot, but more often than not, a lob will be the best option.

Variation

1. Feed point from ad court for work on deuce-court recovery and inside forehands.

40 Short Outside Approach Shot Recovery Game

Purpose

To practice recovering against and neutralizing pressuring down-the-line approach shots.

To practice approaching off short outside groundstrokes.

Time

6-minute games with two 3-minute segments.

Procedure—Full Singles Court

1. With two teams of two players, one team pressuring and the other recovering, players alternate playing singles points beginning with a coach's feed.

2. Recovering players should begin outside the doubles court and may release once the feed is made. Adjust starting position depending on players' abilities.

3. Feeds are from either the deuce or ad court depending on whether working on short outside backhands or forehands.

Note. In this example feeds are from the deuce court.

> Coach: Feeds short outside groundstroke to P1.
>
> P1: Plays feed from three-quarter court and hits 90-degree COD approach shot and closes to the net.
>
> P3: Runs to play P1's shot, ideally passing with no COD.
>
> P1: Looks to end point.
>
> Point is played out.
>
> P2 and P4 play the next point.

Scoring

Keep track of the pressuring team's score only, using one-point scoring. The team with the highest total after the two rotations wins the drill.

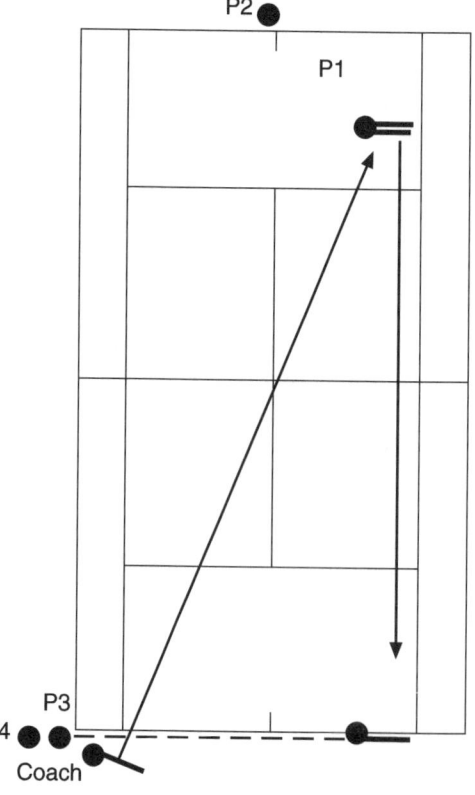

Drill 40 Short Outside Approach Shot Recovery Game

Key Points

- Short outside groundstrokes are the favorite attacking shots for most players. These approach shots should be hit with a 90-degree COD ensuring the ball penetrates the baseline.
- The recovering player should pass down the line, if possible, without changing the direction of the approach shot. Lobs are also an option.

Variation

1. Feed point from ad court for work on deuce-court recovery and short outside backhands.

Singles Play

41 Two-Point Tennis

Purpose

To decrease unforced net or wide errors.

Procedure—Full Singles Court

1. Players play a regular set of singles.

Scoring

One-point scoring except for unforced net or wide errors, which are two-point errors. Double faults are also two-point errors.
For example, P1 nets a ball on the first point of a drill—30-love to P2. P1 serves again to the deuce court. P2 hits next ball deep—30-15 to P2. P1 hits shot wide—game to P2.

Key Points

- Two-Point Tennis is a game players initially dislike. With a little practice, players find they play their normal games without making unforced net or wide errors.
- Players also become more choosy on 90-degree change-of-direction shots—the major source of wide errors.

Variations

1. Server has only one serve, with a missed serve counting as a two-point error.
2. Any missed return of a second serve is a two-point error.

42 Tiebreaker Tournament

Purpose

To practice playing tiebreakers.
To reaffirm/instill various concepts in a game environment (see variations for options and ideas).

Procedure—Full Singles Court

1. Players play tiebreakers to 7 or 11.

Scoring

Regular scoring.

Key Points

- Tiebreakers promote action and intensity as the end is always near and they are quite fun for the players.
- When one court finishes, all the other courts stop, regardless of the score (if score is tied, next point wins).

Variations

1. Net or wide errors are two-point errors.
2. Players have only one serve per point.
3. Servers must serve and volley on first serves.
4. Returners must approach off second serves.
5. Variations three and four combined.
6. Players play by the Directionals (all or some of the guidelines).
7. Pressuring off a first serve or return of a second serve is a two-point winner.
8. Wimbledon Tiebreaker: Players play on or inside the baseline and must approach on balls landing inside the service box.
9. The winning player who finishes first may choose a variation for the next tiebreaker.

43 Eight-Game Pro-Sets

Purpose

To condense match play into one set given time limitations.

Procedure—Full Singles Court

1. Players play sets to 8 with tiebreakers occuring at 8-8.

Scoring

Regular scoring.

Key Points

- Nothing fancy here; eight-game pro-sets are just an extended set of singles.
- Pro-sets are useful if time is a factor in practice.

Variations

1. Net or wide errors are two-point errors.
2. Players have only one serve per point.
3. Servers must serve and volley on first serves.
4. Returners must approach off second serves.
5. Variations three and four combined.
6. Players play by the Directionals (all or some of the guidelines).
7. Pressuring off first serve or return of second serve is a two-point winner.

44 No-Ad Sets

Purpose

To create numerous pressure situations (3-3 points) and to condense match play given time constraints.

Procedure—Full Singles Court

1. Players play sets using no-ad scoring.
2. On 3-3 points the returner chooses which court to return from.

Scoring

Players must win four points to win a game. If the score is tied at 3-3, the next point decides the game but the returner chooses which court to return from. Sets are played to 6 with a tiebreaker at 6-6.

Key Points

- Using no-ad scoring, no-ad sets create numerous pressure points.
- No-ad sets are useful if time is a factor in practice.

Variations

1. Net or wide errors are two-point errors.
2. Players have only one serve per point.
3. Servers must serve and volley on first serves.
4. Returners must approach off second serves.
5. Three and four combined.
6. Players play by the Directionals (all or some of the guidelines).
7. Pressuring off first serve or return of second serve is a two-point winner.
8. Play abbreviated no-ad sets to 4 with a tiebreaker at 4-4.

45 Game-Point Sets

Purpose

To practice closing out games when game point is reached.

Procedure—Full Singles Court

1. Players play a set.
2. If a player fails to win game-point the game score goes back to zero or love.

Scoring

Regular scoring where player goes back to love if he or she fails to capitalize on game point. For example, if P1 leads 40-15, P1 must win the next point and the game or return to love. In this case, if P1 loses the point, the score is love-30 for P2 and the game continues.

Key Points

- A Greg Patton original, Game-Point Sets emphasizes finishing the game when game point is reached. Now is the time!
- Capitalizing on the moment, not letting down or relaxing, and maintaining momentum are the key areas on which to focus.

46 First Four Games

Purpose

To practice playing high-percentage tennis during the first four games of a set or match.

Procedure—Full Singles Court

1. Players play a set of singles.
2. One player can be designated to play strict Directional tennis on the first four games without the opponent knowing.

Scoring

Regular scoring.

Key Points

- To make sure a player gets off to a good start, the coach chooses one player to focus on the first four games of the set. This is done by playing high-percentage Directional tennis (usually limiting 90-degree COD shots).
- Some of my team's best upsets were a direct result of focusing on the first four games of the match. We jumped out to an early lead (3-1, 4-0), won the first set, created doubt in our opponents' minds, and won one of the next two sets. The trick was making our opponents beat us by playing high-percentage error-free tennis.
- Remember, tennis is a game of mistakes, regardless of the level.

Crazy Drills

47 Crazy Groundstrokes

Purpose

To challenge the groundstroker's technique, balance, and footwork with aggressive random feeds.

Time

Two-minute drill with a 1-minute rotation for each player.

Procedure—Full Singles Court

1. Player hits random groundstrokes from the baseline.
2. The feeder feeds from across the net at the service line (from the T), hitting random feeds to the forehand and backhand sides and directly at the player hitting from the baseline.

3. Feeds should be hit with pace and should be challenging, pushing the player to where their technique, balance, and footwork begin to break down.
4. Groundstroker and feeder change places after 1-minute rotation.

Scoring

No score is kept.

Key Points

- Random feeds challenge the baseliner to produce functional groundstrokes.
- The emphasis here is on maintaining proper balance and technique when under pressure.

Variations

1. Use deep, short and wide feeds in a random pattern making the groundstroker play from the whole court.

48 Crazy Returns

Purpose

To challenge the returner with aggressive random serves from close range.

Time

Four-minute drill with a 1-minute rotation from the deuce court and minute from the ad court for each player.

Procedure—Full Singles Court

1. Player hits random service returns from deuce or ad court.
2. The feeder feeds from across the net at the service line (from the T), hitting random serves to the forehand and backhand sides and directly at the player returning.
3. Serves should be hit with pace and should be challenging, pushing the player to where the technique, balance, and footwork begin to break down.
4. Returner and server change places after 1-minute rotation.
5. Allow the returner to reset before each return, but keep the serves coming at a quick rate.

Scoring

No score is kept.

Key Points

Serving from just beyond the service line, the server fires serves that test the returner's range and quickness.

Returners practice moving through returns similar to groundstrokes hit on the run in order to maintain balance through the stroke-and-recovery phase.

49 Crazy Volleys

Purpose

To challenge the volleyer with random passing shots and difficult feeds.

Time

Two-minute drill with 1-minute rotations for each player.

Procedure—Full Singles Court

1. Player hits volleys beginning at the T.
2. The feeder feeds from across the net at the baseline, hitting random shots to the volleyer.
3. Feeds should be hit with pace and should be challenging, pushing the player to where the technique, balance, recovery and footwork begin to break down on the volley.
4. Volleyer and feeder change place after 1-minute rotation.

Scoring

No score is kept.

Key Points

- Feeding rapidly from the baseline, the feeder attempts to stretch out the volleyer with passing shots and difficult feeds.
- The volleyer focuses on moving through the volley, maintaining balance in order to recover and quickly change directions.

50 Crazy Overheads

Purpose

To challenge the overhead hitter with random lobs—low/high, short/deep, and deuce/ad court feeds.

Time

Two-minute drill with 1-minute rotations for each player.

Procedure—Full Singles Court

1. One player feeds lobs from the baseline and the other hits overheads for 1 minute.
2. Feeds should be as crazy as possible, forcing the overhead hitter to hit overheads off low feeds, while on the run, and off lobs over the backhand side.
3. No matter the difficulty, the player must try to hit an overhead.

Scoring

No score is kept.

Key Points

- Feeding rapidly and randomly from the baseline, the feeder attempts to test the overhead hitter.
- The overhead hitter focuses on playing all feeds as overheads, regardless of the difficulty.
- This is an excellent drill for expanding the overhead hitter's range and scope of what can be hit as an overhead.

51 Crazy Overheads and Volleys

Purpose

To challenge the overhead hitter with random lob feeds followed by random volley feeds.

Time

Two-minute drill with 1-minute rotations for each player.

Procedure—Full Singles Court

1. One player feeds from the baseline and the other player hits a series of overhead/volley combinations for 1 minute.
2. Overhead feeds should be as crazy as possible, forcing the overhead hitter to hit overheads off low feeds, while on the run, and off lobs over the backhand side.
3. Volley feeds always follow the overhead.

Scoring

No score is kept.

Key Points

- A combination of Crazy Overheads and Crazy Volleys, this drill focuses on having to recover and maintain balance as quickly as possible after hitting an overhead or volley.
- Proper footwork is essential and must be stressed throughout the drill.
- This drill requires a high work rate.

Variation

1. Have the player complete two 30-second sequences with 15 seconds of rest between them.

7

Doubles Drills

The game of doubles is a dying art and an area clearly neglected in junior tennis. This unfortunate reality is disappointing as doubles training offers tremendous benefits to singles players, especially given today's emphasis on power and pressuring. Doubles skills such as being able to serve and volley and close out points from the midcourt and hit targets with accuracy are invaluable skills transferable to the singles court. It's no coincidence that I often see a direct correlation between doubles and singles improvement with my teams and players. The doubles drills listed below will benefit all players and involve exciting quick exchanges. Players will find the drills challenging, yet fun.

Doubles drills are broken down into three tactical categories:

- First exchanges
- Point building
- Pressuring

First exchanges are the secret to good doubles—the team with the best serves and returns wins. When training doubles teams there is no substitute for a heavy dose of serve-and-return work. The first serve is crucial in doubles, as it sets the tone for the point. Making a high percentage of first serves puts the returning team on the defensive and the serving team in control of the front court. Doubles first serves are different from singles first serves in that the doubles first serve is hit with more spin and less pace. The extra spin results in a higher percentage of first serves in play and gives the server more time to close to the net when serving and volleying. Location of serves is also important, as the serving team tries to involve the server's partner whenever possible.

The returning team has one task, and that is to get the point started. Ideal returns are away from the server's partner and low to the server's feet. Low returns also allow the returner's partner to pick off shots the serving team pops up.

Another area of concentration is point building. With only one doubles point-building drill, Doubles Crosscourts, it should be obvious doubles is not about building the point from the baseline. Of course, whether it is a doubles day or a singles day, practice is not complete without a round or two of Crosscourts.

Making first serves, controlling the net with good court position, and making first volleys and overheads keeps opponents under constant pressure. The pressuring drills focus primarily on volleys, closing to the net, and overheads. There are also two return-team pressuring drills.

Doubles drills involve either two, three, or four players on a court. The advantages of one-versus-one (1v1), two-versus-one (2v1), and two-versus-two (2v2) drills are discussed below.

- **One-versus-one drills.** As almost everyone knows, the key to doubles success is making first serves, returns, and first volleys. These three shots typically involve only two players—the server and the returner. My experience has been that the wisest use of practice time when working on doubles fundamentals is to involve only two players on a court. The number of repetitions is greater, and with fewer distractions, the level of concentration is much better. These drills also offer the baseline player an opportunity to "break down" volleyers by making them hit lots of volleys. Net errors from the baseline are not to be tolerated—make the volleyer volley!

- **Two-versus-one drills.** Introducing team concepts is most effective in 2v1 drills. This is especially true with first-exchange drills and in working on returner's partner and server's partner tactics. Again, 2v1 drills maximize time and personnel and allow doubles teams to focus specifically on their needs.

- **Two-versus-two drills.** With four players on a court, there is a good chance for a game of doubles to break out! Two-versus-two drills are the logical choice for simulating real match play and putting all the tactical pieces together.

- **Doubles play.** Besides playing regular sets and doubles matches in practice, the doubles drills are fun and beneficial alternatives. There is an endless variety of creative ways to play sets and tiebreakers. Remember to keep these drills productive and purposeful.

Doubles First-Exchange Drills

52 Doubles—20 Second Serves/Window Sequence (1v1)

Purpose
To practice the first four shots of a doubles point—the serve, the return, the first volley and the returner's first groundstroke.
To practice hitting through the "window" (the space between doubles partners) off the server's first volley.

Time
Untimed (approximately 15 minutes).

Procedure—Half a Doubles Court (Diagonal)

1. P1, serving and volleying, serves 10 second serves to the deuce court and 10 second serves to the ad court while P2 returns crosscourt.
2. Drill repeats with P2 serving 20 second serves and P1 returning.

   P1: Serves and volleys, hitting a second serve.

   P2: Returns low and crosscourt to server.

   P1: Volleys crosscourt and closes.

   P2: Hits through the "window"—between the server and an imaginary server's partner.

   Point ends after the fourth shot.

Scoring
Record number of serves made. For example, P1 makes 18 out of 20 second serves. My standard for success is for the server to make at least 17 or more serves out of 20.

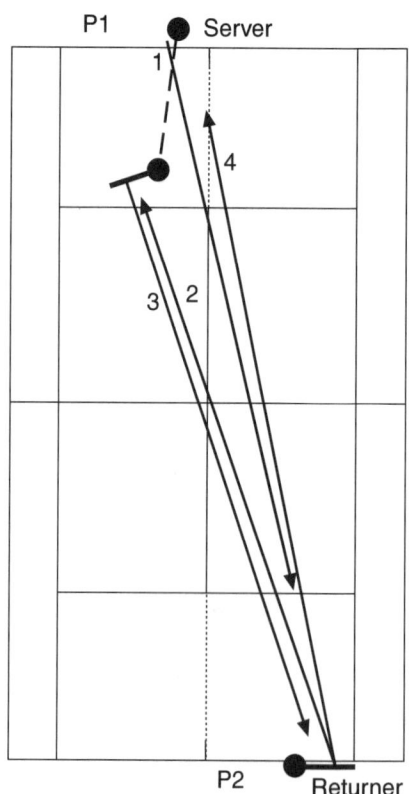

Drill 52 Doubles—20 Second Serves/Window Sequence (1v1)

Key Points

- The returner's first groundstroke should be through what Clemson coach Chuck Kriese calls the "window"—the space between the two net players.
- The returner will have to hit the groundstroke through an imaginary window since there is no server's partner.

Variation

1. Server can be assigned location for serve.

53 Doubles—20 Second Serves/Lob Sequence (1v1)

Purpose

To practice the first four shots of a doubles point—the serve, the return, the first volley and the returner's first reply, in this case a lob.

Time

Untimed (approximately 15 minutes)

Procedure—Half a Doubles Court (Diagonal)

1. P1, serving and volleying, serves 10 second serves to the deuce court and 10 second serves to the ad court while P2 returns crosscourt.
2. Drill repeats with P2 serving 20 second serves and P1 returning.

   P1: Serves and volleys, hitting a second serve.

   P2: Returns low and crosscourt to server.

   P1: Volleys crosscourt and closes.

   P2: Lobs down the line over imaginary server's partner.

   Point ends after the fourth shot.

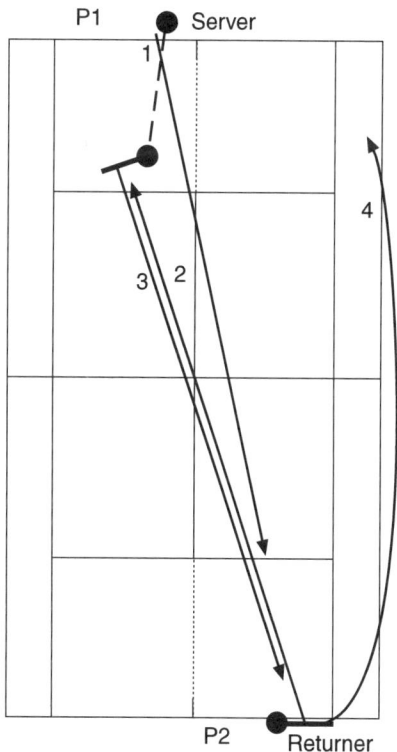

Drill 53 Doubles—20 Second Serves/Lob Sequence (1v1)

Scoring

Record number of serves made. For example, P1 makes 18 out of 20 second serves. My standard for success is for the server to make at least 17 or more serves out of 20.

Key Points

- The returner's lob is over the closest player to the net—the server's partner.
- Since this drill involves only two players, the returner will have to lob over an imaginary server's partner.

Variation

1. Server can be assigned location for serve.

54 Doubles—20 Second Serves/Short-Angle Volley Sequence (1v1)

Purpose

To practice the first five shots of a doubles point—the serve, the return, the first volley, the returner's first groundstroke, and the server's second volley—with emphasis on angling the second volley short.

Time

Untimed (approximately 15 minutes).

Procedure—Half a Doubles Court (Diagonal)

1. P1, serving and volleying, serves 10 second serves to the deuce court and 10 second serves to the ad court while P2 returns crosscourt.
2. Drill repeats with P2 serving 20 second serves and P1 returning.

   P1: Serves and volleys, hitting a second serve.

   P2: Returns low and crosscourt to server.

   P1: Volleys crosscourt and closes.

   P2: Hits P1 an outside volley.

   P1: Short-angle crosscourt volley.

   Point ends after the fifth shot.

Scoring

Record number of serves made. For example, P1 makes 18 out of 20 second serves. My standard for success is for the server to make at least 17 or more serves out of 20.

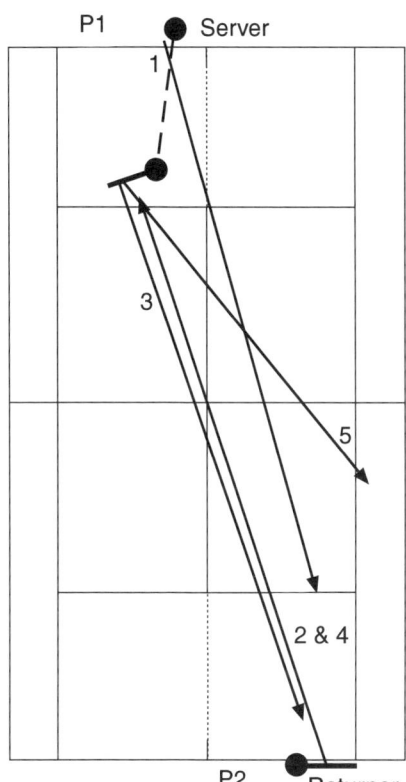

Drill 54 Doubles—20 Second Serves/Short-Angle Volley Sequence (1v1)

Key Points

- The server's second volley is short and angled.
- The returner's role is one of cooperation—making sure the server has good shots to volley.
- Ideally, the returner feeds the volleyer an outside volley to angle short. Excellent drill for simulating having to hit short-angle volleys against a two-back team.

Variation

1. Server can be assigned location for serve.

55 Doubles—20 Second Serves/Returner Approach Sequence (1v1)

Purpose

To practice approaching the net when returning second serves.
To practice defending against returners who approach off second serves.

Time

Untimed (approximately 15 minutes).

Procedure—Half a Doubles Court (Diagonal)

1. P1 serves 10 second serves to the deuce court and 10 second serves to the ad court while P2 returns and approaches net.
2. Drill repeats with P2 serving 20 second serves and P1 returning and approaching.

   P1: Serves second serve and stays at baseline.

   P2: Returns crosscourt and approaches the net.

   P1: Hits groundstroke.

   P2: Hits volley.

   Point ends after the fourth shot.

Scoring

Record number of serves made. For example, P1 makes 18 out of 20 second serves. My standard for success is for the server to make at least 17 or more serves out of 20.

Key Points

- Returner should move through return in order to make it to an advantageous volley position inside the service box.
- Returner can chip and charge in order to create time to close and establish good court position.
- Server should make returner hit a volley or ideally, a half-volley.

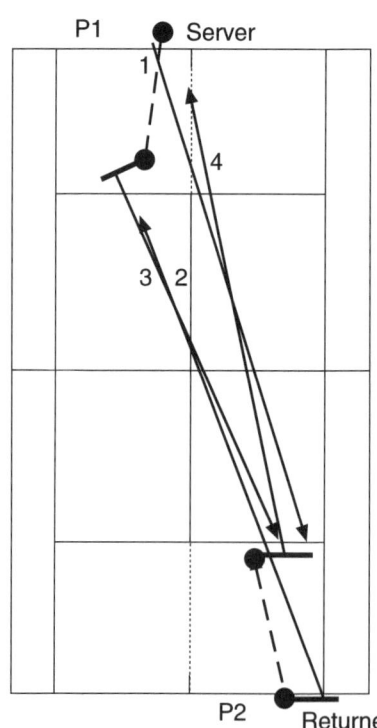

Drill 55 Doubles—20 Second Serves/Returner Approach Sequence (1v1)

Variations

1. Server can be assigned location for serve.
2. Returns are sliced.

56 Doubles Crosscourt Serve and Volley (1v1)

Purpose

To practice the heart and soul of good doubles—making serves, making serve returns and making first volleys.

Time

Three- or 4-minute games.

Procedure—Half a Doubles Court (Diagonal)

1. With only one serve per point, players serve and volley on half a doubles court.
2. P1 serves two points, one to the deuce and one to the ad court, then P2 serves deuce and ad court points.

   P1: Serves and volleys.

   P2: Returns all serves crosscourt.

   P1: Volleys crosscourt.

   Point is played out.

Scoring

One-point scoring.

Key Points

- This drill emphasizes the serve, return, and first volley and is excellent for revealing your team's best doubles players.
- Because the drill is played crosscourt, players have to work the point by playing either low to the feet, high with a lob, at the body, or through the middle.

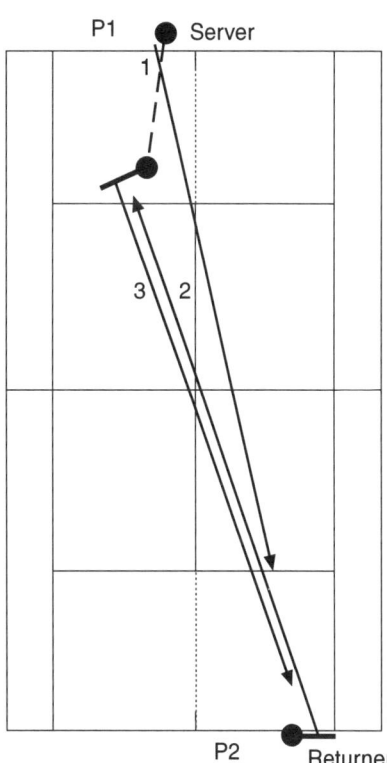

Drill 56 Doubles Crosscourt Serve and Volley (1v1)

Variations

1. Drill can be played as a deuce-court- or an ad-court-only game.
2. Servers allowed two serves.
3. Unforced net errors are two-point errors.
4. Serve, return, or first-volley errors are two-point errors.
5. Returner must come to the net behind the return.
6. Lobs or no lobs can be stipulated.
7. Server can be assigned location for serve.

57 20 Serves With Server's Partner (2v1)

Purpose

To develop the poaching skills of the server's partner.

Time

Untimed (approximately 20 minutes).

Procedure—Full Doubles Court

1. P1 serves 10 second serves to the deuce court and 10 second serves to the ad court while P2 returns over the net center strap and P3 poaches off P2's return.
2. Drill repeats with P2 serving 20 second serves and P3 returning and P1 poaching. (Server becomes poacher, poacher becomes returner, and returner becomes server.)

    P1: Serves second serve.

    P2: Returns serve over the net center strap.

    P3: Poaches return and volleys crosscourt.

    Point ends after third shot.

Scoring

Record number of second serves made.

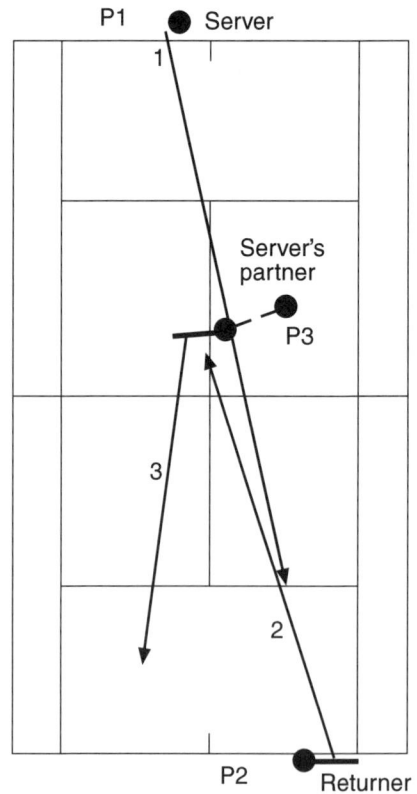

Drill 57 20 Serves With Server's Partner (2v1)

Key Points

- In this variation on the 20 Serves drill, adding the poacher allows doubles teams to work on their movement at the net.
- If doubles partners are on the same court, it makes sense to let them work together as a serving team.
- Poachers should move on the diagonal to the center strap.

Variations

1. Returner turns on inside returns. P3 has to read the situation before moving, based on whether the serve is an inside or outside shot for the returner.
2. Serving team runs plays.
3. The server serves and volleys and the returner may return wherever he or she likes. Server's partner still looks to poach.
4. Server can be assigned location for serve.

58 20 Serves With Returner's Partner (2v1)

Purpose

To develop the poaching and closing skills of the returner's partner. To practice serving and volleying and service returns.

Time

Untimed (approximately 20 minutes).

Procedure—Full Doubles Court

1. P1, serving and volleying, serves 10 second serves to the deuce court and 10 second serves to the ad court while P2 returns crosscourt to the server. The server volleys the return crosscourt aiming over the net center strap. The returner's partner, P3, closes and moves diagonally to the center strap and volleys (poaches) the server's first volley.
2. Drill repeats with P2 serving 20 second serves and P3 returning and P1 becoming the returner's partner. (Server becomes poacher, poacher becomes returner, and returner becomes server.)

   P1: Serves and volleys hitting second serve.

   P2: Returns serve crosscourt back to the server.

   P1: Volleys over the net center strap.

P3: Closes and poaches P1's first volley.

Point ends after fourth shot.

Scoring

Record number of second serves made.

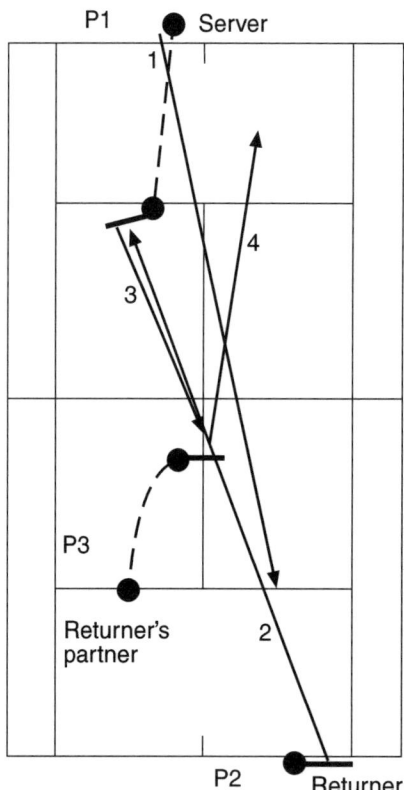

Drill 58 20 Serves With Returner's Partner (2v1)

Key Points

- In this variation on the 20 Serves drill, adding the returner's partner allows doubles teams to work on their movement off returns.
- If doubles partners are on the same court, it makes sense to let them work together.

Variations

1. Server volleys to chosen location. The returner's partner still looks to poach but must respect the server's first volley.
2. Server can be assigned location for serve.

59 Returning Team vs. a Server (2v1)

Purpose
To develop the returning teams' doubles skills with emphasis on setting up the returner's partner at the net.

Time
Nine-minute game with each player taking a 3-minute turn as the server, returner, and returner's partner.

Procedure—Full Doubles Court
1. Server serves and volleys hitting a second serve.
2. Point is played out with the returner able to hit only crosscourt while the server and returner's partner may hit anywhere in the court.
3. Server alternates serving to the deuce and ad courts.

   P1: Serves second serve, serving and volleying.

   P2: Returns crosscourt.

   P3: Closes and looks to poach.

   Point is played out.

Scoring
Count the number of points the server wins.

Key Points
- In this drill, the returning team focuses on working together with an emphasis on making the server volley and on setting up the returner's partner, who closes and poaches.
- The server limits the returner's return angles by serving down the middle.
- The returner must make the server hit a first volley.

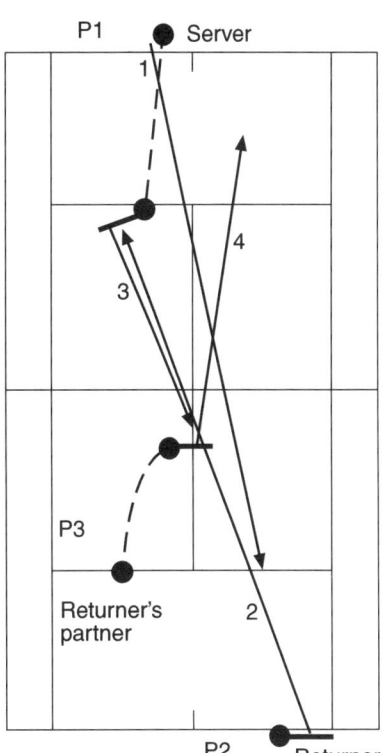

Drill 59 Returning Team vs. a Server (2v1)

Variations

1. Drill is either a deuce or ad court game.
2. Server stays on the baseline and comes forward only on short balls.
3. Server is allowed a first and a second serve.
4. Server is allowed two serves but has only two second serves available per 3-minute game. Once the second serves are used up, the server has only one serve for each point.
5. Returner must approach off the serve.
6. Server can be assigned location for serve.

60 Serving Team vs. a Returner (2v1)

Purpose

To develop the serving team's doubles skills with emphasis on setting up the server's partner at the net.

Time

Nine-minute game with each player taking a 3-minute turn as the server, returner, and server's partner.

Procedure—Full Doubles Court

1. Server serves and volleys hitting a second serve.
2. Point is played out with the server able to hit only crosscourt while the returner and server's partner may hit anywhere in the court.
3. Server alternates serving to the deuce and ad courts.

   P1: Serves second serve, serving and volleying.

   P2: Returns crosscourt.

   P3: Looks to poach.

   Point is played out.

Scoring

Count the number of points the returner wins.

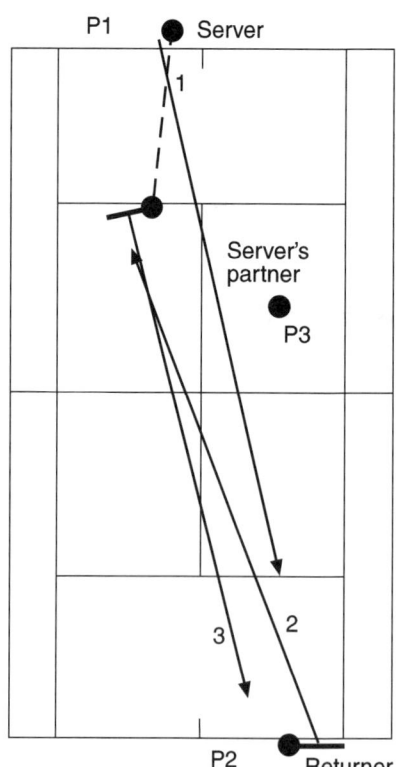

Drill 60 Serving Team vs. a Returner (2v1)

Key Points

- The serving team focuses on working on the plays, with an emphasis on the server serving and volleying and setting up the server's partner, who feints or poaches.
- The returner must make the server hit a first volley and then may lob or hit between members of the serving team to create openings.

Variations

1. Drill is either a deuce or ad court game.
2. Server stays on the baseline and comes forward only on short balls.
3. Server is allowed two serves.
4. Server is allowed two serves but only has two second serves available per 3-minute game. Once the second serves are used up, the server only has one serve for each point.
5. Server can be assigned location for serve.

61 Doubles Serve and Volley vs. Two Back (2v2)

Purpose

To practice serving against a team that returns with both players on the baseline.
To practice returning with both returning partners on the baseline.

Time

Eight-minute games divided into two 4-minute segments.

Procedure—Full Doubles Court

1. Regular doubles points are played out, with the serving team serving and volleying and the returning team playing two back.
2. Each team serves for 4 minutes with each player serving for 2 minutes.

Scoring

One-point scoring.

Key Points

- Good doubles teams must be familiar with playing against teams that play two back when returning.

- Aggressive serve-and-volley teams often find themselves out of sync when playing against the two-back formation because there are no longer targets or lanes at which to aim.
- The serving team works on being patient and opening up the court by initially playing through the middle to create angles and openings.
- The two-back team also must be patient and "break down" the serving team by forcing errors.

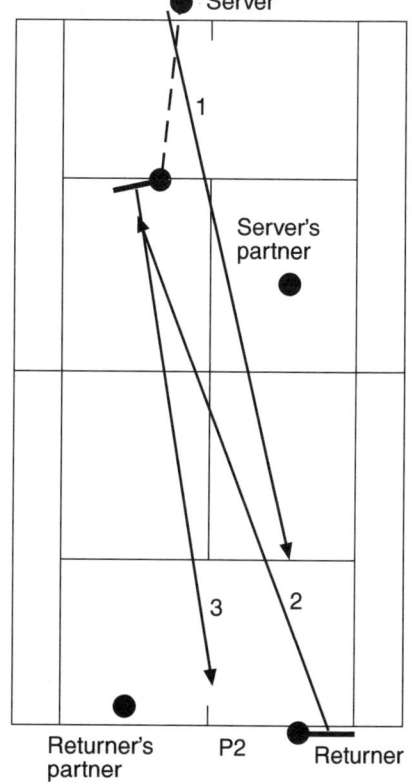

Drill 61 Doubles Serve and Volley vs. Two Back (2v2)

Variations

1. Returning team plays conventional one-up/one-back formation when returning second serves and can even chip and charge off the second serve.
2. Returning team commits two-point errors on unforced netted shots.
3. Feeding pattern can be adjusted to four-point rotations.
4. Server can be assigned location for serve.

Point Building

62 Doubles Crosscourts (1v1)

Purpose

To practice building a doubles point from the baseline.

Time

Three- or 4-minute games.

Procedure—Half a Doubles Court (Diagonal)

1. Points are played out crosscourt from the baseline, with players recovering to a designated chalk mark.
2. Forehands should be hit from the deuce court and backhands from the ad court.
3. Drill is either a deuce or ad court game.
4. One player serves two points, then other player serves two points.
   P1: Serves and stays at the baseline.
   P2: Returns serve crosscourt.
   P1: Hits groundstroke crosscourt.
   Point is played out crosscourt.

Scoring

One-point scoring.

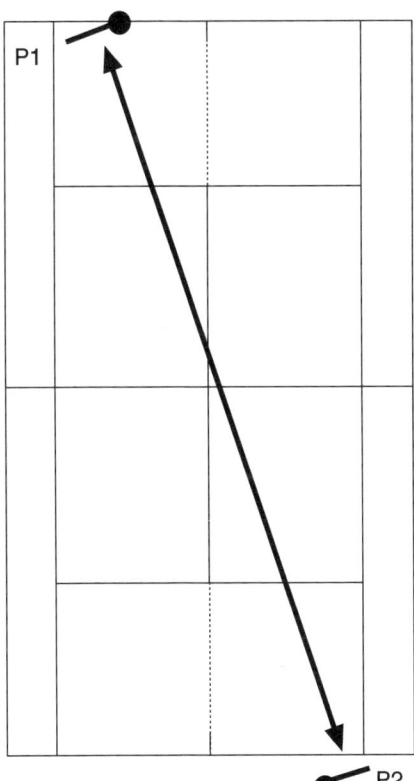

Drill 62 Doubles Crosscourts (1v1)

Key Points

- This drill is similar to Singles Crosscourts but the doubles alleys are in play.
- Doubles Crosscourts familiarizes players with playing from the baseline on a doubles court and makes an excellent early drill during a doubles practice.
- As a reference, the singles sideline can be used as a target.

Variations

1. Wild cards such as serving and volleying, drop shots, chip and charges, and lobs work well in this crosscourt drill.
2. Net errors are two-point errors.
3. Players have a first and second serve.
4. Server can be assigned location for serve.

Pressuring

63 Doubles Two-Touch Crosscourt Serve and Volley (1v1)

Purpose

To practice closing quickly and to develop an aggressive, closing mentality as a server and as a returner.

Time

Three- or 4-minute games.

Procedure—Half a Doubles Court (Diagonal)

1. Points are played out crosscourt with the server having only one serve per point.
2. Servers serve and volley and returners approach net off serve.
3. One player serves two points (one deuce, one ad) then the other player serves two points (one deuce, one ad).
4. The ball is allowed to touch the court only twice—off the serve and off the return. The rest of the point is played out of the air.

   P1: Serves and volleys.

   P2: Returns serve crosscourt and closes.

P1: Volleys or half-volleys crosscourt.

P2: Volleys crosscourt.

Point is played out with the ball not allowed to touch the court.

Scoring

One-point scoring. Ball touching the court after the server's first volley results in loss of point.

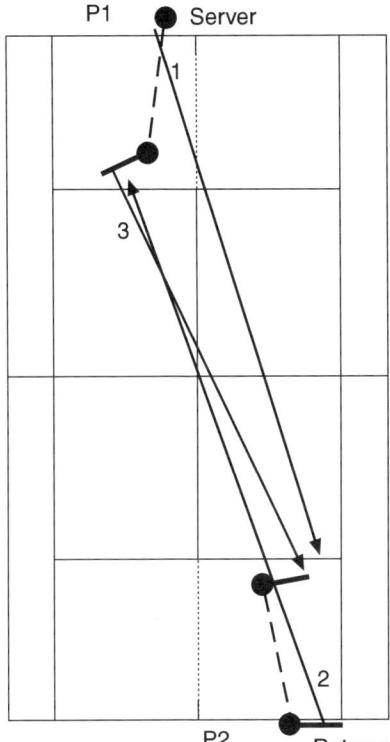

Drill 63 Doubles Two-Touch Crosscourt Serve and Volley (1v1)

Key Points

- This Craig Tiley drill offers excellent practice for aggressive closing. Since players have no choice, the coach will not have to remind the players to close.
- An excellent drill for practicing quick volley exchanges.

Variations

1. Drill can be played as a deuce-court- or an ad-court-only game.
2. Servers allowed two serves.

3. Unforced net errors are two-point errors.
4. Serve, return, or first-volley errors are two-point errors.
5. Lobs or no lobs can be stipulated.
6. Server can be assigned location for serve.

64 Doubles Crosscourt Pinch Volleys (1v1)

Purpose

To practice quick exchange volleys and groundstrokes.
To develop quick hand reactions when "pinched" by deep volleys.

Time

Four-minute game consisting of two 2-minute segments.

Procedure—Half a Doubles Court (Diagonal)

1. P1 begins at the service line with P2 on or inside the baseline.
2. Players switch roles after 2 minutes.
3. Drill is a deuce-court- or an ad-court-only game, but not both.

    P1: Feeds crosscourt and stays on service line.

    P2: Hits P1 a volley.

    P1: Volleys and then closes.

    P2: Plays out point by staying on or inside the baseline. No lobs are allowed.

Scoring

One-point scoring; only the volleyer scores. After each player has a turn, the volleyer with the most points is the winner. Baseline player loses a point if he or she moves behind the baseline. Must always be on or inside baseline.

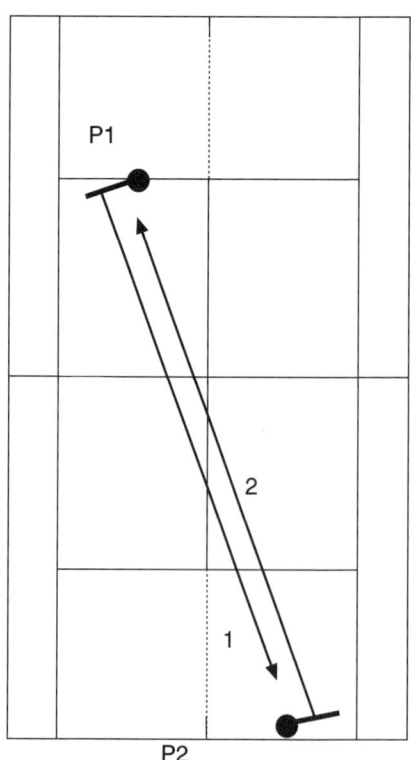

Drill 64 Doubles Crosscourt Pinch Volleys (1v1)

Key Points

- This drill is the same as the singles Pinch Volleys drill except it is played out crosscourt on half a doubles court.
- By playing on or inside the baseline, players practice reacting quickly to deep volleys while maintaining court position.
- Also an excellent drill for practicing controlled volleys during quick exchanges.

Variations

1. Two-point errors for unforced net errors—volleys or groundstrokes.
2. Groundstroker may lob after net player has hit two volleys.
2. Baseline player hits balls to volleyers feet off feed, making them half-volley (good opportunity to practice rolling balls to feet).

65 Doubles One-Player Closing Volleys (1v1)

Purpose

To practice approach shots, first volleys, and point-ending volleys and overheads. To practice neutralizing attacking players.

Time

Three- or 4-minute games.

Procedure—Half a Doubles Court (Diagonal)

1. Both players begin at the baseline.
2. P1, as the baseliner, feeds two points, then P2 feeds two points.
3. Drill is either a deuce-court or an ad-court game.

    P1: Feeds crosscourt to the service line and stays on the baseline.

    P2: Approaches crosscourt back to P1.

    P1: Hits crosscourt groundstroke, making P2 volley or half-volley.

    P2: Volleys and plays out point.

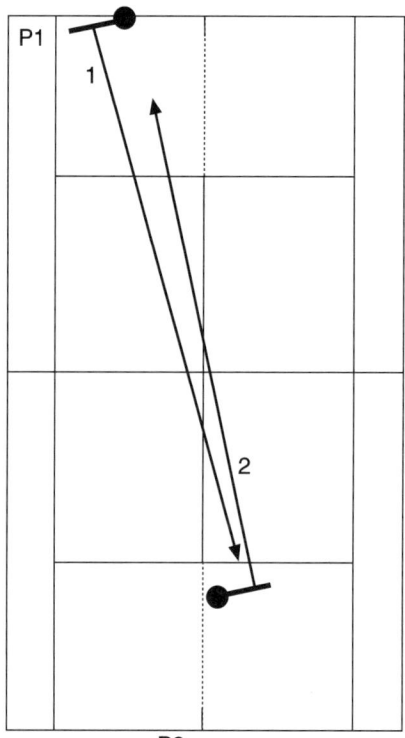

Drill 65 Doubles One-Player Closing Volleys (1v1)

Scoring

One-point scoring.

Key Points

- This drill is the same as the singles One-Player Closing Volleys drill except it is played out crosscourt on half a doubles court.
- Players work on approaching off a short ball.
- Emphasis is on the baseliner making the volleyer hit a first volley and on the volleyer hitting controlled, deep first volleys to establish good court position for a point-ending volley or overhead.

Variations

1. Lobs or no lobs can be stipulated.
2. Baseline net errors are two-point errors.
3. Volleyer slices the approach shot.
4. Instead of feeding, players serve with the returner approaching off the serve.

66 Doubles Two-Player Closing Volleys (1v1)

Purpose

To practice approach shots and quick volley exchanges when closing to the net.

Time

Three- or 4-minute game.

Procedure—Half a Doubles Court (Diagonal)

1. Both players begin at the baseline.
2. P1 feeds two points, then P2 feeds two points.
3. Drill is either a deuce-court or an ad-court game.

    P1: Feeds crosscourt to the service line and closes.

    P2: Approaches crosscourt back to P1. P2 must hit shot at P1 (cannot pass off feed).

    P1: Volleys crosscourt back to P2.

    P2: Volleys and plays out point.

Scoring

One-point scoring.

Key Points

- This drill is the same as the singles Two-Player Closing Volleys drill except it is played out crosscourt on half a doubles court.
- Keeping volleys low is at a premium, as whoever pops up a volley is in serious trouble.

Variations

1. Lobs or no lobs can be stipulated.
2. Player slices approach shot.
3. First volleys must touch the court in front of closing feeder.

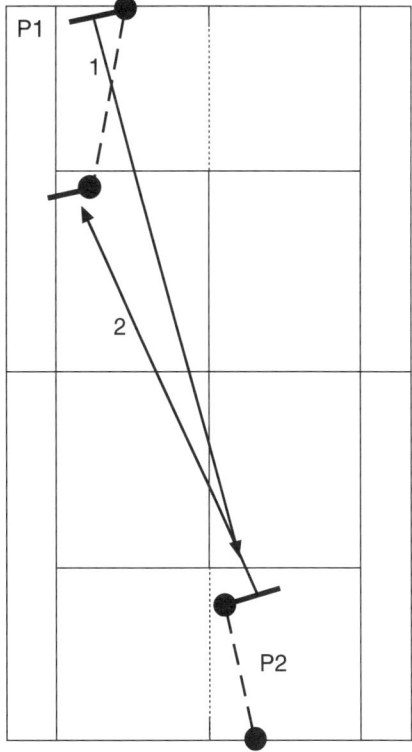

Drill 66 Doubles Two-Player Closing Volleys (1v1)

67 Doubles Overhead Game (2v1)

Purpose

To practice hitting overheads deep and through the middle or wide and angled against a two-back team.

Time

Nine-minute games with three 3-minute segments.

Procedure—Full Doubles Court

1. P1 begins at the service line and P2 and P3 begin at the baseline.

   P1: Feeds either P2 or P3 from the T.

   P2 or P3: Hits P1 a volley.

   P1: Closes and volleys.

   P2 or P3: Lobs P1.

   P1: Hits overhead.

   P2 or P3: Lobs or hits groundstroke.

   Point is played out.

   P2 and P3 must hit all groundstrokes at P1, whereas lobs may be hit anywhere in the court.

2. Once the overhead is struck, the point is played out (P2 and P3 do not have to lob again). If a shot is missed or the lob is unplayable, restart the sequence. Again, the point doesn't officially begin until the overhead is hit.

3. Players rotate clockwise so everyone has a chance to defend from the deuce and ad courts.

Scoring

Count the number of points the overhead hitter wins.

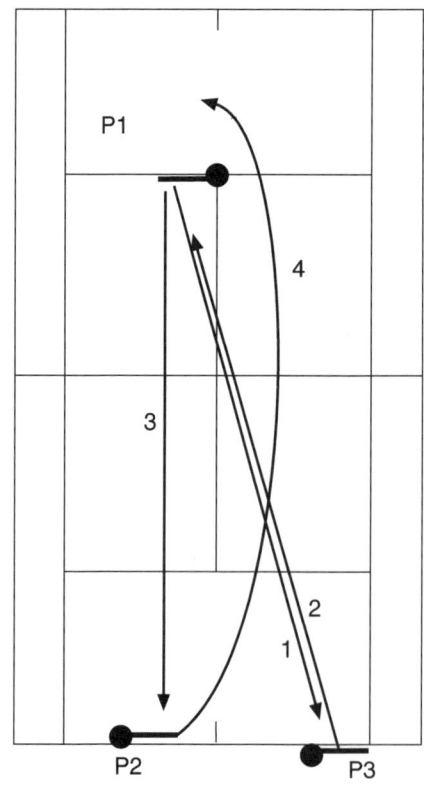

Drill 67 Doubles Overhead Game (2v1)

Key Points

- In this drill, the overhead hitter practices opening up the court against a team playing two back.
- Tactically, it makes sense for the overhead hitter to probe the middle before hitting wide. This is especially true on deep lobs.
- The closer the overhead hitter is to the net, the greater the angle available for put-aways.

Variation

1. After P1 volleys, P2 and P3 must lob for the remainder of the point.

68 Doubles With Returner Pressuring (2v2)

Purpose

To practice taking the net as a team when returning second serves.
To practice defending against a team that approaches off second serves.

Time

Five-minute games.

Procedure—Full Doubles Court

1. Players begin in conventional doubles positions with servers allowed one serve.
2. Servers may serve and volley or stay back.
3. P1 serves four points, then P3 serves four points, followed by P2 and then P4.

   P1: Serves a second serve.

   P3: Returns crosscourt and approaches the net.

   P1: Volleys or hits groundstroke.

   Point is played out.

Scoring

One-point scoring.

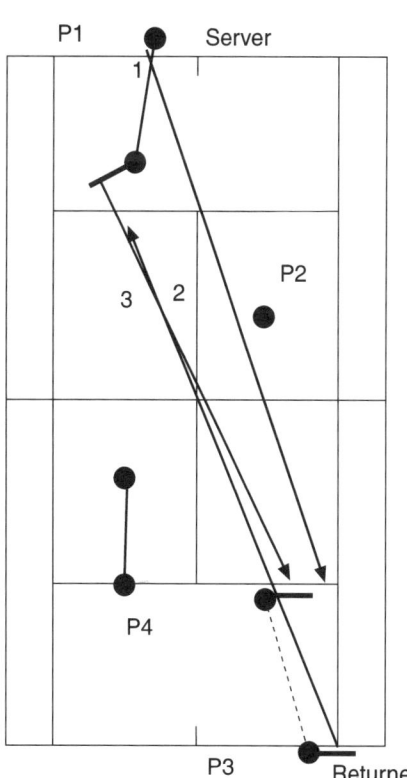

Drill 68 Doubles With Returner Pressuring (2v2)

Key Points

- This drill emphasizes the returner pressuring by coming forward off the second-serve return.
- Low returns to the serve-and-volleyer's feet are desired. Again, the focus is on the returner, so the drill should be tailored to meet the returner's needs.
- Slicing the return allows the returner time to close to an advantageous first-volley position.

Variations

1. Server stays back.
2. Returner's partner poaches.
3. Two points for executed poaching play—serving or returning team.
4. Returner chips lob over server's partner and moves forward.
5. Server can be assigned location for serve.

69 Doubles With Returner's Partner Poaching (2v2)

Purpose

To practice as a team setting up the returner's partner when returning second serves.

To practice defending against a team whereby the returner's partner closes and poaches.

Time

Five-minute games.

Procedure—Full Doubles Court

1. Players begin in conventional doubles positions with servers allowed one serve.
2. Servers may serve and volley or stay back.
3. P1 serves four points, then P3 serves four points, followed by P2 and then P4.

   P1: Serves and volleys.

   P3: Returns crosscourt to server.

   P1: Volleys or hits groundstroke crosscourt.

   P4: Closes and poaches.

   Point is played out.

Scoring

One-point scoring.

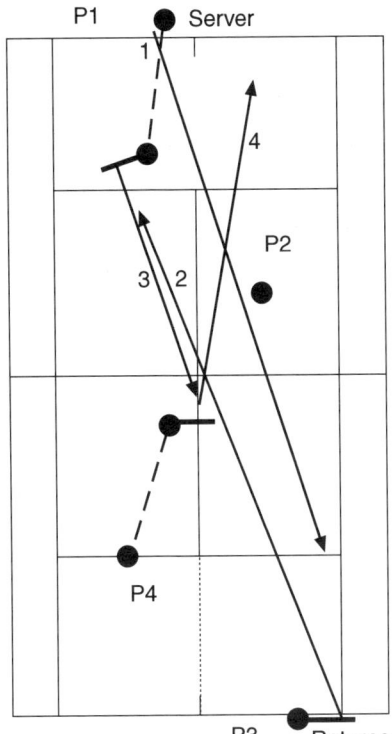

Drill 69 Doubles With Returner's Partner Poaching (2v2)

Key Points

- This drill emphasizes the returner's partner poaching by coming forward off the second-serve return and then releasing to the center strap.
- The success of the drill depends on the returner returning low to the server if serving and volleying, or deep if the server stays back. The returner's aim is to set up his partner.
- Once again, the returner's partner moves forward and then releases to the center strap. The returner's partner should be close enough to the net to be able to touch it with the racket after the move.

Variations

1. Server stays back.
2. Returner closes behind return.
3. Two points for executed poach play.
4. Server can be assigned location for serve.

70 Doubles Quick Volleys (2v2)

Purpose

To develop and practice quick exchange volleys, and moving and working together as a team.

Time

Three-, 4-, or 5-minute games.

Procedure—Full Doubles Court

1. All four players begin at the service line.
2. Each player holds two to three balls, with each feeding all their balls in the following order: P1, P3, P2, P4. When all the balls have been fed, players reload for another round until time expires.
3. Players return to the service line after each point.

   P1: Feeds to P3 or P4 (feed should be at least knee high).

   P3 or P4: Volleys back to P1 or P2.

   Point is played out.

Scoring

One-point scoring.

Key Points

- With both teams beginning at the service line, quick volleys emphasize moving and covering the court as a team, maintaining the point of attack, and hitting reflex volleys.
- Players can also be tethered together with 8 feet of surgical tubing to promote teamwork.

Variations

1. Coach feeds to start points.
2. Use singles court.
3. Lobs or no lobs can be stipulated.

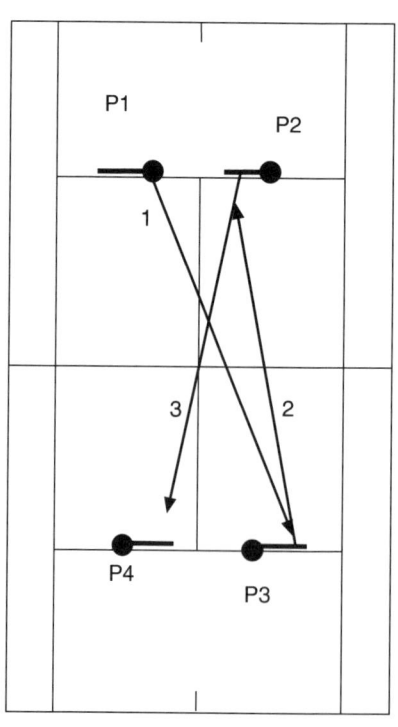

Drill 70 Doubles Quick Volleys (2v2)

71 Doubles One-Player Closing Volleys (2v2)

Purpose

To practice as a one-up/one-back team against a team at the net. To practice developing a point against a one-up/one-back team.

Time

Five-minute games.

Procedure—Full Doubles Court

1. Players begin in conventional doubles positions.
2. Four-point feeding patterns. P1, as the baseliner, feeds two deuce-court points, then P2 becomes the baseliner and feeds two ad-court points. P3 and P4 then each feed two points.

   P1: Feeds crosscourt to the service line and stays on the baseline.

   P3: Approaches crosscourt back to P1.

   P1: Hits groundstroke, making P3 volley or half-volley.

   Point is played out.

Scoring

One-point scoring.

Key Points

- This drill simulates playing doubles with two players at the net versus a one-up/one-back formation.
- Net players learn to maintain the point of attack until at least the second volley or a point-ending opportunity is created.
- The one baseline player should look to hit between the net players or hit low and crosscourt to force the net players to volley up and involve the baseliner's partner at the net.
- Tactically, lobs are effective after closing player hits a first volley.

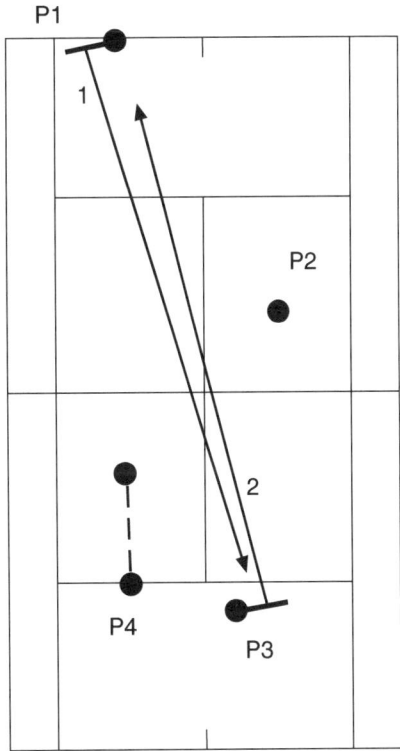

Drill 71 Doubles One-Team Closing Volleys (2v2)

Variations

1. Lobs or no lobs can be stipulated.
2. Baseline net errors are two-point errors.
3. Approaching player slices the approach shot.

72 Doubles One-Team Closing Volleys (2v2)

Purpose

To practice approaching the net as a team and developing the point against a two-back team.
To learn how to defend and neutralize the point against an attacking team when playing two-back doubles.

Time

Five-minute games.

Procedure—Full Doubles Court

1. Both teams begin on the baseline.
2. Using crosscourt feeds, each team rotates feeding four points—2 deuce and 2 ad court feeds.

   P1: Feeds crosscourt to the service line and stays on the baseline.

   P3: Approaches through the middle and closes with P4 to the net.

   P1 or P2: Hits groundstroke, making P3 or P4 volley or half-volley.

   Point is played out.

Scoring

One-point scoring.

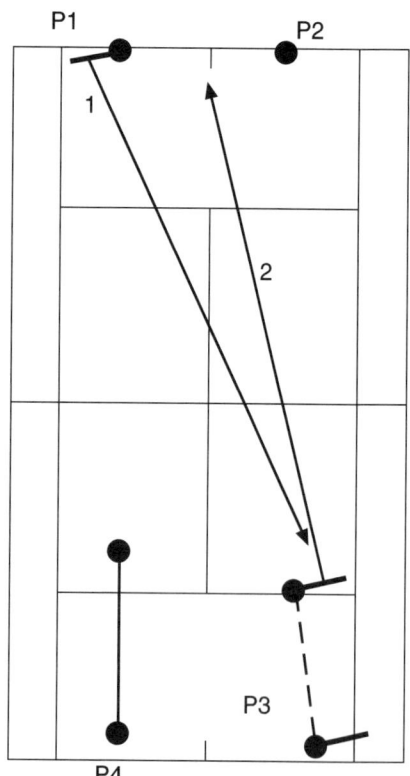

Drill 72 Doubles One-Team Closing Volleys (2v2)

Key Points

- This drill simulates playing with two players at the net versus a two-back formation.
- Net players practice probing the middle, playing between the baseliners, volleying short and wide, maintaining patience at the net, and isolating on one player.
- Tactically, lobs are effective against the attacking team after the team has hit a first volley.

Variations

1. Lobs or no lobs can be stipulated.
2. Baseline net errors are two-point errors.
3. Approaching player slices the approach shot.

73 Doubles Overhead Game (2v2)

Purpose

To control and end points as a team with overheads against a two-back team.

Time

Four- or 6-minute games with two segments of 2 or 3 minutes.

Procedure—Full Doubles Court

1. Feeding team plays against a two-back team.
2. P1 feeds two points, then P2 feeds two points, alternating until their time allotment is up.
3. Teams reverse roles with overhead team becoming the two-back team.

   P1: Feeds crosscourt from three-quarter court and closes.

   P3: Hits crosscourt groundstroke to P1.

   P1: Volleys through the middle.

   P3 or P4: Lobs (point now begins).

   P1 or P2: Hits overheads.

   Point is played out.

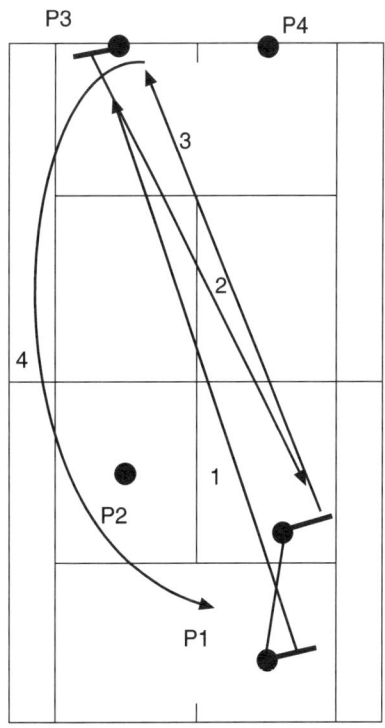

Drill 73 Doubles Overhead Game (2v2)

Scoring

One-point scoring.

Key Points

- Tactically, it makes sense for the overhead hitter to probe the middle before hitting wide. This is especially true on deep lobs. The closer the overhead hitter is to the net, the greater the angle available.
- Short-angled volleys are very effective against a two-back team.

Variations

1. Two-back team lobs all shots after first volley.
2. Two-back team can make net team hit one or two volleys before lobbing (keeps the net team honest and the drill less predictable).
3. Points are scored only after an overhead has been hit.

Doubles Play

The following doubles games involve either set play or tiebreaker play. Each game has numerous variations that are used to isolate specific team and individual needs. The coach can also assign different variations to different teams on the same court to highlight areas of strength or weakness. For instance, one team has to serve and volley while the other team has only one serve per point.

74 1v1 Sets

Purpose

To reveal and develop serve and volley, return, and first-volley strengths.

Procedure—Half a Doubles Court (Diagonal)

1. Two-player doubles sets are played crosscourt with an imaginary boundary line down the middle of the court.
2. Regular scoring is used.

Key Points

- These sets are an excellent way to evaluate the strengths and weaknesses of your doubles players.
- Primary focus is on serving and volleying, returning, and first volleys.

Variations

1. Regular or no-ad scoring can be used.
2. Net errors are two-point errors.
3. Players have only one serve per point.
4. Players have only two second serves per service game.
5. Returner must move forward off return.
6. Players must serve and volley.
7. Two-touch doubles (ball bounces only twice—off serve and off return).
8. Server can be assigned location for serve.
9. Play 1v1 tiebreakers instead of sets.

75 Two-Touch Doubles (2v2)

Purpose

To practice aggressive closing and pressuring as a server and as a returner.

Procedure—Full Doubles Court

1. Teams play a set of doubles.
2. The ball may touch the court only twice—off the serve and off the return.
3. Any other touch results in the loss of a point.

Key Points

- This Craig Tiley original forces both teams to play aggressive, attacking doubles.
- Players should attempt to play to the feet of their opponents as often as possible.

Variations

1. Regular or no-ad scoring can be used.
2. Players have only one serve per point.
3. Players have only two second serves per service game.
4. Server can be assigned location for serve.
5. No lobs are allowed.

76 Doubles Sets (2v2)

Purpose

To practice doubles under match conditions.

Procedure—Full Doubles Court

1. Teams play a regular or eight-game pro-set of doubles.

Scoring

Regular scoring.

Key Points

- Use stipulations and variations to keep players alert and focused and to work on strengths and weaknesses.

Variations

1. Returners play two back only on first serves or on both first and second serves.
2. Returner's partner must look to poach off all second serves.
3. Returner must move forward off return.
4. Returning team moves forward (variations 2 and 3 combined).
5. Regular or no-ad scoring can be used.
6. Unforced net errors are two-point errors.
7. Players have only one serve per point.
8. Players have only two second serves per service game.
9. Players must serve and volley.
10. Two-touch doubles (ball bounces only twice—off serve and off return).
11. Server can be assigned location for serve.

77 Doubles Tiebreakers (2v2)

Purpose

To practice doubles tiebreakers.
To practice playing doubles with stipulations and to focus on various tactical concepts.

Procedure—Full Doubles Court

1. Teams play a tiebreaker.
2. When one court finishes, all the other courts stop, regardless of the score.

Scoring

Tiebreakers can be played to 7 or 11.

Key Points

- Tiebreakers are fun and exciting, and keep all four players focused and intense as the end is always near.
- Tiebreakers are excellent for focusing on different aspects of doubles (see the variations listed below).

Variations

1. Returners play two back.
2. Returner's partner must look to poach off all second serves.
3. Returner must move forward off return.
4. Returning team moves forward (variations 2 and 3 combined).
5. Unforced net errors are two-point errors.
6. Players have only one serve per point.
7. Players have only two second serves per tiebreaker.
8. Servers must serve and volley.
9. Two-touch doubles (ball bounces only twice—off serve and off return).
10. Server can be assigned location for serve.
11. Winners choose the variation for the next tiebreaker.

8

Warm-Up Drills

A proper on-court warm-up is important in order to be physically and mentally prepared for an intense and focused practice session. On-court warm-ups can also be used for teaching and reviewing tactical and technical concepts and, in general, setting the tone for the upcoming practice. Because pressure training practices are highly structured and disciplined, I like the warm up to prepare the players for the type of practice to follow. For example, if it is a doubles day in practice, players should warm-up by hitting volleys and groundstrokes off volleys and by hitting serves down the middle and returns crosscourt. As the example shows, the warm up exercises can also serve to create and enhance a doubles mind-set or attitude before the pressure drills begin.

Important reminders:

- On-court warm-ups should be preceded by jogging and stretching so that the player is actually physically warmed up before taking the court.
- Warm-ups are cooperative, not competitive, as no one likes to play with someone trying to win a warm-up.
- Always make sure players have a chance to warm up their serves before beginning a drill requiring serves.

The following warm-ups can also be combined and ordered to meet your daily needs.

A Five-Minute Warm-Up

In tournament and match play, players are often given only 5 minutes to warm up, including serves. The 5-Minute Warm-Up is adequate for a general warm-up and serves as a good lead-in to crosscourt groundstroke games. Players like the 5-Minute Warm-Up because it allows them the freedom to warm up as they choose.

Variation

1. Warm up more than 5 minutes to a maximum of 10 minutes. Useful if practicing after a layoff of two or more days.

B Topspin Warm-Up

Excellent for working on net clearance and topspin, the Topspin Warm-Up begins with a deuce-court warm-up as both players hit topspin outside groundstrokes crosscourt from:

1. the service line.
2. three-quarter court.
3. the baseline.

Have players practice hitting at a target.

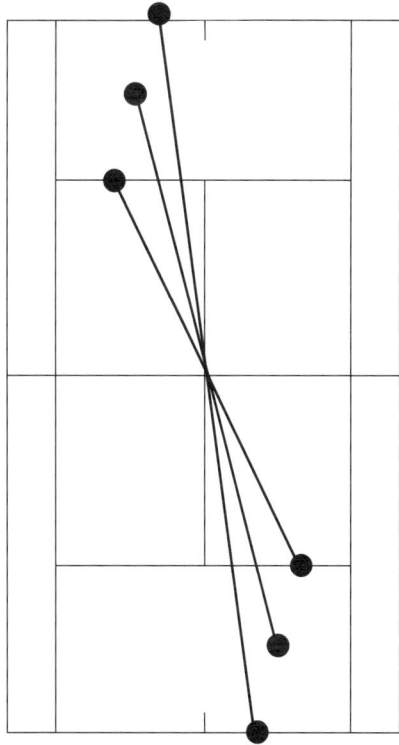

Figure 8.1 Topspin warm-up

After the deuce-court sequence is complete, the topspin sequence is repeated from the ad court. Targets (small disk cones) are useful in this warm-up as they encourage players to focus on location and topspin.

Allow at least 1 minute for each rally. For example, players will rally for 1 minute from the service line and 1 minute from three-quarter court. The drill will require a minimum of 6 minutes of rallying. Again, all strokes are outside topspin groundstrokes.

Variations

1. Each player has one ball and must run forward to retrieve the ball if a net error occurs.
2. Allow more time for the baseline rally segment, e.g., 2 minutes.

Note. Give players 2 minutes to warm up serves.

C Volley Warm-Up

Similar in structure to the Topspin Warm-Up, the Volley Warm-Up has players volleying crosscourt from three different areas—the front court, the service line, and three-quarter court. The player rallying with the volleyer hits crosscourt from the baseline. The Volley Warm-Up begins with a deuce-court warm-up as the volleyer volleys from:

1. the front court.
2. the service line.
3. three-quarter court.

After the deuce-court sequence is complete, the volley sequence is repeated from the ad court. Allow at least 1 minute for each rally. For example, the volleyer rallies for 1 minute from the deuce court service line and 1 minute from three-quarter court in the deuce court. The drill requires a minimum of 6 minutes of volleying for each player, for a total of 12 minutes. A target placed in front of the groundstroker at three-quarter court encourages the volleyer to hit controlled and accurate volleys.

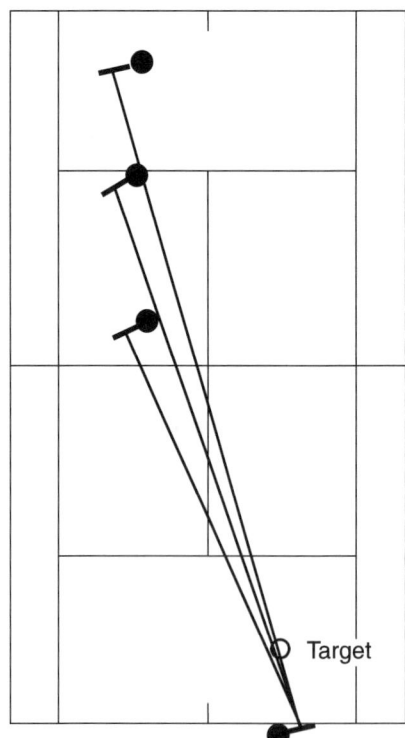

Figure 8.2 Volley warm-up

Note. Give players 2 minutes to warm up serves.

D One-Up/One-Back Warm-Up

This volley/groundstroke warm-up is excellent preparation for a doubles day. With one player volleying and the other player groundstroking from the baseline, both players hit only crosscourt outside shots. Having to hit only outside groundstrokes definitely requires a concentrated effort by both players. A target is useful for the volleyer to aim at and should be placed at the three-quarter-court mark. The volleyer begins each rally from the service line, closing after the first volley. Players volley at least 2 minutes from the deuce court and 2 minutes from the ad court. The volleyer and groundstroker switch roles, making the warm-up a minimum of 8 minutes.

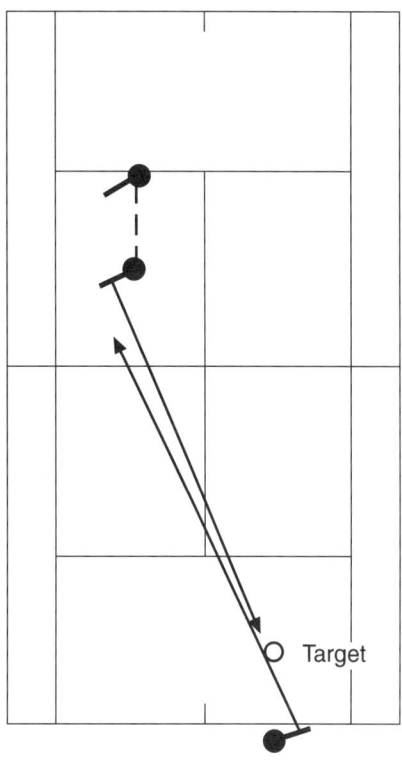

Figure 8.3 One-up/one-back warm-up

Variation

1. Groundstroker takes one pace forward after each groundstroke. Volleyer volleys in front of groundstroker and has to aim for a new spot on each volley as groundstroker closes.

Note. Give players 2 minutes to warm up serves.

E Directional Minitennis

Minitennis is an excellent warm-up and ideal for practicing tactical patterns. The players, playing on half a doubles court and rallying from the service line, follow a set routine emphasizing the Directionals with minitennis groundstrokes and volleys. Slice or topspin should be stipulated before starting the warm-up. For maximum benefit, stress footwork and constant movement. Targets are beneficial, especially when first learning the patterns, as players tend to groundstroke and volley too deep. After all, it is mini-tennis. Both players begin on the service line and execute the following 1-minute segments:

Segment 1: Outside forehand to outside forehand rally (figure 8.4a)
Segment 2: Outside backhand to outside backhand rally (figure 8.4b)

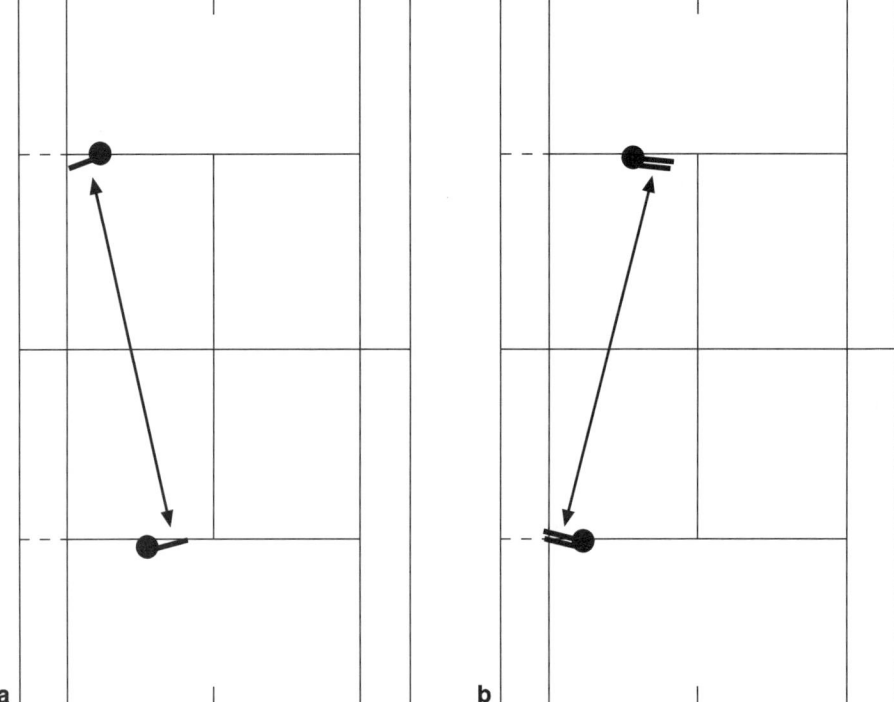

Figure 8.4 Directional minitennis—outside rally

Segment 3: P1 feeds P2 an inside backhand, P2 hits the inside shot crosscourt (figure 8.5a)

The rally continues with P1 hitting P2 an inside forehand which P2 hits crosscourt. Sequence continues. Players switch roles and the sequence is repeated (figure 8.5b).

The next phase involves one player at the net and one player at the service line. Again, each segment lasts 1 minute.

Segment 4: Outside forehand volley to outside forehand groundstroke (figure 8.6a)

Segment 5: Outside backhand volley to outside backhand groundstroke (figure 8.6b)

Segment 6: P1 feeds P2 an inside backhand volley, P2 changes direction on the volley (figure 8.7a)

The rally continues with P1 hitting P2 an inside forehand volley. P2 hits inside volley crosscourt. Sequence continues. Players switch roles and the sequence is repeated (figure 8.7b).

Warm-Up Drills 153

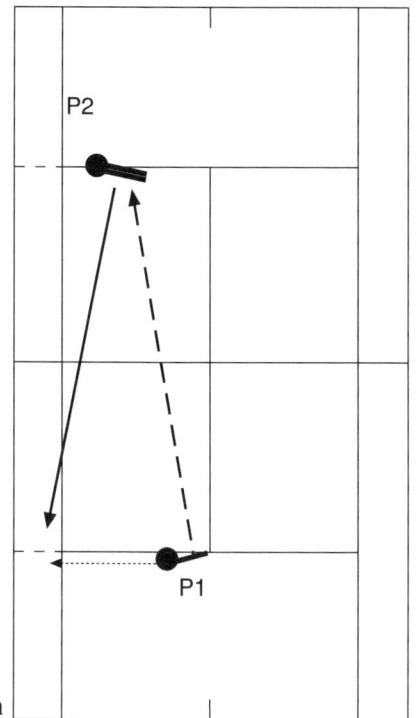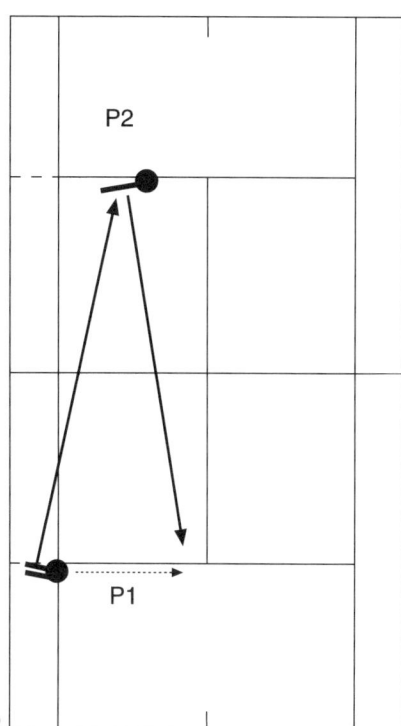

Figure 8.5 Directional minitennis inside rally

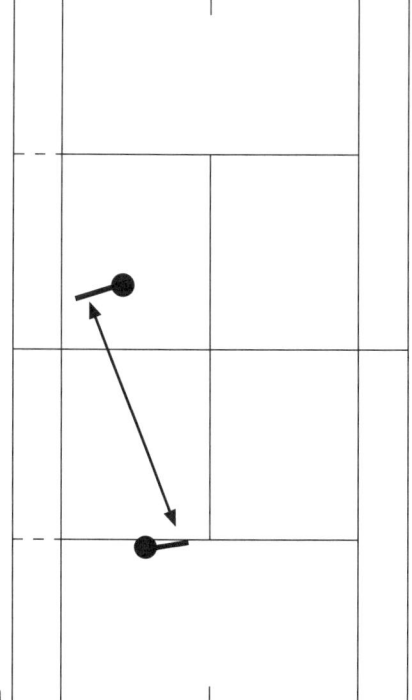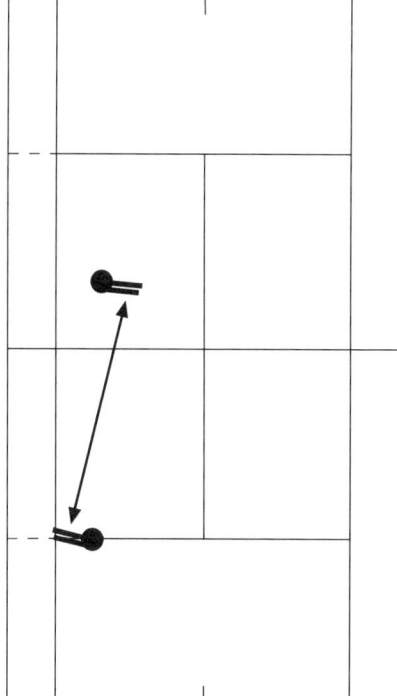

Figure 8.6 Directional minitennis volleys

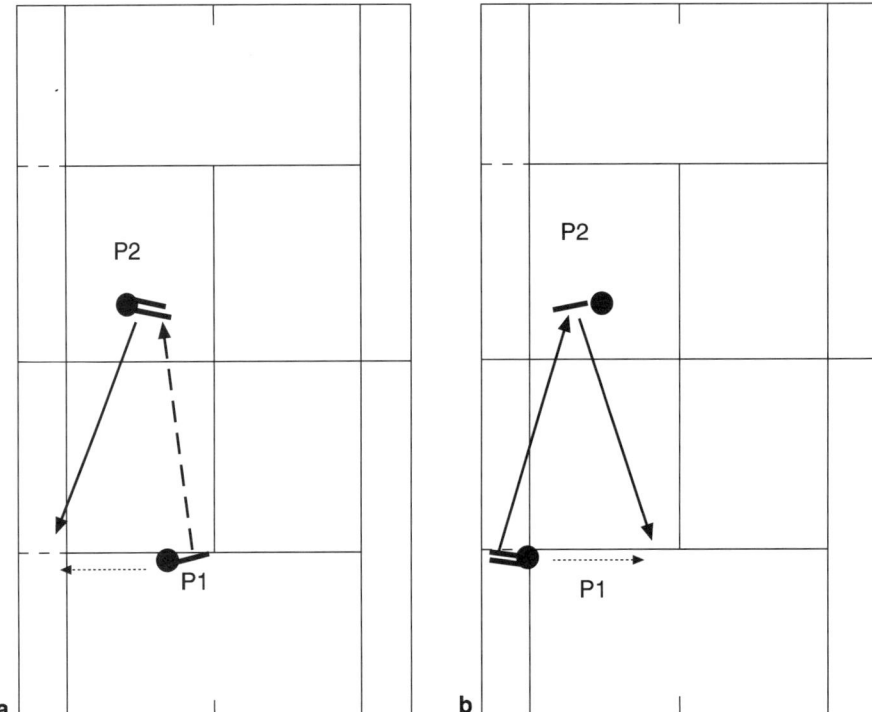

Figure 8.7 Directional minitennis inside volley

Variation

1. Begin the warm-up with one player at the net and one player on the service line. Emphasizing volley technique and footwork, players complete volley segments 4, 5, and 6.

Note. Follow Directional Minitennis with the 5-Minute Warm-Up.

F Soft-Toss Drills

Here's another drill I learned from Jeff Moore. Soft-Toss Drills are ideal for warming up strokes, reviewing tactics, and focusing on racket acceleration and footwork patterns. Feeders stand roughly 5 to 10 feet in front of the player and toss balls underhand to a designated area. Players must recover to the center mark or starting spot after each stroke. Coaches and players may act as feeders. Having players feed allows the coaches to roam and coach more than one court. Here are some soft-toss options.

Pattern 1: Coach feeds outside forehand soft-tosses (figure 8.8a)

Pattern 2: Coach feeds outside backhand soft-tosses (figure 8.8b)

Pattern 3: Coach feeds inside backhand soft-tosses (figure 8.9a)

Pattern 4: Coach feeds inside forehand soft-tosses (figure 8.9b)

Warm-Up Drills 155

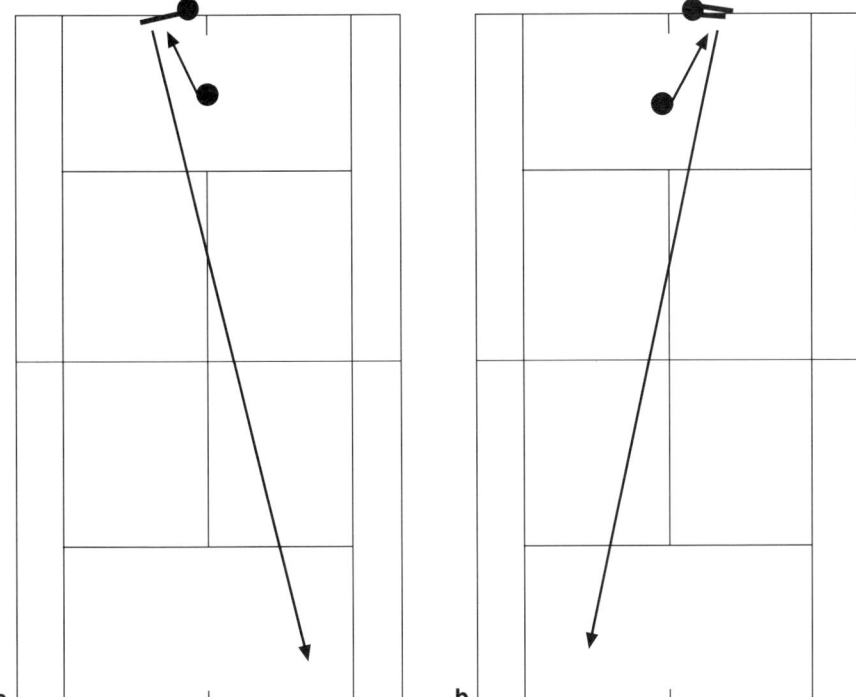

Figure 8.8 Soft-toss feeds for outside forehands and backhands

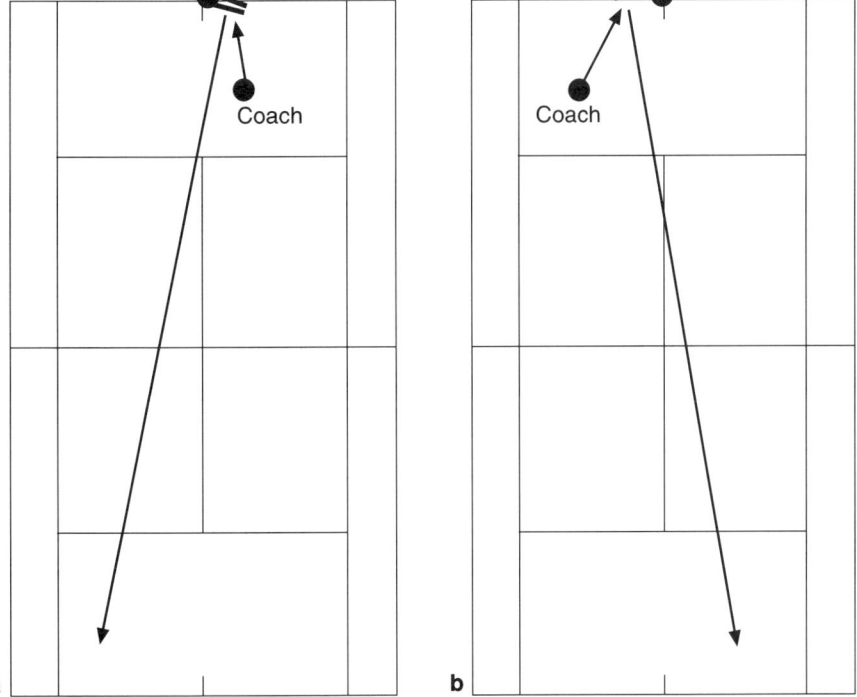

Figure 8.9 Soft-toss feeds for inside backhands and forehands

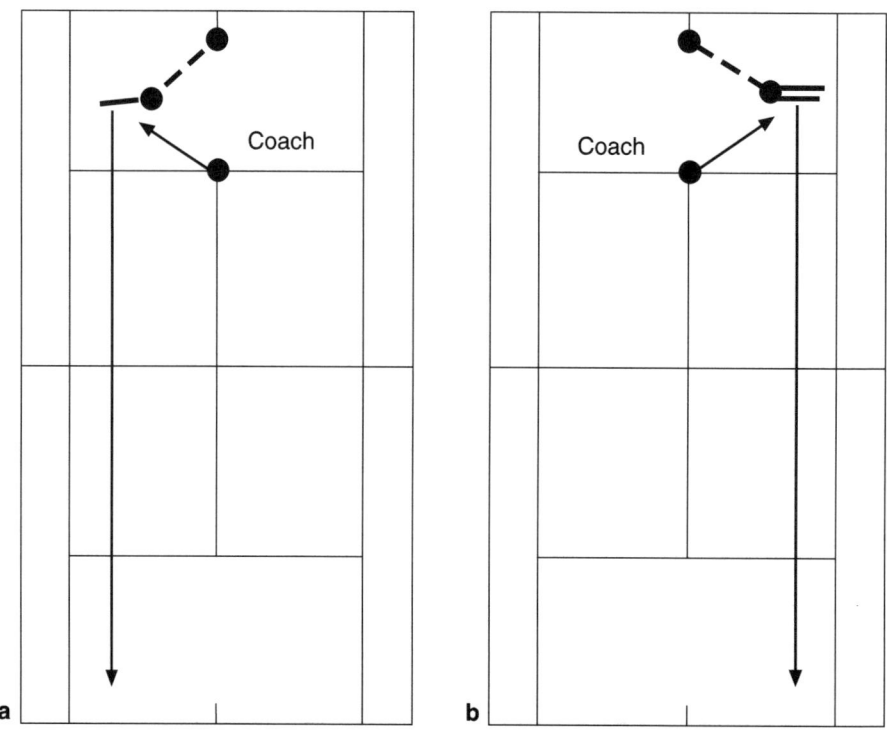

Figure 8.10 Soft-toss feeds for outside forehand and backhand approaches

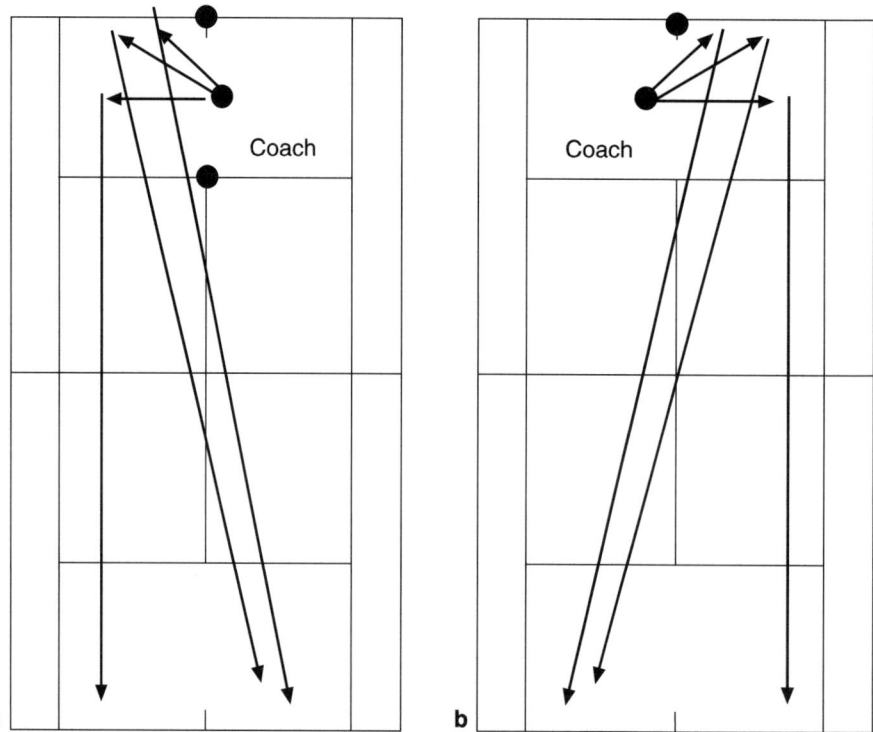

Figure 8.11 Soft-toss feeds for outside groundstroke sequences with outside approaches

Pattern 5: Coach feeds outside forehand approaches (figure 8.10a) and outside backhand approaches (figure 8.10b)

Pattern 6: Coach feeds outside forehand sequence with forehand approach shot (figure 8.11a)

Pattern 7: Coach feeds outside backhand sequence with backhand approach shot (figure 8.11b)

G Soft-Toss Sequences

Sequence 1: Coach feeds outside forehand, outside forehand, outside forehand approach (sequence applies to backhands as well) (figure 8.12)

Sequence 2: Coach feeds outside backhand, outside backhand, inside forehand (sequence applies to backhands as well) (figure 8.13)

Sequence 3: Coach feeds inside-out forehand, inside-out forehand, inside forehand 90-degree COD (figure 8.14)

Sequence 4: Coach feeds forehand volley, recover to T, backhand volley (figure 8.15)

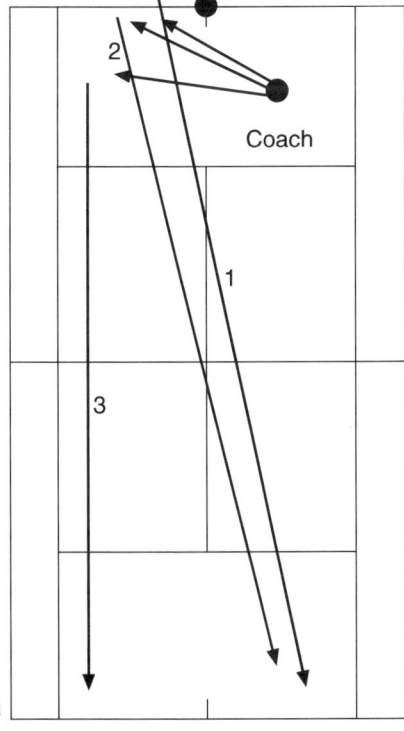

Figure 8.12 Sequence 1

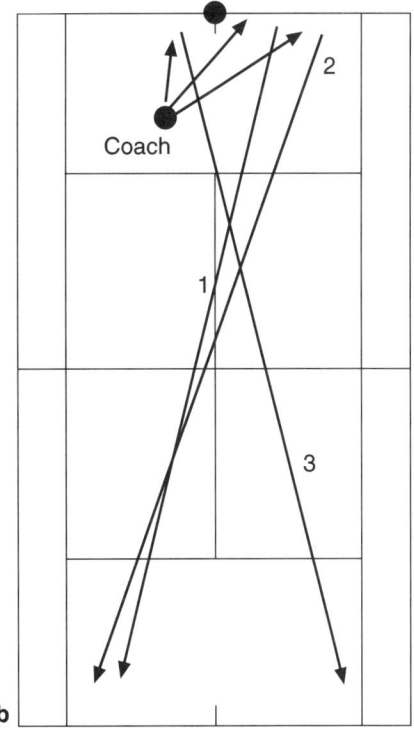

Figure 8.13 Sequence 2

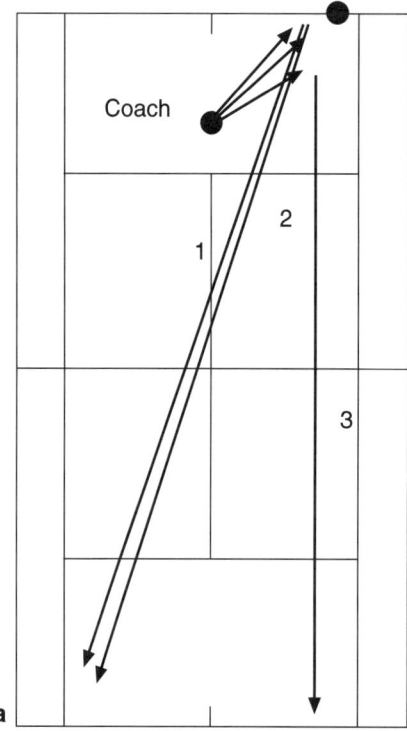 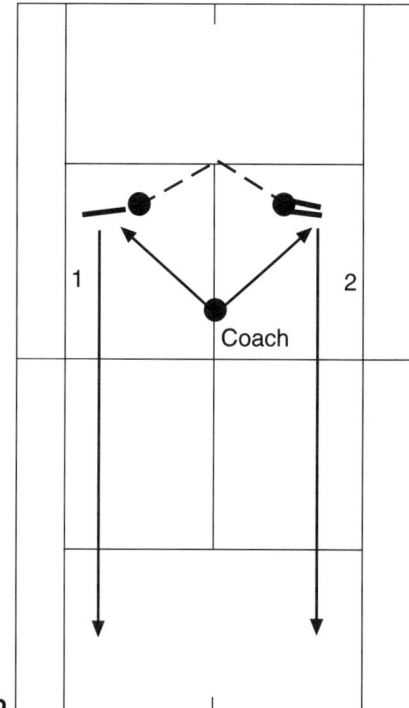

Figure 8.14 Sequence 3 **Figure 8.15** Sequence 4

Doubles Warm-Up

From Craig Tiley at the University of Illinois, this four-player doubles warm-up starts with two balls being fed crosscourt simultaneously. When one crosscourt rally ends, all four players join in to finish out the remaining rally, playing it as a doubles point.

P1 and P2: Both feed crosscourt to the service line at the same time.

P3 and P4: Both approach crosscourt.

P1 and P2: Both hit groundstrokes crosscourt.

P3 and P4: Both volley.

Points are played out crosscourt. When a rally ends, the two players without a ball become involved in the remaining rally. The point now becomes a doubles point, with all four players playing the remaining ball.

Rotation

Warm-up lasts 8 minutes. Deuce- and ad-court players exchange places after 2 minutes. Feeders switch roles after 4 minutes (two 2-minute segments).

Variation

1. Point begins with two crosscourt groundstroke rallies with both teams at the baseline. When one of the baseline rallies ends, the point is played out with either team allowed to take the net.

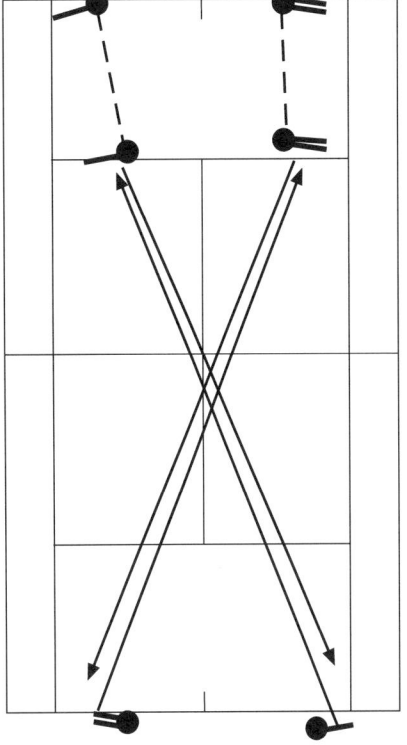

Figure 8.16 Doubles warm-up

9

The Performance Index

An important difference between match play and practice is immediacy. What happens in a match has immediate consequences, whereas practices are preparation for a future event. Without the sense of immediacy or urgency that today matters, practice lacks the physical, mental, and emotional demands of match play. The simple solution is to create immediacy by making practice count, by creating an environment where every ball hit has a purpose and value. Immediacy can only be created when there is accountability—when players know they have to produce because they are being measured by their practice performance. This is where the Performance Index comes in.

The Performance Index is an objective tool for measuring a player's daily practice performance relative to other team members and established standards. Since each pressure drill is a game that is won or lost, I record a "+" for a win and a "-" for a loss. For example, you may receive a "+" for winning a crosscourt forehand drill against your teammate or for reaching an established standard such as making 19 of 20 second serves. After recording the outcome of each drill during practice, results are totaled by drill type—groundstroke drills, air drills (volleys and overheads), and serve drills. A final summation of the three drill types is totaled under the category "Drill Totals."

It will be helpful to go through a sample practice session to better understand how to use the Performance Index.

Sample Practice from October 2:

1. 20 Second Serves With Returns (one round) {serve drill}
2. Crosscourt Groundstrokes (two rounds of deuce court, two rounds of ad court) {groundstroke drill}
3. Directionals (one round) {groundstroke drill}
4. Singles Points (one round) {groundstroke drill}
5. Closing Volleys (two rounds) {air drill}

The first practice drill, 20 Serves With Returns, involves competition between a player and a standard. My standard for a "+" for 20 second serves is 17 or higher. Each player serves 20 second serves (10 to the deuce court and 10 to the ad court), and their totals are recorded on a daily sheet (see figure 9.1).

Since my standard for a "+" in this drill is 17 or more out of 20 serves, Alex receives a "+" for making 17 second serves. On drills where players compete against a standard, I record their score in addition to the "+" or "-" so I know where they stand in relation to the standard. Of the eight players, only Alex, Leslie, and Jane received a "+" by reaching the team standard of 17 or more second serves made out of 20.

The second practice drill, Crosscourt Groundstrokes (indicated by the "cc" in the second drill column in figure 9.2), involves competition between two players. The matchups might have been: Natalie/Leslie, Patty/Jane, Alex/Ruth, and Caroline/Katy. Since winners receive a "+", we know Alex, Caroline, Leslie, and Patty won their crosscourt games.

Daily Performance Index
Friday, October 2, 1998

Name	20s
1. Alex	17+
2. Natalie	16-
3. Caroline	16-
4. Katy	16-
5. Leslie	18+
6. Patty	16-
7. Jane	17+
8. Ruth	14-

Figure 9.1 The daily performance index

At the end of a practice, the chart will look like the one in figure 9.3, with players receiving a "+" or "-" for each drill in which they compete. The nine columns after the names are the players' drill results.

The final eight columns on the chart in figure 9.3 are for win and loss totals. "GS" stands for groundstroke drill totals, "A" stands for air drill totals, and "S" stands for serve drill totals. The last two columns designated by "T" are a summation of all the drill totals. Looking at the first player's results, we see that Alex won five groundstroke drills and lost one. She won zero air drills and lost two and won her only service drill. Alex's drill total for the day was six wins and three losses.

These daily practice results are then recorded on a Weekly Performance Index sheet, which accommodates up to six practice sessions. The weekly totals are also added to a Season Performance Index sheet. I've automated my Performance Index on a computer using a spreadsheet program, so I need only to enter the daily practice results, and the spreadsheet automatically tabulates the weekly and season results. In addition to wins and losses, the Performance Index has winning percentages for each drill category. Examples of Weekly and Season Performance Index sheets are shown in figures 9.4 and 9.5.

Daily Performance Index
Friday, October 2, 1998

Name	20s	cc
1. Alex	17+	+
2. Natalie	16-	-
3. Caroline	16-	+
4. Katy	16-	-
5. Leslie	18+	+
6. Patty	16-	+
7. Jane	17+	-
8. Ruth	14-	-

Figure 9.2 Crosscourt groundstrokes recorded in the daily performance index

Note. Players will move up or down a court after drills that involve competition between players. Moving up or down a court allows everyone the opportunity to practice with each other on a daily basis. I designate at the beginning of practice which court will be the top court and which the bottom court. Drills like 20 Second Serves, which involve competition against a standard, do not lend themselves to moving up or down a court, as it is possible for all the players to receive a "+" by making 17 or more serves.

Daily Performance Index

		20s	cc	cc	cc	cc	D	sp	cv	cv	GS W	GS L	A W	A L	S W	S L	T W	T L
1.	Alex	17+	+	+	+	-	+	+	-	-	5	1	0	2	1	0	6	3
2.	Natalie	16-	-	-	+	-	+	-	-	-	2	4	0	2	0	1	2	7
3.	Caroline	16-	+	+	-	+	-	+	+	-	4	2	1	1	0	1	5	4
4.	Katy	16-	-	-	-	-	+	-	-	-	1	5	0	2	0	1	1	8
5.	Leslie	18+	+	-	-	-	+	-	-	+	2	4	1	1	1	0	4	5
6.	Patty	16-	+	-	+	+	-	+	+	+	4	2	2	0	0	1	6	3
7.	Jane	17+	-	+	+	+	-	+	+	+	4	2	2	0	1	0	7	2
8.	Ruth	14-	-	+	-	+	-	-	+	+	2	4	2	0	0	1	4	5

Figure 9.3 The daily performance index at the end of practice

Weekly Performance Index

Total drill results — Week Three

		2 Oct. W	2 Oct. L	3 Oct. W	3 Oct. L	4 Oct. W	4 Oct. L	5 Oct. W	5 Oct. L	6 Oct. W	6 Oct. L	7 Oct. W	7 Oct. L	Totals W	Totals L	Win Pct.
1.	Alex	6	3	7	2	15	7	8	0	7	1	7	3	50	16	0.76
2.	Natalie	2	7	4	5	15	7	4	4	6	2	4	6	35	31	0.53
3.	Caroline	5	4	6	3	14	8	3	5	5	3	6	4	39	27	0.59
4.	Katy	1	8	2	7	8	14	5	3	3	5	5	5	24	42	0.36
5.	Leslie	4	5	3	6	8	14	4	4	3	5	8	2	30	36	0.45
6.	Patty	6	3	5	4	12	10	1	7	6	2	6	4	36	30	0.55
7.	Jane	7	2	4	5	8	14	4	4	4	4	5	5	32	34	0.48
8.	Ruth	4	5	4	5	11	11	5	3	3	5	5	5	32	34	0.48

Groundstroke drills

		2 Oct. W	2 Oct. L	3 Oct. W	3 Oct. L	4 Oct. W	4 Oct. L	5 Oct. W	5 Oct. L	6 Oct. W	6 Oct. L	7 Oct. W	7 Oct. L	Totals W	Totals L	Win Pct.
1.	Alex	5	1	5	1	6	1	2	0	1	1			19	4	0.83
2.	Natalie	2	4	3	3	3	4	0	2	1	1			9	14	0.39
3.	Caroline	4	2	4	2	5	2	1	1	2	0			16	7	0.70
4.	Katy	1	5	1	5	2	5	1	1	1	1			6	17	0.26
5.	Leslie	2	4	2	4	2	5	1	1	1	1			8	15	0.35
6.	Patty	4	2	3	3	4	3	0	2	2	0			13	10	0.57
7.	Jane	4	2	2	4	3	4	1	1	1	1			11	12	0.48
8.	Ruth	2	4	2	4	4	3	1	1	0	2			9	14	0.39

Air drills

	2 Oct.		3 Oct.		4 Oct.		5 Oct.		6 Oct.		7 Oct.		Totals		Win
	W	L	W	L	W	L	W	L	W	L	W	L	W	L	Pct.
1. Alex	0	2	1	1	5	4	5	0	3	0	4	2	18	9	0.67
2. Natalie	0	2	1	1	7	2	3	2	2	1	2	4	15	12	0.56
3. Caroline	1	1	2	0	6	3	2	3	1	2	4	2	16	11	0.59
4. Katy	0	2	1	1	3	6	2	3	2	1	3	3	11	16	0.41
5. Leslie	1	1	0	2	4	5	3	2	1	2	4	2	13	14	0.48
6. Patty	2	0	1	1	5	4	1	4	2	1	4	2	15	12	0.56
7. Jane	2	0	2	0	3	6	2	3	1	2	2	4	12	15	0.44
8. Ruth	2	0	1	1	4	5	3	2	2	1	3	3	15	12	0.56

Figure 9.4 Weekly performance index

Serve drills

	2 Oct.		3 Oct.		4 Oct.		5 Oct.		6 Oct.		7 Oct.		Totals		Win
	W	L	W	L	W	L	W	L	W	L	W	L	W	L	Pct.
1. Alex	1	0	1	0	4	2	1	0	3	0	3	1	13	3	0.81
2. Natalie	0	1	0	1	5	1	1	0	3	0	2	2	11	5	0.69
3. Caroline	0	1	0	1	3	3	0	1	2	1	2	2	7	9	0.44
4. Katy	0	1	0	1	3	3	1	0	0	3	2	2	6	10	0.38
5. Leslie	1	0	1	0	2	4	0	1	1	2	4	0	9	7	0.56
6. Patty	0	1	1	0	3	3	0	1	2	1	2	2	8	8	0.50
7. Jane	1	0	0	1	2	4	1	0	2	1	3	1	9	7	0.56
8. Ruth	0	1	1	0	3	3	1	0	1	2	2	2	8	8	0.50

Season Performance Index

Total drill results *Weeks One–Four*

	WK1		WK2		WK3		WK4		Totals		Win
	W	L	W	L	W	L	W	L	W	L	Pct.
1. Alex	40	22	36	33	50	16	44	18	170	89	0.66
2. Natalie	41	21	31	34	35	31	27	32	134	118	0.53
3. Caroline	35	26	42	23	39	27	31	30	147	106	0.58
4. Katy	17	39	30	28	24	42	10	14	81	123	0.40
5. Leslie	7	32	21	27	30	36	13	22	71	117	0.38
6. Patty	33	29	33	35	36	30	28	36	130	130	0.50
7. Jane	30	32	26	39	32	34	26	33	114	138	0.45
8. Ruth	28	34	25	33	32	34	35	38	120	139	0.46

Groundstroke drills

	WK1		WK2		WK3		WK4		Totals		Win
	W	L	W	L	W	L	W	L	W	L	Pct.
1. Alex	28	15	21	12	19	4	29	10	97	41	0.70
2. Natalie	29	14	18	15	9	14	21	18	77	61	0.56
3. Caroline	26	16	18	15	16	7	21	17	81	55	0.60
4. Katy	11	29	15	16	6	17	10	4	42	66	0.39
5. Leslie	6	24	9	13	8	15	11	12	34	64	0.35
6. Patty	19	21	17	14	13	10	18	19	67	64	0.51
7. Jane	23	20	15	18	11	12	16	23	65	73	0.47
8. Ruth	21	22	13	18	9	14	19	20	62	74	0.46

Air drills

	WK1		WK2		WK3		WK4		Totals		Win
	W	L	W	L	W	L	W	L	W	L	Pct.
1. Alex	8	5	12	21	18	9	9	7	47	42	0.53
2. Natalie	8	5	13	16	15	12	5	11	41	44	0.48
3. Caroline	7	6	21	8	16	11	5	11	49	36	0.58
4. Katy	4	7	13	12	11	16	5	3	33	38	0.46
5. Leslie	1	5	12	13	13	14	3	4	29	36	0.45
6. Patty	7	6	14	15	15	12	8	7	44	40	0.52
7. Jane	6	7	10	19	12	15	10	5	38	46	0.45
8. Ruth	5	8	16	13	15	12	8	7	44	40	0.52

Serve drills

	WK1		WK2		WK3		WK4		Totals		Win
	W	L	W	L	W	L	W	L	W	L	Pct.
1. Alex	3	3	7	3	13	3	14	5	37	14	0.73
2. Natalie	3	3	3	7	11	5	11	8	28	23	0.55
3. Caroline	2	4	9	1	7	9	10	10	28	24	0.54
4. Katy	2	3	3	3	6	10	2	4	13	20	0.39
5. Leslie	1	3	2	6	9	7	2	10	14	26	0.35
6. Patty	1	3	2	6	8	8	2	10	13	27	0.33
7. Jane	1	5	3	7	9	7	9	10	22	29	0.43
8. Ruth	2	3	5	5	8	8	8	11	23	27	0.46

Figure 9.5 Season performance index

Note. Over the course of a semester, players may miss drills due to injury, class schedules, or special practice needs. Since missed drills will cause players to have varying drill amounts, the winning percentage for each type of drill is your guide for comparing players.

Coach's Perspective

Having a Performance Index will definitely change a coach's practice experience. While players learn and adapt to pressure training, the coach should also expect resistance which is a natural by-product of change. The coach must be firm in his/her commitment to training under pressure as players experience initial discomfort and voice their concerns.

From the coach's perspective, the Performance Index is an invaluable tool that assists with many important tasks.

- **Evaluating players objectively.** As a coach, how can you accurately evaluate 8 or even 12 players at practice? Just watching athletes play a few points here and there gives you only a glimpse of how they are hitting the ball and does not really tell you how they're playing. I find myself watching a player in practice and thinking she is playing well based on a few good points or shots, then later find out she has lost most of her drills on that day. She appeared to play well (based on how she hit the ball), but the Performance Index contradicted my perception. Since practice is preparation for match play, I need to know how my players are playing! The Performance Index indicates playing proficiency and makes evaluations objective.

- **Communicating and training with facts.** Having facts from the Performance Index when discussing a player's game or team lineup results in open and positive lines of communication. The Performance Index clearly points out a player's deficiencies compared with teammates or a standard and reinforces a coach's analysis of a player's with strengths and weaknesses. The facts will speak for themselves.

- **Training players how to reflect on their performance.** Understanding how their rating came about gives players an opportunity to be reflective. I am always amazed at the revealing insights players have regarding their own play. Using the Performance Index as a catalyst for probing questions, ask players to critique their practice performance. What are the obstacles for improvement, and what are the solutions? Helping players develop reflective skills bolsters communication between coach and player and taps into the valuable insights players have to offer.

- **Spotting trends.** Positive and negative trends for a player can develop over a few days, a week, or a semester. Dramatic drops in practice performance may indicate personal or academic difficulties or may simply point out motivational problems with tennis. Spotting negative trends early can help alleviate a problem while it is still in its infancy. Of course, positive trends should be pointed out and celebrated.

- **Deciding the lineup.** I choose my team's lineup based on criteria such as
    1. match play against opponents,
    2. match play against teammates,

3. the Performance Index, and
4. coachability.

It's amazing how closely the Performance Index mirrors our lineup almost every year.

• **Motivating players.** Ideally, my player's results will fall within a winning percentage of 40 to 60 percent. A range this narrow indicates very competitive practices and signifies team depth. If players fall below this range, their contribution to practice is questionable. If a player has a 60-percent winning percentage or higher, you probably have a player much stronger than the others and one most likely in need of more practice competition. Challenge the rest of the team to play to your top player's standards. Having a player who can "raise the bar" for the rest of the team is invaluable.

Player's Perspective

Having a Peformance Index changes how a practice is viewed by the players. Initially players are very uncomfortable with a Performance Index. Pressure training is contrary to the way they've grown up practicing and having to be accountable is often disconcerting. A 2-week adjustment period for the players is quite normal. However, once the players are accustomed to having their practice results recorded in a Performance Index, numerous benefits are revealed from the player's perspective.

• **Learning to handle pressure.** Players need to learn to handle pressure. Competitive practices offer numerous situations where you have to play pressure points. For example, the drill score may be tied at 3-all and the point you are playing decides whether or not you win the drill. How do you respond to the pressure? Knowing the outcome is being recorded and you will either move up or down a court gives the point value and makes it important. Having a sense of immediacy in practice, knowing that now matters, is the only way to prepare for the pressure of these match-deciding situations.

• **Taking responsibility for practice performance.** Players need to be able to say, "I am responsible for my Performance Index." Your coaches and teammates are there to help you improve by working with you and challenging you during each drill. Accepting your positive or negative results as being of your own making is the first step in becoming the best player you can be.

• **Seeking together.** Remember, competition means "seeking together." The best thing you can do for teammates is to play your best and push them to be their best. In every sport, all top players have been pushed to greatness by a teammate or an opponent. Ideally, your best effort will make your teammates better and ultimately your team. Practice is not just about *you;* it's about making everyone around you better. When a team and its members take responsibility for player-to-player and player-to-team relationships, you know you have a "real" team.

- **Learning strengths and weaknesses.** Pay attention to your strengths and weaknesses as indicated by the Performance Index. You may think your volley is a strength, but your practice performance may indicate otherwise.
- **Giving an inspired effort.** Knowing that you are being held accountable for your practice performance offers tremendous daily inspiration to give your best effort.
- **Learning how to play.** Since the drills are games, you are playing games throughout practice. The Performance Index measures how you play relative to your teammates. Pressure training practices are more about how you are playing as opposed to how you are hitting the ball. Learning to play productively even when you are not hitting as well as you would like is a major hurdle for you as a player. Champions play well even when not hitting well (a prime example of being comfortable with the uncomfortable).
- **Practicing in your range.** Because you play like you practice, you must play in your range in practice. Playing in your range is simply hitting your shots as aggressively as possible and in the court. Players play out of their range by hitting too cautiously (trying for too little) or too aggressively (trying for too much). Hitting cautiously allows your opponent to force the action, whereas being too aggressive produces too many errors. You have your own range for each shot, and you are usually aware when you are playing too cautiously or too aggressively. Practicing out of your range will definitely produce a poor Performance Index.
- **Asking for help.** After learning about your strengths and weaknesses, ask your coach for assistance. Taking an active role in your own development is a major step in taking ownership of your game. The only way to have a better Performance Index is to improve.
- **Reflecting on your performance.** Understanding how your rating came about is an opportunity to be reflective. What can I do to improve? How do I play the pressure points? What obstacles block my development? Since the goal is to be the best player you can be, focus on what is holding you back. Players have a deep pool of experience to draw from. Their insights are often as valuable as the coaches'.
- **Acting like a champion.** Practice acting like a champion when winning or losing a drill or playing a pressure point. As sports psychologist Jim Loehr points out, it is normal to be nervous or scared before pressure points. The trick is not to act like you are nervous or scared. Also, champions maintain their composure when things go wrong. After losing a drill or big point, you might demonstrate anger or tanking behavior. Champions accept the challenge by trying to do better in the next drill or point. Act like a champion!

- **Doing your best.** Control what you can control—your effort and attitude. Being completely engaged mentally, physically, and emotionally leads to outstanding performances. Play your best, and the results will follow.
- **Controlling your impulses.** Tennis is definitely a game where controlling your impulses and resisting various temptations are imperative for success. Examples of lack of impulse control might be always going for aces or always hitting to the open court. These temptations rear their ugly heads even for top pro players. Knowing that you are responsible for your practice performance forces you to resist these temptations and focus on playing productively, not impulsively. Delaying gratification in our microwave age definitely takes a lot of self-control and practice!

The Technical Dilemma

I am often asked how players can work on technical changes in a pressure practice if they are worried about winning a drill. As a college coach, I work with my players individually. Individual lessons allow for technical work to take place in a noncompetitive environment where the player can focus on specific technique without having to worry about results. However, the players eventually have to go to a team practice where their Performance Indexes can be affected if they are in the process of changing a stroke.

My solution is to give the player the green light in a team practice to concentrate on the new stroke rather than focusing on just winning the drill. With this in mind, it may make sense not to record results for drills affected by the new technique. Common sense and communication between player and coach allow productive technical work to take place in a pressure practice environment. At some point, the player will have to test the new stroke under competitive fire. Until that time, punishing a player for trying to improve technically is counterproductive.

Recording the Data

Recording the data takes very little time during practice. After a drill, I watch who moves up a court and fill in a "+" for those players on my practice result sheet. Everyone else receives a "-". When I first started using the Performance Index at Kenyon College, I recorded and entered all the data myself. At the University of Iowa, I now have the luxury of hiring a student manager who actually runs practice and records all the data on a laptop computer. My assistant and I are completely free to roam practice, observing and coaching. Obviously I prefer my Iowa arrangement, but the effort involved in recording data is minimal if you are prepared and organized. The improved atmosphere and productive environment in practice more than make up for the additional time spent organizing and recording a Performance Index.

Evaluating Players With the Performance Index

Due to its objectivity, the Performance Index is a tremendous tool for instructing and motivating players. The results do not lie. However, for maximum instructive value to occur, a well-thought-out method of evaluation is important. I learned the hard way during my first year of using the Performance Index in 1992. I was so excited to have all this revealing data that I simply posted the weekly and semester indexes in the locker room, as if that were enough. The players read their results but weren't equipped to understand what their deficiencies were or what they could do to improve. Valuable teaching opportunities were definitely wasted that first year. Maybe this was why Kenyon lost the 1992 national championship 5-4 in the finals. I guess I'll never know!

As I learned, evaluations are most beneficial given the following conditions:

- **Mentor the player.** A mentoring relationship is built on service. How can the coach best serve the player? The coach's ego must take a back seat to the needs of the player for nonjudgmental and nondefensive dialogue to take place. You will be amazed how players take ownership for their deficiencies in a true mentoring relationship.
- **Meet one-on-one.** Meet with each player to discuss the practice performance. Private meetings avoid confusion, embarrassment, and ambiguity and allow players and coaches to work together. The coach's message can be clear and to the point while allowing for discussion and feedback from the player. Rotate the meeting place, frequently choosing locations most familiar to the player rather than the coach (Freud's suggestion).
- **Define the problem.** Why is the player doing poorly in serve games? It's not enough to say he needs work on his serve. Encourage the player to analyze the situation first. Work together and come up with specific reasons, which might involve technique, tactics, mental approach, or more practice.
- **Devise a solution.** Brainstorm with the player on possible solutions that also include a plan of action. For example, the player's second serve is too flat, so the player suggests working on the second serve right before practice to learn how to generate more spin. Again, addressing specific rather than general remedies is essential for clarity of action and growth.

Looking back on my coaching career, it is clear that my teams and players began reaching their potential once I started using a Performance Index. Four of my last five years at Kenyon saw the teams enter the national championships as the number-one seeds, capturing three national titles. Most recently, my Iowa team is off to a great start as players make steady progress and we continue to climb in the Big Ten and national rankings. My teams' consistent performance is directly attributable to the practice environment where players are held accountable for their performance. I'm confident that using a Performance Index will immediately take any practice session and team to a new level.

10

Planning a Pressure Practice

As a young coach, I quickly planned practice by listing drills in a rough outline form, allowing for numerous changes during practice, depending on how I felt the session was going. These practices usually lacked focus and structure and created an atmosphere deficient in discipline and purpose. As I've now learned, planning a successful pressure practice requires much forethought and preparation. By following a simple practice outline and the suggestions below, your practices will be instructional, challenging, engaging, and fun.

Practice Preparation Strategies

The following five items should be kept in mind when preparing practices.

- **Plan the week.** Set aside time at the beginning of the week to outline what you would like to accomplish during the week's practices. Of course, also plan on being flexible to meet needs that might arise during the week.
- **Type practices and results.** Type or computerize your practice plans for ease of use, legibility, and uniformity. Typed practice sessions can be posted in the team locker room and kept for review after a semester or season. Being able to look back on your practice plans allows you to spot trends and compile an overview of how you approached the season.
- **Visualize the session from a player's perspective.** Remember what it's like to be a player when

planning your practice. I always visualize how the session will progress from the player's perspective. When thinking like a player, I often discover a drill sequence is out of order for maximum effectiveness and flow.

- **Rest.** Train your team intelligently by making rest an important part of your tennis program. I clearly remember the temptation to overtrain when I first began coaching. "So many things to cover, so little time!" Taking a day off midweek or periodically shortening a practice session allows players to recharge their mental and physical energy systems, making practice time matchlike, focused, and most important, productive.
- **Think in three-day blocks.** Pressure training is mentally and physically taxing. Players remain fresh and focused in practice if pressure training is limited to no more than three consecutive days. After the third day of pressure training, I make sure to change the routine by having a match day, a shortened practice, a team-building session, a practice geared toward individual needs, or even a day off.

Practice Outline

When designing a pressure practice, I use three guiding principles.

1. Each practice session must focus on a central theme or concept. From beginning to end, the practice theme is emphasized by drills that build upon one another in a progressive manner.
2. Time must be set aside each session for work on fundamentals, which I call base work.
3. Each practice must end with an opportunity for play.

The first step in creating a productive training environment is to have a clear picture of what you want to accomplish at each practice. With that in mind, you can organize drills to reach your objective. A well-designed practice will weave the day's point of emphasis throughout the session—from warm-up to base work to an area of emphasis to play. Understanding the three guiding principles helps you better comprehend how the sample practices are organized and offers an outline for planning future practice sessions.

Area of Emphasis

Each day's practice stresses one or two themes or concepts to be emphasized. Having a clearly defined purpose in practice helps players understand why particular drills are used and increases motivation, because things are done for a reason and as part of a big picture. It's very important to spend 5 to 10 minutes before practice discussing the aim of the session and how the drills will accomplish your teaching goals.

By emphasizing one or two aspects, drills can build progressively off each other and be organized in a logical progression. For instance, if the emphasis in practice is on volleying, a sample drill sequence might be as follows:

1. Minitennis Volleys
2. One-Up/One-Back Warm-Up
3. Pinch Volleys
4. One-Player Closing Volleys

Minitennis Volleys and One-Up/One-Back Warm-Up are volley technique drills in preparation for drills 3 and 4. Pinch Volleys and One-Player Closing Volleys are point situation drills emphasizing the volley. The practice goes from simple volley technique focusing on footwork and racket work to complex match-condition volleys. The sample practice follows a logical progression, as each drill incorporates key aspects from the previous drill.

Emphasis Considerations

- **Three-week practice cycles.** I look at practice in three-week time periods. Each three-week cycle begins with a heavy dose of base work in singles and doubles followed by practices that emphasize current needs. Using a three-week practice cycle ensures that the team continues to strengthen and deepen its base while allowing for further growth in other areas. Do not lose sight of your base, regardless of how much progress the team makes.

- **Time of year.** There are several things to consider when planning what to emphasize in practice. The first is time of year. A tennis season can be broken down into three segments: preseason, competitive season, and postseason competition. During the preseason, emphasis is on fundamentals and base work. Early practices offer the opportunity to teach and reinstill how your team practices and plays. This is especially useful if new players have joined the team.

Once you've established a technical and tactical base, more advanced concepts can be addressed and developed throughout the competitive season. The three-week practice cycle ensures that base work is revisited consistently during the competitive season.

Finally comes the postseason competition. Conference, state, regional, and national tournaments test our preparation from the competitive season. Typically, there is little practice time between the regular season and the postseason; thus, teams need to enter the postseason confident and focused on playing their game. Postseason practices should emphasize sharpening skills and team and individual strengths. Again, base work is invaluable. Postseason play is pressure packed, and when the pressure is on, there is no substitute for a solid foundation.

- **Level of team.** Points of emphasis in practice must take into consideration the abilities of your players. Asking your players to compete in drills that are too difficult will only lead to frustration. Good coaches strike a balance by selecting drills that develop and challenge their teams but also allow for success.
- **Singles or doubles.** I prefer to focus a practice session on either singles or doubles concepts, and very rarely will I combine the two unless we are having a general review the day before a match. Players learn and retain information better when they are able to focus on only a few aspects. This is especially true in a typical 2-hour practice session. Experience has taught me that it's mostly either a singles day or a doubles day in practice.
- **Match play dictates needs.** Once match play begins against other teams, individual and team strengths and weaknesses become clearer and will guide you in practice planning. During match play, I note areas of need in a journal. The match journal is a great source of information in planning future practices. There's no better practice-planning resource than match play.

Base Work

Establishing a base to play from is essential and necessary for further development. Base work in practice covers all aspects related to high-percentage tennis and sound technique. Having a solid foundation allows players and teams to build their games while having a position of strength, security, and reliability to fall back on.

Building a base is really about being good at what happens over and over

Don't try to focus a practice on both singles and doubles. Work on one concept at a time.

throughout a match. Watch a tennis match. What shots are hit most often? Points begin with serves and returns, and most rallies take place crosscourt. It makes sense then that base work places a heavy emphasis on crosscourt groundstrokes and first exchanges (serves and returns). Additionally, the three main tactical considerations—change-of-direction decisions, shot selection, and court position—are integrated when building and strengthening a base.

I learned firsthand the value of developing a solid base after graduating my top five players from Kenyon College's 1993 national championship team. Coaching a team of freshmen and sophomores with little college tennis experience in 1994 left me with no choice but to focus solely on developing a high-percentage foundation. We basically hit all our groundstrokes crosscourt (outside groundstrokes, no change of direction; inside groundstrokes, change of direction) and made all our second serves and returns. While playing from a strong base, the team finished a respectable 11th nationally. Building off the base established in 1994, the 1995 team captured a national championship, winning two pressure-packed matches in the semifinals and finals by identical 5-4 scores. The 1995 championship was a direct result of our ability to play confident all-court tennis, a confidence instilled by knowing we had a rock-solid foundation to fall back on. When the pressure was on, the team responded by playing to our strength—our base.

A word to the wise: A player's or team's base can always improve. Avoid the temptation to move beyond basic fundamentals too quickly, and always include base work in every practice. You'll find that having a base to play from is the most effective way to handle pressure.

End Your Practice With Play

Players should always play at the end of every practice session. As I've mentioned before, practice is preparation for play. The team has worked hard during practice; now it's time to reward them with play. Play can be a set or match, a tiebreaker tournament, or numerous other creative yet functional types of play. Keep the following in mind.

- **Have fun.** There's no better way to end a practice session than by having fun—let the players play. Scheduling play time at the end allows players to finish the day doing what they love—playing tennis.

- **Incorporate emphasized concepts.** Players should be encouraged to put into practice the concepts emphasized during the training session. Restrictions and "rules of play" can be used to ensure emphasized concepts are practiced when playing. For example, if serve and volley is the emphasized concept, stipulate that each server has to serve and volley on first serves in a set of singles. As shown in chapters 6 and 7, there are endless creative ways to play that emphasize concepts covered in practice.

Make sure tennis is fun for your players.

- **Compete when you are fatigued.** A major benefit to playing at the end of practice is that players begin playing after an hour or more of practice. Beginning a set when the players are mentally and physically fatigued simulates what it is like to play a third set after two tough sets.
- **Coach just as you would in a match.** The play portion of practice is an ideal time to practice coaching players just as you would coach them in a match. Make sure you balance your coaching time among players so no one feels at a disadvantage.

Planning a successful pressure practice requires much forethought and preparation. By following a simple practice outline and the suggestions above, practices will be instructional, challenging, engaging, and fun.

11

Proven Pressure Practice Plans

The pressure practices included here are actual practices used with my teams since 1997. I have included the sample practices to give a better idea of how I organize and run a training session and to help assist coaches in learning how to pressure train their teams or players. It is important to remember each session was designed to meet my teams' needs on that particular day and time of season. These sessions are by no means the definitive way to organize a practice as team and player needs will vary day to day and year to year. In fact, I never use the same practice plan more than once as my team's needs change and evolve and new ideas are integrated into the program. Use the practices as a guide, as is, or modify them to suit your own needs.

The practice plans are organized and grouped by the following common themes or points of emphasis:

1. Point Building
2. Pressuring—Inside Groundstrokes
3. Pressuring—Outside Groundstrokes (90-Degree COD)
4. Pressuring—First Serves and Returns of Second Serves
5. Court Position
6. Spin
7. Air Raid—Volleys and Overheads
8. Doubles Serves and Returns
9. Doubles Serve and Volley

10. Doubles Volleys
11. Prematch Sessions
12. One-Hour Practices

Each practice averages seven to eight drills per 2-hour session usually including time for play at the end. The drills and warm-ups used are explained in detail in chapters 6, 7, and 8. Just a reminder: COD stands for change of direction.

Timed drills may have four different notations:

1. (1 × 3 minutes) = one round of 3 minutes in length.
2. (2 × 2/2 minutes) = two rounds of 4 minutes in length, but in this case each round is divided into two 2-minute segments. This occurs in drills, for example, whereby one player hits a slice while the other drives the ball for 2 minutes and then players switch roles for the remaining 2 minutes.
3. (2/2 × 3 minutes) = two 3-minute rounds in the deuce court and two 3-minute rounds in the ad court for a total drill time of 12 minutes. Crosscourt drills have this unique time notation since the drills take place in both the deuce and ad court.
4. (1/1 × 3/3 minutes) = each player has one 3-minute deuce round and one 3-minute ad round for a total drill time of 12 minutes. This notation occurs only in warm-ups like the Volley Warm-up where each player volleys for 3 minutes from the deuce and ad courts.

Point Building

Purpose: To develop a strong foundation from the baseline. To become proficient hitting aggressive high-percentage groundstrokes.

Developing a proper foundation is the chief aim of the point-building practice sessions. Playing from on or behind the baseline, players build points with aggressive topspin shots until a pressuring opportunity arises. Players adopt a can't-miss aggressive attitude, hitting shots with high net clearance that penetrate the baseline—reducing most net and wide errors. No matter how advanced the player or team, there's always a need to refine point-building skills.

Point Building With Inside Groundstrokes and Inside-Out Forehands

1. Directional Minitennis
2. Five-Minute Warm-Up
3. Crosscourts—Deuce and Ad Court (3/3 × 3 minutes)

4. Four-Shot 20 Second Serves With Returns; serve and volley at least once every 10 serves; directional returns
5. Directionals—Inside Groundstroke COD (2 × 5 minutes)
6. Crosscourts—Inside-Out Forehands (Ad Court) (1 × 2/2 minutes)
7. Directionals—Forehands Are Wild (2 × 5 minutes)
8. Tiebreakers with two serves (3 ×); rotate when a court finishes

Net-Free Point Building

1. Topspin Warm-Up (8 minutes)
2. Crosscourts—Deuce and Ad Court (3/3 × 4 minutes)
3. Directionals—Inside Groundstroke COD (3 × 5 minutes)
4. Two-Shot 20 Second Serves With Returns
5. Singles (two sets of two-point tennis with one serve)

Note. All net errors are two-point errors for each drill.

Point Building With a Weapon

1. Topspin Warm-Up (8 minutes)
2. Crosscourts—Deuce and Ad Court (1/1 × 3 minutes)
3. Crosscourts With 90-Degree COD (1/1 × 3 minutes)
4. Crosscourts—Inside-Out Forehands (Ad Court) (2 × 2/2 minutes)
5. Directionals—Inside Groundstroke COD (1 × 5 minutes)
6. Directionals—Inside-Out Forehands (2 × 5 minutes)
7. First-Strike Game (2 × 3/3 minutes)
8. Singles Tiebreakers

Point Building and Court Position

1. Five-Minute Warm-Up
2. Crosscourts—Deuce and Ad Court (2/2 × 3 minutes)
3. Directionals—Inside and 90-Degree COD (2 × 5 minutes); 90-degree COD with good court position
4. Singles Tiebreakers (3 ×); focus on maintaining good court position
5. One-Player Closing Volleys (2 × 3 minutes)
6. First-Serve Game (1 × 5/5 minutes)
7. Singles (one set)

Point Building With 90-Degree COD

1. Directional Minitennis
2. Five-Minute Warm-Up

3. Crosscourts—Deuce and Ad Court (2/2 × 3 minutes)
4. Directionals—Inside Groundstroke COD (1 × 5 minutes)
5. Crosscourts With 90-Degree COD (3/3 × 3 minutes); 90-Degree COD with good court position
6. Directionals—Inside and 90-Degree COD (2 × 5 minutes); 90-Degree COD with good court position
7. One-Player Closing Volleys (2 × 3 minutes)
8. Four-Shot 20 Service Points
9. Tiebreaker Tournament

Directionals With Two Serves

1. One-Up/One-Back Warm-Up (1/1 × 3/3 minutes)
2. Two-Shot 20 Second Serves With Returns
3. Crosscourts—Deuce and Ad Court (2/2 × 4 minutes)
4. Drive vs. Slice (2 × 2/2 minutes)
5. Directionals—Inside Groundstroke COD (1 × 5 minutes); first and second serves
6. Directionals—Inside and 90-Degree COD (2 × 5 minutes); first and second serves
7. Pressuring Serve/Return Game (2 × 5 minutes)
8. Singles (one set)

Point Building With Inside Groundstrokes

1. Topspin Warm-Up (8 minutes)
2. Soft Toss (backhands, 3 minutes); focus on left hand with backhand
3. Crosscourts—Deuce and Ad Court (1/1 × 3 minutes)
4. Crosscourts With Inside Groundstroke COD (2/2 × 3 minutes)
5. Four-Shot 20 Second Serves With Returns; serve and volley at least once every 10 serves. Directional returns.
6. Outside/Middle Drill (2 × 2/2 minutes)
7. Directionals—Inside Groundstroke COD (1 × 5 minutes); first and second serves
8. Directionals—Inside and 90-Degree COD (1 × 5 minutes); first and second serves; outside 90-Degree COD errors are two-point errors
9. Inside Groundstroke Recovery Drill (2 × 3/3 minutes)

Point-Building Tune-Up

1. Topspin Warm-Up (8 minutes)
2. Crosscourts—Deuce and Ad Court (1/1 × 3 minutes)

3. Crosscourts With Inside Groundstroke COD (1/1 × 3 minutes)
4. One-Player Closing Volleys (2 × 3 minutes)
5. Directionals—Inside Groundstroke COD (1 × 5 minutes); first and second serves
6. Directionals—Inside and 90-Degree COD (1 × 5 minutes); first and second serves, 90-Degree COD is two-point error
7. Singles (two sets)

Point Building and Serving With Location

1. Directional Minitennis
2. Soft Toss (forehands and backhands, one-half basket each)
3. Two-Shot 20 Second Serves With Returns
4. Crosscourts—Deuce and Ad Court (3/3 × 4 minutes)
5. Directionals—Inside Groundstroke COD (2 × 5 minutes)
6. Instruction; wide serve and T serve (5 minutes to deuce court, 5 minutes to ad court)
7. First-Strike Game (1 × 5/5 minutes); location: wide and T
8. Singles (one set); focus on hitting first serves with location (wide or T)

Pressuring—Inside Groundstrokes

Purpose: To learn how to create inside groundstroke opportunities. To become proficient hitting inside groundstrokes.

The inside shot is usually the first opportunity to pressure during a baseline rally. Unfortunately, few players or teams practice capitalizing on these offensive openings. Learning to create the inside shot and to effectively make this pressuring shot is the aim of these sample practice sessions.

Defending Against the Inside Groundstroke

1. Five-Minute Warm-Up
2. Four-Shot 20 Second Serves With Drop-Shot Returns
3. Crosscourts—Deuce and Ad Court (2/2 × 3 minutes)
4. Offense/Defense (3 × 2/2 minutes)
5. Outside/Middle Drill (2 × 2/2 minutes)
6. Inside Groundstroke Recovery Drill (2 × 3/3 minutes)
7. Singles (one set)

Pressuring With Inside Groundstrokes

1. Five-Minute Warm-Up (1-minute forehand/backhand)
2. Soft Toss (inside feeds, 1-minute deuce/ad)

3. Four-Shot Pressuring Returns (X Marks the Spot)
4. Crosscourts—Deuce and Ad Court (1/1 × 3 minutes)
5. Crosscourts With Inside Groundstroke COD (1/1 × 3 minutes)
6. Directionals—Inside and 90-Degree COD (2 × 5 minutes); two-point error for 90-degree COD errors
7. Pressuring Serve/Return Game (1 × 5 minutes)
8. Singles (one set)

Pressuring From the Middle Third

1. Five-Minute Warm-Up
2. Crosscourts—Deuce and Ad Court (3/3 × 3 minutes)
3. Four-Shot 20 Second Serves With Returns
4. Soft Toss (inside feeds, one-half basket forehands and backhands)
5. Outside/Middle Drill (2 × 3/3 minutes)
6. First-Serve Game (1 × 5/5 minutes); location: wide and T
7. Singles (one set); first-serve location: wide or T

Approaching off the Inside Ball

1. Topspin Warm-Up (8 minutes)
2. Soft Toss (inside forehands and backhands, one-half basket each)
3. Crosscourts—Deuce and Ad Court (1/1 × 3 minutes); serve and volley once
4. Crosscourts With Inside Groundstroke COD (1/1 × 3 minutes); serve and volley once
5. Crosscourts With Inside Groundstroke COD (1/1 × 3 minutes); must approach off inside groundstroke
6. Inside Groundstroke Recovery Drill (2 × 3/3 minutes)
7. Directionals—Inside Groundstroke COD (3 × 5 minutes); must approach on inside ball
8. Four-Shot Pressuring Returns (X Marks the Spot)
9. Pressuring Serve/Return Game—(2 × 5 minutes)
10. Singles Tiebreakers (3 ×) Games to 11.

Pressuring With Inside Groundstrokes, Serves, and Returns

1. Topspin Warm-Up (8 minutes)
2. Crosscourts—Deuce and Ad Court (2/2 × 3 minutes)
3. Inside Groundstroke Recovery Drill (2 × 3/3 minutes)

4. Directionals—Inside and 90-Degree COD (3 × 5 minutes); 90-Degree COD only when approaching
5. Four-Shot Pressuring Returns (X Marks the Spot)
6. First-Strike Game (2 × 3/3 minutes)
7. Singles (one set)

Inside Groundstrokes and Court Position

1. Directional Minitennis
2. Five-Minute Warm-Up
3. Crosscourts—Deuce and Ad Court (3/3 × 3 minutes)
4. Wimbledon Points (3 × 3 minutes)
5. Directionals—Inside Groundstroke COD (3 × 5 minutes); must approach on inside ball
6. Inside Groundstroke Recovery Drill (2 × 3/3 minutes)
7. Four-Shot 20 Service Points
8. First-Serve Game (2 × 3/3 minutes)
9. Singles (one set)

Inside and Inside-Out Groundstrokes

1. Soft Toss (forehands and backhands, 2 × 3 minutes); two outside/one inside sequence
2. Four-Shot 20 Second Serves With Returns
3. Inside Groundstroke Recovery Drill (2 × 3/3 minutes)
4. Crosscourts—Deuce and Ad Court (2/2 × 3 minutes)
5. Crosscourts With Inside Groundstroke COD (1/1 × 3 minutes)
6. Directionals—Inside Groundstroke COD (2 × 5 minutes)
7. Directionals—Inside-Out Forehands (1 × 5 minutes)
8. Pressuring Serve/Return Game (1 × 3/3 minutes)
9. Singles Tiebreakers

Inside Groundstroke Weapon

1. Directional Minitennis
2. Five-Minute Warm-Up
3. Soft Toss—Three-shot sequence: inside-out forehand, inside-out forehand/inside forehand (one-half basket)
4. Crosscourts—Deuce and Ad Court (2/2 × 3 minutes)
5. Crosscourts—Inside-Out Forehands (Ad Court) (2 × 2/2 minutes)
6. Directionals—Inside-Out Forehands (3 × 5 minutes)
7. Singles (one set); service winners worth two points

Inside Groundstroke Pressure

1. Five-Minute Warm-Up
2. Soft Toss (inside forehands and backhands; half basket each)
3. Crosscourts—Deuce and Ad Court (2/2 × 3 minutes)
4. One-Player Closing Volleys (2 × 4 minutes)
5. Outside/Middle Drill (2 × 2/2 minutes)
6. Inside Groundstroke Recovery Drill (2 × 3/3 minutes)
7. First-Serve Game (2 × 3/3 minutes)
8. Singles Tiebreakers (3 ×)

Inside Pressuring From the Ground and Out of the Air

1. Directional Minitennis
2. Five-Minute Warm-Up
3. Crosscourts—Deuce and Ad Court (1/1 × 3 minutes); must serve and volley once a game
4. Crosscourts—Inside-Out Forehands (Ad Court) (2 × 2/2 minutes)
5. Directionals—Inside-Out Forehands (2 × 5 minutes)
6. One-Player Closing Volleys (2 × 4 minutes)
7. Inside Groundstroke Recovery Drill (1 × 3/3 minutes); ad-court lob feeds
8. Inside Groundstroke Recovery Drill (2 × 3/3 minutes); deuce-court lob or groundstroke feeds
9. Overhead Game (1 ×)
10. Singles Tiebreaker Tournament

Pressuring—Outside Groundstrokes (90-Degree COD)

Purpose: To learn to judge when to change direction on outside groundstrokes. To become proficient hitting 90-degree change-of-direction shots.

I normally prefer my players to be on or inside the baseline when attempting down-the-line shots and to follow the 90-degree COD guidelines. All players must be aware of their own down-the-line limitations and what constitutes a good pressuring opportunity. Temptations will constantly arise—to change or not to change direction, this will be the question!

Attacking Down the Line

1. Topspin Warm-Up (8 minutes)
2. Soft Toss (90-Degree COD feeds, 1/1 × 2/2 minutes)

3. Crosscourts With 90-Degree COD (2/2 × 3 minutes); must serve and volley once a game
4. Directionals—Inside and 90-Degree COD (2 × 5 minutes)
5. Offense/Defense (2 × 2/2 minutes); singles court
6. First-Serve Game (3 × 5 minutes)
7. Singles (one set)

Long-Line Pressuring

1. Five-Minute Warm-Ups
2. Soft Toss (90-Degree COD feeds, 1/1 × 2/2)
3. Crosscourts With 90-Degree COD (2/2 × 3 minutes); stress court position when changing direction
4. Short Outside Approach Shot Recovery Drill (2 × 3/3 minutes)
5. One-Player Closing Volleys (3 × 3 minutes)
6. First-Strike Game (1 × 3/3 minutes)
7. Singles (one set)

90-Degree Change of Direction

1. Directional Minitennis
2. Five-Minute Warm-Up
3. Crosscourts—Deuce and Ad Court (2/2 × 3 minutes)
4. Short Outside Approach Shot Recovery Drill (2 × 3/3 minutes)
5. Crosscourts With 90-Degree COD (2/2 × 3 minutes); stress court position when changing direction
6. Directionals—Inside and 90-Degree COD (2 × 5 minutes)
7. Directionals—Forehands Are Wild (2 × 5 minutes)
8. Four-Shot 20 Second Serves With Returns
9. Singles (one set)

Pressuring—First Serves and Returns of Second Serves

Purpose: To take control of points with the first serve or return of the second serve. To create an aggressive attitude when serving first serves and returning second serves.

Serving with a purpose, taking control of the point with an aggressive return and looking to immediately apply pressure is the aim of these practice sessions. With each point in tennis beginning with a serve and return, the outcome usually rides on who strikes first—the server or the returner. Adopting an attacking attitude is essential in modern tennis!

Serves and Returns

1. Topspin Warm-Up (8 minutes)
2. Crosscourts—Deuce and Ad Court (2/2 × 3 minutes)
3. Directionals—Inside Groundstroke COD (2 × 5 minutes)
4. Two-Shot 20 Second Serves With Returns; wide location
5. First-Serve Game (2 × 6 minutes); emphasize wide location
6. Singles (two sets)

Quick Strike

1. One-Up/One-Back (2/2 × 3/3 minutes)
2. Four-Shot 20 Second Serves (X marks the spot)
3. Crosscourts—Deuce and Ad Court (1/1 × 3 minutes); serve and volley once; ad-court returns must be forehands
4. One-Player Closing Volleys (2 × 3 minutes)
5. Offense/Defense (2 × 2/2 minutes)
6. First-Serve Game (3 × 5 minutes)
7. Singles (one set)

Serve and Volley

1. Topspin Warm-Up (8 minutes)
2. Crosscourts—Deuce and Ad Court (1/1 × 3 minutes); serve and volley once
3. Directionals—Inside and 90-Degree COD (2 × 5 minutes); serve and volley on first serves
4. One-Player Closing Volleys (2 × 3 minutes)
5. Singles Serve and Volley (2 × 4 minutes); two serves with Directional Returns
6. Singles (one set)

Pressuring Serves and Returns

1. Five-Minute Warm-Up
2. Soft Toss (forehands and backhands, one-half basket each)
3. 20 Second Serves; no returners, both serving at same time
4. Four-Shot Pressuring Returns (X Marks the Spot)
5. Crosscourts—Deuce and Ad Court (1/1 × 3 minutes)

6. Crosscourts With 90-Degree COD (2/2 × 3 minutes); COD errors are two-point errors
7. Crazy Overheads
8. Pressuring Serve/Return Game (4 × 6 minutes)

Court Position

Purpose: To create awareness of the tactical value of court position. To pressure opponents with aggressive court position.

One of the most subtle and effective forms of pressuring is establishing good court position on or inside the baseline. Players have a feel for the time they desire between baseline shots and the spacing they feel comfortable with between themselves and their opponents. If one player moves up, the other player moves back. The player moving back ends up hitting shorter, has less angle to use, and is limited to a retrieving/defensive style of play. Good court postion leads to exciting, attacking, all-court play. As they say, it is better to give than to receive.

Playing on or Inside the Baseline

1. Directional Minitennis
2. Soft Toss (forehand and backhand approaches, one-half basket each)
3. Four-Shot Pressuring Returns (X Marks the Spot)
4. Crosscourts—Deuce and Ad Court (2/2 × 4 minutes)
5. One-Player Closing Volleys (3 × 3 minutes)
6. Wimbledon Points (3 × 3 minutes)
7. Tiebreakers (3 ×); full-court Wimbledon tiebreakers
8. Singles (one set)

Wimbledon Directionals

1. Five-Minute Warm-Up
2. Soft Toss (wide backhands—half basket each), maintain court position on or inside baseline
3. Crosscourts—Deuce and Ad Court (2/2 × 3 minutes); serve and volley once a game
4. Wimbledon Directionals (2 × 5 minutes); 90-degree COD and inside-out forehands allowed
5. Singles Serve and Volley (2 × 4 minutes); Directional returns, two serves
6. Pressuring Serve/Return Game (1 × 5 minutes); wide and T serves
7. Singles (one set)

Wimbledon Tennis

1. One-Up/One-Back Warm-Up (1/1 × 3/3 minutes)
2. Crosscourts—Deuce and Ad Court (1/1 × 3 minutes)
3. Wimbledon Points (2 × 4 minutes)
4. One-Player Closing Volleys (3 × 3 minutes)
5. Four-Shot Pressuring Returns (X Marks the Spot)
6. First-Strike Game (2 × 3/3 minutes)
7. Tiebreakers (3×)—Wimbledon tiebreakers
8. Singles (one set)

Spin

Purpose: To practice hitting shots outside (above and below) an opponent's hitting zone. To become proficient at hitting drives, slices, and loops.

While everyone loves to hit the big forehand drive, it's the mature player who understands the subtlety of mixing spins and playing shots outside an opponent's hitting zone. Learning to effectively use a variety of spins takes constant practice and requires numerous reminders. As with most baseball pitchers, tennis success arises when more than one spin (pitch) is mastered.

Slice-O-Rama

1. Directional Minitennis
2. Five-Minute Warm-Up
3. Crosscourts—Deuce and Ad Court (3/3 × 3 minutes); serve and volley once
4. Soft Toss (slice backhands, one-half basket)
5. Slice vs. Slice (2 × 3 minutes); ad court
6. Drive vs. Slice (2 × 2/2 minutes)
7. First-Strike Game (1 × 3/3 minutes)
8. Short Outside Approach Shot Recovery Drill (1 × 3/3 minutes); deuce court feed only
9. Singles (one set)

Loop/Slice/Drive

1. Directional Minitennis (all slice)
2. Crosscourts—Deuce and Ad Court (1/1 × 3 minutes); serve and volley once
3. Slice vs. Slice (1 × 4 minutes); full court

4. Drive vs. Loop (1 × 2/2 minutes)
5. Drive vs. Slice (1 × 2/2 minutes)
6. Singles (two sets)

Slice Approaches and Drop Shots

1. Directional Minitennis
2. Crosscourts—Deuce and Ad Court (2/2 × 3 minutes)
3. Slice vs. Slice (2 × 3 minutes); singles court; two points if point won because of drop shot
4. Wimbledon Points (2 × 3 minutes); slice approaches
5. Inside Groundstroke Recovery Drill (2 × 3/3 minutes); slice approaches
6. Singles (two sets)

Playing Out of the Strike Zone

1. Five-Minute Warm-Up
2. Crosscourts—Deuce and Ad Court (2/2 × 3 minutes)
3. Slice vs. Slice (2 × 4 minutes)
4. Loop vs. Loop (2 × 4 minutes)
5. Drive vs. Loop (2 × 2/2 minutes)
6. Drive vs. Slice (2 × 2/2 minutes)
7. Tiebreakers to 11 points (2 ×); two serves

Drive vs. Spin

1. Directional Minitennis
2. Five-Minute Warm-Up
3. Crosscourts—Deuce and Ad Court (2/2 × 3 minutes)
4. Drive vs. Loop (2 × 2/2 minutes)
5. Drive vs. Slice (2 × 2/2 minutes)
6. Offense/Defense (2 × 2/2 minutes)
7. First-Strike Game (2 × 3/3 minutes)
8. Singles (two sets)

Slice Backhands

1. One-Up/One-Back Warm-Up (1/1 × 3/3 minutes)
2. Crosscourts—Deuce and Ad Court (2/1 × 3 minutes)
3. One-Player Closing Volleys (3 × 3 minutes)
4. Soft Toss (slice backhand feeds, one-half basket)

5. Drive vs. Slice (2 × 2/2 minutes)
6. Slice vs. Slice (1 × 3 minutes); ad court, backhand to backhand
7. Tiebreakers with one serve (3 ×); slice backhands unless passing
8. First-Serve Game (2 × 5 minutes); location: wide and T
9. Singles (one set); first-serve location: wide or T

Air Raid—Volleys and Overheads

Purpose: To become proficient playing shots out of the air from the pressuring and point-ending zones.

These are fun practices. Tons of balls are played out of the air with lots of exciting action requiring a high work rate. Air Raid practices clearly reveal who the best doubles and attacking players are. Always a team favorite!

Closing Volleys

1. Five-Minute Warm-Up
2. Pinch Volleys (2 × 2/2 minutes)
3. One-Player Closing Volleys (2 × 3 minutes)
4. Two-Player Closing Volleys (3 × 3 minutes)
5. Overhead Game (seven points)
6. First-Strike Game (1 × 5/5 minutes)
7. Tiebreakers (4 ×); must serve and volley

Pressuring Volleys

1. Topspin Warm-Up (8 minutes)
2. Crosscourts—Deuce and Ad Court (2/2 × 3 minutes); serve and volley once
3. Three-Quarter-Court Closing Volleys (2 × 4 minutes)
4. Inside Groundstroke Recovery Drill (2 × 3/3 minutes)
5. Pinch Volleys (2 × 2/2 minutes)
6. One-Player Closing Volleys (2 × 3 minutes)
7. Serve-and-Volley Points (2 × 4 minutes); two serves
8. Singles (one set)

Volley Day

1. Volley Warm-Up (1/1 × 3/3 minutes)
2. Crosscourts—Deuce and Ad Court (1/1 × 3 minutes); serve and volley once
3. Doubles 20 Second Serves/Window Sequence

4. Pinch Volleys (3 × 2/2 minutes)
5. One-Player Closing Volleys (2 × 3 minutes)
6. Two-Player Closing Volleys (2 × 3 minutes)
7. First-Strike Game (2 × 3/3 minutes)
8. Singles Tiebreakers (3 ×)

Volleys and Overheads

1. Directional Minitennis
2. Crosscourts—Deuce and Ad Court (2/2 × 3 minutes)
3. Pinch Volleys (2 × 2/2 minutes)
4. One-Player Closing Volleys (2 × 3 minutes)
5. Two-Player Closing Volleys (1 × 3 minutes)
6. Overhead Game; game to 11 points with three-feed rotation
7. Doubles 20 Second Serves/Window Sequence
8. Singles (one set)

Air Raid

1. Five-Minute Warm-Up
2. Five-Shot 20 Second Serves—Serve and Volley
3. Crosscourts—Deuce and Ad Court (2/2 × 3 minutes); serve and volley once a rotation
4. Tiebreakers (3 ×); serve and volley once a breaker
5. One-Player Closing Volleys (3 × 3 minutes)
6. Crazy Overheads (1 minute)
7. Crazy Overheads and Volleys (1 minute)
8. Overhead Game (seven points)
9. Singles (one set)

Doubles Serves and Returns

Purpose: To focus on the two keys to good doubles—making the first serve and making the return.

Tactically, doubles is simple—make first serves and put returns in play. Making the first serve puts tremendous pressure on the returning team and allows the server's partner to become immediately involved in the point. Making the return challenges the serving team to make a first volley and creates opportunities for the returner's partner to poach. Doubles servers sacrifice pace for spin and location while returners drive returns with an occasional lob return for variety.

Starting a Doubles Point

1. One-Up/One-Back Warm-Up (1/1 × 3/3 minutes)
2. Doubles 20 Second Serves/Window Sequence
3. Doubles 20 Second Serves/Lob Sequence
4. Doubles 20 Second Serves/Short-Angle Volley Sequence
5. 20 Serves With Server's Partner (2v1)
6. 20 Serves with Returner's Partner (2v1)
7. Doubles Tiebreakers to 11 points (3 ×)

Doubles Returns

1. Five-Minute Warm-Up
2. Doubles Crosscourts (2/2 × 3 minutes)
3. Doubles One-Player Closing Volleys (1v1) (2/2 × 3 minutes)
4. Doubles 20 Second Serves/Lob Sequence
5. Doubles Crosscourt Serve and Volley (1v1) (2/2 × 3 minutes)
6. Doubles Tiebreakers (2v2) to 11 points; returners two back on first serves, conventional on second serves
7. Doubles (one set)

Serves and Returns

1. One-Up/One-Back Warm-Up (1/1 × 3/3 minutes)
2. 20 Serves With Returner's Partner (2v1)
3. Crazy Overheads (1 minute)
4. Doubles 20 Second Serves/Window Sequence
5. Crosscourts—Deuce and Ad Court (2/2 × 3 minutes); serve and volley once
6. Two-Player Closing Volleys (3 × 5 minutes)
7. Returning Team vs. a Server (2v1) (3 × 3 minutes)
8. Doubles (one set); only two second serves per game; unforced volley error is a two-point error

Doubles Serve and Volley

Purpose: To become proficient serving with aggressive spin, making first volleys, and in general setting up the point for the serving team.

Successfully serving and volleying allows the serving team to take control of the net and control of the point. I recommend outside first volleys to be volleyed back deep to the returner and inside volleys to be aimed at the T.

Making doubles first serves and first volleys makes for an unbeatable combination—aggressive, high-percentage doubles at its best.

Server and Returner Closing Volleys

1. Doubles Warm-Up (1/1 × 2/2 minutes)
2. Doubles 20 Second Serves/Window Sequence
3. Doubles Crosscourts—Deuce and Ad Court (1/1 × 3 minutes); serve and volley once
4. Doubles Crosscourt Serve and Volley (1v1) (2 × 4 minutes); one serve
5. Doubles Crosscourt Serve and Volley (1v1) (2 × 4 minutes); one serve and returner must come in behind return
6. Doubles Two-Touch Crosscourt Serve and Volley (1v1) (2 × 4 minutes); one serve
7. Doubles Serve and Volley vs. Two Back (2v2) (2 × 5 minutes)
8. Doubles—Pro-Set

Aggressive Doubles

1. One-Up/One-Back Warm-Up (1/1 × 3/3 minutes)
2. Doubles Crosscourts (1/1 × 3 minutes); serve and volley once
3. Doubles Crosscourt Serve and Volley (1v1) (2 × 4 minutes); one serve
4. Doubles Crosscourt Serve and Volley (1v1) (2 × 4 minutes); one serve, returner approaches off return
5. Doubles Two-Touch Crosscourt Serve and Volley (1v1) (2 × 4 minutes); one serve
6. Doubles Overhead Game (2v2) (eight points)
7. Doubles Quick Volleys (2v2) (2 × 2/2 minutes); coach feeds
8. Doubles (one set)

Doubles First Volleys

1. One-Up/One-Back Warm-Up (1/1 × 3/3 minutes)
2. Doubles Crosscourts (1/1 × 3 minutes)
3. Doubles Crosscourts (2 × 3 minutes); may approach with proper court position
4. Doubles Crosscourt Serve and Volley (2 × 3 minutes)
5. Doubles 20 Second Serves/Short-Angle Volley Sequence
6. Doubles Serve and Volley vs. Two Back (2v2) (2 × 4/4 minutes)
7. Doubles (one set)

Classic Doubles

1. Five-Minute Warm-Up
2. Doubles 20 Second Serves/Window Sequence
3. Crosscourts—Deuce and Ad Court (2/2 × 3 minutes); serve and volley once
4. Doubles One-Player Closing Volleys (1v1) (2 × 4 minutes)
5. Doubles Crosscourt Serve and Volley (1v1) (2/2 × 4 minutes)
6. Doubles Two-Touch Crosscourt Serve and Volley (1v1) (2 × 3 minutes)
7. Doubles—Pro-Set

First Three Shots

1. Doubles Warm-Up (1/1 × 3/3 minutes)
2. Crazy Volleys (1 minute)
3. Crazy Overheads and Volleys (1 minute)
4. 20 Serves With Server's Partner (2v1)
5. Crosscourts—Deuce and Ad Court (1/1 × 4 minutes); serve and volley once
6. Doubles Crosscourt Serve and Volley (1v1) (1/1 × 3 minutes); second serves
7. Doubles Crosscourt Serve and Volley (1v1) (2/2 × 4 minutes); first and second serves
8. Overhead Game (seven point)
9. Doubles (one set)

Doubles Serve and Volley

1. Soft Toss (forehands and backhands, one-half basket each)
2. Crosscourts—Deuce and Ad Court (2/2 × 3 minutes); serve and volley once
3. Slice vs. Slice (2 × 3 minutes); ad court, backhand to backhand
4. One-Player Closing Volleys (2 × 3 minutes)
5. Doubles Crosscourt Serve and Volley (1v1) (1/1 × 4 minutes); one serve
6. Doubles Crosscourt Serve and Volley (1v1) 1/1 × 4 minutes); two serves
7. Doubles (one set)

Doubles Volleys

Purpose: To develop strong doubles second volleys and closing volleys. The first volley's been made and now the doubles team is in position to play the point from inside the service line. Learning to move and cover the court together, learning where to aim volleys, and learning how to close out a doubles point is the focus of these practice sessions.

Second Volleys

1. Volley Warm-Up (2/2 × 3/3 minutes)
2. Doubles Crosscourts (2/2 × 3 minutes)
3. Doubles 20 Second Serves/Window Sequence
4. Doubles Crosscourt Pinch Volleys (1v1) (2 × 2/2 minutes)
5. Doubles Two-Player Closing Volleys (1v1) (1/1 × 3 minutes)
6. Doubles (two sets)

Quick Volleys

1. Volley Warm-Up (2/2 × 3/3 minutes)
2. Doubles Crosscourts (1/1 × 3 minutes)
3. Doubles Crosscourt Serve and Volley (1v1) (1/1 × 4 minutes); one serve
4. Doubles Two-Touch Crosscourt Serve and Volley (1v1) (1/1 × 3 minutes); one serve
5. Doubles Quick Volleys (2v2) (2 × 3 minutes); one round singles court, one round doubles court
6. Doubles (one set)

Pinch Volleys

1. Directional Minitennis—Volley Warm-Up
2. One-Up/One-Back Warm-Up (1/1 × 2/2 minutes)
3. Doubles 20 Second Serves/Short-Angle Volley Sequence
4. Crosscourts—Deuce and Ad Court (2/2 × 3 minutes); serve and volley once
5. Doubles Pinch Volleys (1v1) (3 × 2/2 minutes); two-point errors in effect for unforced volleys and netted groundstrokes
6. Doubles One-Player Closing Volleys (1v1) (2/2 × 4 minutes)
7. Doubles (one set); two second serves per game

Finishing the Point

1. Directional Minitennis—Volley Warm-Up
2. One-Up/One-Back Warm-Up (1/1 × 2/2 minutes)
3. Doubles 20 Second Serves/Short-Angle Volley Sequence

4. Crosscourts—Deuce and Ad Court (1/1 × 3 minutes); serve and volley once
5. Crazy Overheads (1 minute)
6. Doubles Crosscourt Serve and Volley (1v1) (1/1 × 4 minutes); second serves
7. Doubles One-Player Closing Volleys (1v1) (2/2 × 3 minutes)
8. Doubles Two-Player Closing Volleys (1v1) (1/1 × 3 minutes)
9. Doubles (one set)

Doubles Volleys

1. One-Up/One-Back Warm-Up (1/1 × 3/3 minutes)
2. Crazy Overheads (1 minute)
3. Crazy Overheads and Volleys (1 minute)
4. Doubles 20 Second Serves/Short-Angle Volley Sequence
5. Crosscourts—Deuce and Ad Court (1/1 × 3 minutes); serve and volley once
6. Doubles One-Player Closing Volleys (2v2) (3 × 5 minutes)
7. Doubles Two-Touch Crosscourt Serve and Volley (3 × 4 minutes)
8. Doubles (one set); only two second serves per game; unforced volley error is a two-point error

Prematch Practices

Purpose: To sharpen players' skills and confidence before a match. To focus on key singles and doubles essentials.

Usually I prefer to have separate singles and doubles practices but there is always the exception to the rule. Practice sessions the day before a match are good opportunities to review singles and doubles concepts and to sharpen players' strengths and ultimately, their confidence.

Directionals

1. Five-Minute Warm-Up
2. Four-Shot Pressuring Returns (X Marks the Spot)
3. Doubles Crosscourts—Deuce and Ad Court (1/1 × 3 minutes)
4. Directionals—Inside Groundstroke COD (1 × 5 minutes)
5. Directionals—Forehands Are Wild (1 × 5 minutes)
6. Doubles One-Player Closing Volleys (1v1) (1/1 × 4 minutes)
7. Doubles Crosscourt Serve and Volley (1v1) (1/1 × 4 minutes)

8. Overhead Game (seven points)
9. Doubles Tiebreakers (3 ×); 1v1 crosscourt serve and volley

Point Building and Serve and Volley

1. One-Up/One-Back Warm-Up (1/1 × 3/3 minutes)
2. Crazy Volleys (1 minute)
3. Doubles Two-Player Closing Volleys (1v1) (1/1 × 3 minutes)
4. Crosscourts—Deuce and Ad Court (1/1 × 4 minutes); serve and volley once
5. Big Targets Game (1 × 4 minutes)
6. Doubles Crosscourt Serve and Volley (1v1) (1/1 × 3 minutes); one serve
7. Doubles Crosscourt Serve and Volley (1v1) (1/1 × 4 minutes); two serves
8. Overhead Game (seven points)
9. Singles Tiebreakers (2 ×)
10. Doubles (one set)

Approach Shots and Volleys

1. One-Up/One-Back Warm-Up (1/1 × 3/3 minutes)
2. Crosscourts—Deuce and Ad Court (2/2 × 3 minutes); serve and volley once
3. Doubles Crosscourt Serve and Volley (1v1) (1/1 × 4 minutes)
4. One-Player Closing Volleys (1 × 4 minutes)
5. Two-Player Closing Volleys (1 × 4 minutes)
6. Doubles (one set)
7. Singles (one set)

Attacking Play

1. One-Up/One-Back Warm-Up (1/1 × 3/3 minutes)
2. Crosscourts—Deuce and Ad Court (2/2 × 3 minutes)
3. Doubles One-Player Closing Volleys (1v1) (2 × 3 minutes)
4. Singles Tiebreakers (3 ×); first and second serves
5. Doubles Crosscourt Serve and Volley (1v1) (3 × 3 minutes)
6. Doubles Quick Volleys (2v2) (2 × 2/2 minutes)
7. Doubles Tiebreakers (2 ×)

Change-of-Direction Pressure

1. Topspin Warm-Up (8 minutes)
2. Crosscourts With 90-Degree COD (1/1 × 3 minutes); serve and volley once a game
3. Directionals—Inside Groundstroke COD (2 × 5 minutes)
4. First-Strike Game (2 × 5 minutes)
5. One-Player Closing Volleys (2 × 3 minutes); may lob after first volley
6. Doubles 20 Second Serves/Window Sequence
7. Doubles—Eight-Game Pro-Set

Slice and Set Play

1. One-Up/One-Back Warm-Up (1/1 × 3/3 minutes)
2. Crosscourts—Deuce and Ad Court (1/1 × 3 minutes)
3. Slice vs. Slice (2 × 3 minutes)
4. Offense/Defense (1 × 3/3 minutes); slice backhands
5. Doubles (one set)
6. Singles (one set)

Spin and Set Play

1. Topspin Warm-Up (8 minutes)
2. Crosscourts—Deuce and Ad Court (2/2 × 3 minutes)
3. Drive vs. Slice (1 × 2/2 minutes)
4. Drive vs. Loop (1 × 2/2 minutes); singles court
5. Five-Minute Warm-Up
6. Doubles (one set)
7. Singles (one set)

Inside Groundstrokes and Set Play

1. One-Up/One-Back Warm-Up (1/1 × 3/3 minutes)
2. Crosscourts—Deuce and Ad Court (2/2 × 3 minutes)
3. Directionals—Inside Groundstroke COD (1 × 5 minutes); two serves
4. Inside Groundstroke Recovery Drill (1 × 3/3 minutes)
5. Short Outside Approach Shot Recovery Drill (1 × 3/3 minutes)
6. Doubles (one set)
7. Singles (one set)

Pressuring

1. Five-Minute Warm-Up
2. Crosscourts—Deuce and Ad Court (2/2 × 3 minutes)
3. Drive vs. Slice (2 × 2/2 minutes, ad court)
4. Directionals—Inside and 90-Degree COD (2 × 5 minutes)
5. One-Player Closing Volleys (2 × 4 minutes)
6. Doubles Crosscourt Serve and Volley (1v1) (1/1 × 4 minutes)
7. First-Strike Game (1 × 5/5 minutes)
8. Singles (one set)

Quick Strike

1. 20-Minute Warm-Up
2. Four-Shot Pressuring Returns (X Marks the Spot)
3. Crosscourts—Deuce and Ad Court (1/1 × 3 minutes)
4. Crosscourts With 90-Degree COD (1/1 × 3 minutes)
5. Crazy Overheads (1 minute)
6. One-Player Closing Volleys (2 × 4 minutes)
7. Pressuring Serve/Return Game (2 × 5 minutes)
8. Singles (one set)

Directionals and Doubles

1. Topspin Warm-Up (8 minutes)
2. Four-Shot 20 Second Serves With Returns
3. Crosscourts—Deuce and Ad Court (1/1 × 3 minutes)
4. Crosscourts With 90-Degree COD (1/1 × 3 minutes)
5. Directionals—Inside Groundstroke COD (1 × 5 minutes); two serves
6. Singles Tiebreakers (2 ×)
7. Doubles Two-Player Closing Volleys (1v1) (1/1 × 3 minutes)
8. Doubles (eight games)

One-Hour Practices

Purpose: To give players a structured 1-hour practice session when training on their own.

One-Hour Practices were originally created for players who needed guidance when practicing on their own and in the off-season. The structured part of a 1-Hour Practice lasts an hour, followed by an opportunity to play. The five practice sessions cover base work, spin, pressuring, offense/defense and doubles/air drills.

Base Work

1. Directional Minitennis
2. Crosscourts—Deuce and Ad Court (3/3 × 3 minutes)
3. Directionals With Inside COD (3 × 5 minutes)
4. Four-Shot 20 Second Serves With Returns
5. First-Strike Game
6. Play; think high percentage—good shot selection and change-of-direction decisions

Spin

1. Directional Minitennis; use slice
2. Crosscourts—Deuce and Ad Court (1/1 × 4 minutes); must serve and volley once
3. Slice vs. Slice (2 × 3 minutes); singles court
4. Drive vs. Loop (2 × 2/2 minutes)
5. Drive vs. Slice (2 × 2/2 minutes)
6. Tiebreakers with two serves (3 ×)

    a. all slice

    b. variety—no two spins hit consecutively

    c. regular—no stipulations (still think variety of spin)
7. Play; think variety—hit out of your opponent's strike zone

Pressuring

1. Topspin Warm-Up (8 minutes)
2. Crosscourts—Deuce and Ad Court (1/1 × 4 minutes); must serve and volley once
3. Directionals—Inside Groundstroke COD (2 × 5 minutes); must serve and volley once per rotation
4. Pinch Volleys (2 × 2/2 minutes); half a doubles court
5. Inside Groundstroke Recovery Drill (2 × 3/3 minutes)
6. Short Outside Approach Shot Recovery Drill (2 × 3/3 minutes)
7. Play

Offense/Defense

1. Soft Toss (forehands and backhands, one-half basket each)
2. Crosscourts—Deuce and Ad Court (1/1 × 4 minutes); must serve and volley once

3. Offense/Defense (3 × 2/2 minutes)
4. Outside/Middle (2 × 3/3 minutes)
5. First-Strike Game (2 × 3/3 minutes)
6. Play

Doubles/Air Drills

1. Volley Warm-Up (1/1 × 3/3 minutes)
2. Crosscourts—Deuce and Ad Court (1/1 × 4 minutes); must serve and volley once
3. One-Player Closing Volleys (1 × 3 minutes)
4. Two-Player Closing Volleys (2 × 3 minutes)
5. Doubles Crosscourt Serve and Volley (1v1)
    a. returner must stay back (1/1 × 4 minutes)
    b. returner attacks—must come in behind return (1/1 × 4 minutes)
    c. returner's choice—come in or stay back (1/1 × 4 minutes)
6. Play; focus on returns and first volleys

ABOUT THE AUTHOR

Paul Wardlaw has worked his way up to the top of the tennis coaching ranks. In the early 1990s, he turned Division III Kenyon College into a national powerhouse, leading them to three NCAA National Team Championships. In recognition of his outstanding coaching skills, Wardlaw received the Wilson/Intercollegiate Tennis Association's National Coach of the Year Award.

Wardlaw then turned his attention to the University of Iowa women's tennis program. In just two short years as head coach, he increased the team's standing to its highest ranking ever and led them to their first NCAA tournament bid and a trip to the Sweet 16. Wardlaw has written "The Wardlaw Directionals," which appeared in the book *Coaching Tennis* and will be featured in the upcoming Human Kinetics video *High-Percentage Tennis*. He resides in Iowa City with his wife and two daughters.

Wardlaw can be reached via email at paul-wardlaw@uiowa.edu

See Wardlaw's "directionals" in action

Take the advantage on the court! In *High-Percentage Tennis*, coach Paul Wardlaw presents his winning system of play, called the "directionals," that he's used throughout his 14 successful seasons at the college level. By learning and mastering his tactical system, you will respond instinctively to game situations, minimizing errors and making your play more consistent.

In the *High-Percentage Tennis* video, expert players demonstrate

- where to hit the ball based on their opponent's position on the court,
- when—and when not to—change the direction of the ball,
- how to minimize errors by selecting shots based on the relationship of the ball to the player, and
- how to better recognize offensive opportunities as well as recover from defensive positions.

Wardlaw also teaches you when and where to hit high-percentage groundstrokes, service returns, passing shots, volleys, and approaches. Progressive drills for practicing the directionals are included, helping you develop the techniques and tactics to play directional tennis. You will also see the directionals in action with footage of top pros like Andre Agassi, Todd Martin, Martina Hingis, and Venus Williams making high-percentage shots.

Make the directionals an integral part of your program, and in no time, you will be playing high-percentage tennis and consistently winning—game, set, and match!

(Approx 40 minute videotape)
ISBN 0-7360-3110-3
$29.95 ($44.95 Canadian)

To place your order, U.S. customers call

TOLL FREE 1-800-747-4457.

Customers outside the U.S. place your order using the appropriate telephone number/address shown in the front of this book.

Prices are subject to change.

HUMAN KINEICS
The Premier Publisher for Sports & Fitness
P.O. Box 5076, Champaign, IL 61825-5076
www.humankinetics.com

Three great resources for improving your game!

Become a complete tennis player with the instruction found in *Serious Tennis*. Internationally known instructor Scott Williams, in conjunction with 20 of the top tennis minds in the world, presents the same techniques, conditioning, mental training, and strategy tips used to develop the world's best players.

If you're dedicated to becoming a better player, you owe it to yourself to get the best instruction in the game. Get *Serious Tennis* and become the kind of player you've always wanted to be.

ISBN 0-88011-913-6 • $19.95 ($29.95 Canadian)

In acquiring and mastering sports skills, a picture is often worth a thousand words. Research shows most athletes learn skills better through *visual* demonstration than through *verbal* instruction. If you're a visual learner, *Visual Tennis* may be the most natural and effective way to improve your game.

Visual Tennis provides more than 200 photographs—including many of top stars like Pete Sampras, Martina Hingis, Andre Agassi, and Steffi Graf. Leading teaching pro John Yandell shares his proven method, which has helped thousands of players realize their potential and raise their game to new levels.

ISBN 0-88011-803-2 • $19.95 ($29.95 Canadian)

Raise your game to the next level with *Competitive Tennis* and the USTA's National Tennis Rating Program (NTRP).

Inside this book you'll find drills and strategies for both singles and doubles, geared specifically to your ability. If you're already playing USTA league tennis, this book will speed your climb up the NTRP ladder. If you're new to the NTRP, you'll find the tools to rate yourself and advice to benefit from the most effective handicapping system in tennis.

No matter what level you're starting at, *Competitive Tennis* has everything you need to improve you performance on the court.

ISBN 0-88011-755-9 • $17.95 ($25.95 Canadian)

Develop winning physical and mental skills!

Train to play like the pros by specifically conditioning each fitness component to meet the physical demands of tennis.

Complete Conditioning for Tennis improves your strength, power, agility, flexibility, quickness, and stamina. Experts from the United States Tennis Association provide the very best training exercises and drills, sample workouts from the game's top players, and sample programs to maximize your tennis performance. You'll finish strong in every match.

ISBN 0-88011-734-6 • $15.95 ($23.95 Canadian)

Pressure: It's inherent to the game, and it can make or break a tennis player. *Playing Better Tennis Under Pressure* shares the findings of sports psychologists and experts at the USTA's Player Development Center to help you recognize common pressure points and develop ways to handle game-time stress.

Plus, you'll see examples of Pete Sampras, Michael Chang, Lindsay Davenport, Monica Seles, and other top players working through pressure situations. The *Playing Better Tennis Under Pressure* video will help you play through pressure like a pro.

(30 minute videotape)
ISBN 0-88011-743-5 • $19.95 ($29.95 Canadian)

Coaches, instructors, and players alike will appreciate the *USTA's 10 Keys to Mastering Tennis* video. Ron Woods of the United States Tennis Association and coaches Nick Saviano, Lynne Rolley, Kathy Woods, and Lew Brewer present a series of drills designed to help players learn skills faster, retain them better, and perform them under pressure.

In addition to full explanations and drills that demonstrate each key, footage from the U.S. Open and vivid graphics underscore the most important teaching points.

(25 minute videotape)
ISBN 0-99-001779-6 • $24.95 ($37.50 Canadian)

To place your order, U.S. customers call

TOLL FREE 1-800-747-4457.

Customers outside the U.S. place your order using the appropriate telephone number/address shown in the front of this book.

Prices are subject to change.

HUMAN KINETICS
The Premier Publisher for Sports & Fitness
P.O. Box 5076, Champaign, IL 61825-5076
www.humankinetics.com